THE NORTH WOODS WIL

OLIFE REGION
St. Lawrence R.
GASPE PENINSULA
ANTICOSTI IS.
NEWFOUNDLAND
PRINCE EDWARD IS.
CAPE BRETON. ISLAND
EBEC
NEW BRUNSWICK
NOVA SCOTIA
MAINE
VERMONT
N. HAMPSHIRE
YORK
MASS.
CONN.
NIA
N. JERSEY
DEL.
C. Conrader

Plate 1. Climax maple and white pine forest.

THE NORTHWOODS WILDLIFE REGION

Jay M. Conrader

Illustrated by

Constance Conrader

Photographs by the author

Naturegraph Publishers, Inc.

Library of Congress Cataloging in Publication Data

Conrader, Jay M., 1910-
The Northwoods wildlife region.

Includes index.
1. Natural history—Great Lakes Region. 2. Natural history—Canada, Eastern. I. Conrader, Constance. II. Title.
QH104.5.G7C67 1983 508.713 83-6257
ISBN 0-87961-126-X
ISBN 0-87961-127-8 (pbk.)

Books for a better world

Naturegraph Publishers, Inc.
P. O. Box 1075
Happy Camp, California 96039

Contents

Plate 2. Opening and forest edge, where spruce trees are beginning to invade an abandoned field.

Plate 3. Water-sculptured Pre-Cambrian sandstone of the Canadian Shield, in the Lake Superior basin.

Plate 4. Rock polypody and tree sapling, growing in rocks beside a waterfall.

Plate 5. Arethusa standing among cranberry and sedge on an open sphagnum bog.

Plate 6. Indian-pipes on a mossy hillside in a pine woods.

Plate 7. Mossy interior of a black spruce forest on the Canadian Shield.

Introduction to the Northwoods Region

Reaching across the northern Great Lakes states and southern Canada, from southeastern Manitoba to the Atlantic coast, is a region of great natural beauty known as the Northwoods to those acquainted with its wild solitude. The purpose of this book is to provide simple descriptions of its indigenous plants and animals, and characteristic habitats, so that they may be recognized and called by name, and so that the intrinsic wonder and beauty of this unique region may be better understood and appreciated.

Because nature is complex and variable, and because plants and animals are not necessarily confined within precise geographic limits, the boundaries of the Northwoods are only approximated. Yet this region possesses enough unity in its physical and biological qualities to make this approximation useful to students of nature. In this book the boundaries are established as follows: on the north, by the northern extent of red pine and white pine; on the south, by the limit to which plants typical of the coniferous forest are found in noticeable numbers; on the west, by the meeting of forest with prairie; and on the east, by the inland reach of marine flora.

Within these boundaries are three major geologic subdivisions.

The most extensive area lies in the north and west where the Northwoods Region cuts across the lower edge of the vast Canadian Shield, a unique and complex structure consisting of granites, gneisses, sedimentary, conglomerate, other igneous, and volcanic formations. The ancient Pre-Cambrian rocks forming the Canadian Shield are among the oldest known on earth, their age being measured in billions of years. They contribute much to the interest of the region, and from them the soil in this area has been derived.

The second area lies southeast of the Canadian Shield, in the Great Lakes and St. Lawrence basin. This fertile lowland of nearly undisturbed sandstone, shale and limestone, was laid down during the Mid-Paleozoic Era, when sediments washed from the surrounding uplands settled into ancient seas.

The third area, which shows the most geologic disturbance, is the Appalachian highland. Here sediments of sandstone, shale, and limestone thousands of feet thick were folded, broken, and thrust upward in a series of orogenies during the Paleozoic Era. Much of the sediment has since been worn down, and time has reduced the former rugged contour to a series of round-topped mountains and ridges, broad benchlands, and sheltered valleys. However, hard granitic rock intruded during the upheavals remain as the highest crests of the Appalachian range.

Although the basic geologic features of the Northwoods Region were established over two hundred million years ago, most of the present surface features were shaped more recently by glaciers which plowed up the former surface, moved it about as an unassorted mixture of sand, gravel and clay, and redeposited it as drumlins, moraines, eskers, and sand and clay plains. New lakes were added to the already numerous depressions in the Canadian Shield, new river courses formed, and rocky barrens scoured on exposed uplands.

The Northwoods can be divided into two main forest types: the coniferous forest, with an intermixture of a few subordinate deciduous trees; and the northern hardwood forest with an intermixture of coniferous trees which, with the exception of hemlock and white pine, occur mostly as subordinate members of the community. Although in general the coniferous forest occurs on the Canadian Shield and Appalachian heights, and the hardwood forest in the Great Lakes, St. Lawrence and Maritime lowlands, the two types of forest blend into each other so that it is hardly possible to draw a single line to show their separation.

The Northwoods is a region of cool temperate, moist climate, with short summers and long cold winters—the severity of winter coldness moderated by deep and lasting snow. The soils which develop in such a climate, on the geologic foundations, and under the forest cover described above, are characteristic of all cool-moist forest regions. These soils are of two major types, podzol and podzolic.

Podzol soil is distinguished by a brown surface layer of several inches of undecomposed forest litter, or "raw humus." Beneath this is an ashy-gray or white layer of leached sand, loam or clay, which is nearly or totally devoid of incorporated humus. Underlying the whole, at a depth of from one to four feet is a cemented layer of hardpan through which tree roots penetrate with great difficulty, if at all. This type of soil is strongly acid, comparatively infertile, and supports a limited but distinctive vegetation.

Podzolic soil differs from podzol in having a layer several inches deep in which humus is incorporated with soil particles, lying between the surface litter and the leached layer. Also, it shows an incompletely cemented layer at the bottom which permits the penetration of tree roots. This type of soil is more fertile than podzol, and supports a richer, more varied vegetation.

In addition to these two major soils, there are many areas of peat and muck soils, rocky outcrops, and windblown sands. All of these support distinctive plant and animal life.

The Northwoods is predominantly a forest region. Under natural conditions, the forest would give way only to areas covered by water, rocky barrens, sand dunes, or openings created by natural catastrophies. If a natural forest area is reduced to an opening, it tends to revert to forest through a series of definite and predictable stages over a period of time. When the forest reaches its final stage of development, the "climax" stage, it will perpetuate itself in this condition unless some catastrophe again reduces it to an opening.

In nature, the openings in a forested region are relatively few and mostly temporary. However, since the coming of European man to this continent, the natural condition of the land has been much altered. The great primeval forest that clothed the continent from sea to prairie was leveled in careless haste, and what we now call the Northwoods became a vast opening of slash, smoldering fire, and marginal farmland, with only a few isolated stands of forest left to show its former grandeur. In more recent years, people have begun to learn the value of forested land in its natural condition, and are fostering more and more the reestablishment and conservation of forests in regions such as the Northwoods.

As a result of this awakened sense of values, a visitor to the Northwoods today may see many stages of forest development—from bracken-grown openings where seedling shrubs and trees are beginning the slow march back to woodland, through all degrees of second growth, up to climax forest.

To discuss all the variations in the forest growth of the Northwoods would be impossible in a book of this scope. The reader should be aware, therefore, that the following descriptions of the forest types, and the other habitats as well, have been simplified. Probably no single area will look exactly like the typical habitat described. Yet there is a harmony of relationship between the elements that make up each type of habitat. The discovery of this harmony is one of the satisfactions of field study.

8/NORTHWOODS WILDLIFE REGION

In any natural community, the character of the plant-cover is determined largely by physical, chemical, and climatic conditions. The animal population, in turn, depends upon the kinds of plants available for food and shelter. Each element of the natural community is part of an interdependent, coordinated whole which is far from being fully understood. Until our understanding is complete, wild things ask only that we appreciate them as essential parts of the living earth.

> *That land is a community is the basic concept of ecology, but that land is to be loved and respected is an extension of ethics.*
>
> Aldo Leopold

The Coniferous Forest

Deep wet moss and cool blue shadows
Beneath a bending fir;
And the purple solitude of mountains
When only the dark owls stir.

Lew Sarett

Nowhere in the Northwoods are the qualities of this region more clearly expressed than in the coniferous forest. Here is an evergreen land, where the essence of spruce and balsam fir pervades the air, and where moist, deep moss carpets the springy duff of the forest floor. Beneath a close evergreen canopy, in a land shaded, cool, and blanketed with snow for more than half the year, the marten and lynx find seclusion. Slender spruce spires, strummed by

Fig. 1. A spruce forest presents a solid front of spires to the roadside.

the wind, play a soft accompaniment to the mellow flute-song of the thrush, while from the forest edge the moose bawls his challenge across lake and sedge marsh.

The coniferous forest as considered in this book coincides with the southeastern extensions of that great boreal forest of conifers that fans out across the continent from Newfoundland to Alaska. In the eastern United States, as one travels northward toward the Canadian border he discovers an area in which the northern cone-bearing trees—the pines, spruces, and their kin—become noticeable in the landscape. Here he is entering the Northwoods Region. Continuing northward, he finds that these trees become more and more prominent, and the species of deciduous trees fall away one by one, until finally there is a point at which the vision is bounded on all sides by a serrated horizon of dark green spires. This forest of spires, the coniferous forest, covers the northern part of the Northwoods and the mountain areas southward, and it extends far beyond the northern boundary of this region, to the tundra.

Fig. 2. The interior of a spruce forest. The tree trunks bristle with stiff remnants of dead lower branches covered with lichens, but the forest floor is verdant and soft with deep mosses; here bunchberry and airy wood horsetail are growing under the moving sun and shadow cast by the trees' needle canopy high above.

Fig. 3. Sphagnum moss, nearly universal in cold moist conifer forests, is shown here on a decaying arbor vitae log.

Fig. 4. Creeping snowberry is abundant in mossy conifer forests, and in the east it can often be found in extensive beds.

The approximate southern boundary of unbroken coniferous forest reaches from Lake of the Woods in Ontario, to the north shore of Lake Superior near Port Arthur. It moves eastward in an irregular course across Ontario and Quebec to the vicinity of Beaupré on the St. Lawrence River, and continues up both shores of the St. Lawrence estuary, detouring around the Saguenay River and Lake St. John basin on the north shore.

Across the estuary in the Maritime Provinces, the forest cover is largely a specialized mixture of conifers and northern hardwoods, but there are areas of coniferous forest on the highlands in Gaspé, New Brunswick, and Cape Breton, and in a coastal belt around the Bay of Fundy and the south and southeast coast of Nova Scotia.

In New England, the coniferous forest is found in northern Maine, and on the mountainsides elsewhere; and a restricted association of red spruce and balsam fir clothes the crests of the Appalachian Mountains as far south as North Carolina.

Small outposts of coniferous forest may also be found here and there throughout the southern part of the region, particularly in bogs and swamps.

There are two major types of coniferous forest here: those in which spruce and balsam fir are dominant; and those in which jack pine is dominant. Each of these major types has variations determined by the geographic location, the topography, and the soil.

In the spruce forests, any of the three species of spruce may be

Fig. 5. One-flowered wintergreen, among the daintiest of flowers, is hardly larger than its companion moss. Here its pure white flowers stand above dark decaying wood in a wet conifer forest.

found in pure stands, or in mixture with one another. They may also be mixed with other conifers and the few deciduous trees—such as paper birch, aspen, and balsam poplar—that are able to thrive in the severe climate and on the infertile podzol soil of the far north. Black spruce occurs throughout the region, but white spruce does not occur south of central New England, and red spruce is not found north or west of New Brunswick and southeastern Quebec. On the poorly drained lowlands and cold bogs which cover so much of the Northwoods area, black spruce is the dominant tree, companioned by the equally cold-loving tamarack in the bogs, and by tamarack and balsam fir in swamps and other wet places. On better drained soils, white spruce and red spruce are dominant in their respective ranges. From low woods and river shores, to wind-swept mountain-sides up to timberline, these two spruces are accompanied by the ubiquitous balsam fir.

Jack pine forests, commonly referred to as "barrens," may be found either on sterile sand plains or granitic rock. In many places throughout the Northwoods, receding lakes and streams of the glacial age deposited quantities of sand in level plains and out-washes. In other places large areas of Canadian Shield rock are exposed. In both cases, the soil is still in early stages of formation, and has not developed depth or richness sufficient to support other conifers or hardwoods. On these immature soils, the hardy jack pine holds undisputed sway. In still other areas, unwise use of the land has forced an ecological regression from productive forest soil back to sterile unproductive soil. In such areas, jack pine enters to begin the slow work of nursing the land back to maturity, for it is the only conifer in this region which can thrive on either burned out or eroded sandy soil.

Jack pine's humble associates in the more southern parts of the region are a scrub form of red oak and a ground cover of bracken, sweet fern, and blueberry. On slightly better soils, red pine, aspen, and paper birch may be found with the jack pine. These barrens occur locally in the eastern part of the Northwoods Region, but they are most extensive in the western part. In central Michigan and Wisconsin, and in a vast area reaching from above Lake Huron westward to Minnesota and Lake of the Woods, jack pine forests cover thousands of square miles of dry upland wilderness.

Fig. 6. Formerly a forest of white pine and red pine, this area has been reduced by logging and fire to a jack pine barrens with a ground layer of bracken.

The Northern Hardwood Forest

Underfoot and overhead the heartbeat of the world,
Wild, oh wild and solitary.

August Derleth

South of the coniferous forest, and blending with it, is the northern hardwood forest of mixed hardwoods and conifers, a more complex community than the former, with a greater variety of plants and animals. This type of forest covers the Great Lakes and St.

Fig. 7. A mature forest of maple and hemlock showing its open shrub-free character. The ground is covered with maple seedlings.

Fig. 8. Fringed polygala in association with barren strawberry and aromatic wintergreen in a mixed woodland of hardwoods and pine.

Fig. 9. Spotlighted in a shaft of sunlight, twinflower trails across the forest duff. Though delicate appearing, this plant is hardy and at home in both hardwood and conifer forests.

Fig. 10. Spinulose wood fern is one of the forest's evergreen ferns. It is growing here with wild sarsaparilla.

Lawrence basin, and lowlands of the Maritime Provinces; the growing season is longer, and climatic conditions are less severe than in the coniferous areas.

A characteristic mature hardwood forest is spacious and majestic, reposeful in its solitude. Its green dome, borne on lofty trunks high above a springy carpet of humus, filters the sun's rays, softening the light in the forest even at midday. In spring, during the brief period before leaves develop fully on the trees, the ground is abloom with starflowers, wild lilies-of-the-valley, fringed polygalas, and bunchberries. Where ferns arch green sprays above the cool moist humus, clintonia may hang its pale yellow bells beside a mosaic of goldthread on a fallen hemlock log. Later, after the rush of bloom is past, the fruits of some of these plants provide a bonus of food for squirrels, chipmunks and woodland mice, adding variety to their principal diet of tree seeds. The forest is verdant throughout the year, since many of its trees are conifers and much of its ground cover remains green under the deep snows.

An upland hardwood forest is usually composed of a variable combination of sugar maple, yellow birch, hemlock, and white

Fig. 11. A moist lowland forest with shrub edge bordering a marshy pond, the kind of habitat favorable to a variety of animals and birds.

Fig. 12. A mother raccoon rests on the stub of a mature oak tree, guarding her young ones hidden in the hollow below her hand.

pine. The understory consists of balsam fir, white spruce and, in some areas, a scattering of shade-tolerant shrubs such as ground hemlock and fly honeysuckle. Intermixed with these species, depending upon the geographic location of the forest and the type and condition of the soil, are such trees as beech, red spruce, basswood, and oak. The large trees, lavish in their production of seeds, provide the staple food of the forest's small mammals. Black bears may come from some distance away to feast on beech nuts in autumn. Porcupines feed on the bark of both hardwoods and conifers. Blackburnian warblers are like tiny flames darting among the high branches of dark pines and hemlocks. For the most part, however, there are fewer birds and mammals in the interior of a mature forest than in other habitats, because it lacks the kind of shrubby cover preferred by the majority of species.

One is more likely to see wildlife in the younger woodlands, the moist lowlands, or the edges of the forest, where there are more

Fig. 13. A burned-over area where the climax hardwood forest has been replaced by aspen, birch, and a ground layer of thimbleberry.

plants to give food and cover to a greater variety of animals. In such areas there is an understory of small hardwoods and conifers as well as a shrub layer of such species as beaked hazel, dogwood, shadbush, and elder crowding beneath and around the large trees. Songbirds find summer food in the fleshy fruits of the shrubs. Hollow trees near water areas harbor raccoons and wood ducks. Game trails cut across the wilderness between water and feeding grounds; if the area is remote from civilization, there may be sign of the gray wolf where this rare animal ranges the forest in restless search for food. Deer rest watchfully in thickets on the border between forest and opening; most of the animals of the hardwood forest may be found at some time under the protective cover of the forest edge.

On land where lumbering has destroyed the virgin forest, and repeated fires have depleted the soil, extensive groves of hawthorn, pincherry, aspen, paper birch or gray birch have replaced the magnificent hemlocks, pines, and maples. These secondary trees deserve a higher regard than is usually accorded them; not only are they attractive in themselves, but they serve as nurse trees in the hardwood areas, just as jack pine, aspen, and paper birch do in coniferous areas.

Freshwater Areas

A lonely lake, a lonely shore,
A lone pine leaning on the moon;
All night the water-beating wings
Of a solitary loon.

Lew Sarett

The Northwoods is a land of clear inland waters. From awesome Lake Superior to the most remote woodland pond, its quiet waters are held in a vital net of flowing rivers and tumbling cascades. These lakes and rivers give rise, in the working of nature's plan, to marshes and swamplands rich in wildlife.

The waters have played an important part in the human population of the region. Over them, like a morning mist, hangs the memory of silent Indian canoes, gay French-Canadian voyageur

Fig. 14. Throughout the Northwoods, rivers and streams spill down rocky courses in cataracts and cascades of all sizes, seeking the lowlands, coming to rest at last in lakes and ponds.

songs, and boisterous lumbermen's shouts. Northwoods waters are still important to people, but in a different way. Accessible as they are to the most densely populated area of North America, they offer to city man an opportunity to relearn a lost wisdom. They offer the challenge of adventure on white water, the refreshment of clear running streams, the peace of quiet lakes mirroring silent conifers.

For the purposes of this book, water habitats will include rivers and lakes and their shores, marshes, swamps, and bogs. All common vertebrate animals except fishes will be considered, and those plants whose flowering parts grow above the surface of the water.

Water itself is a habitat for plants and animals. At the same time it provides sites for animals and birds that choose to live in the rushes and cattails just off shore, or among the tangle of rocks and roots at the water's edge, or in nearby trees and shrubs. In addition, water acts as a magnet that draws wildlife to itself, and animals come from farther inland for food and drink. Thus, a wildlife enthusiast afloat in a canoe has an excellent opportunity to observe a wide variety of birds and animals.

Fig. 15. A black duck eyes canoeist from a quiet lake shore bordered with alder.

Fig. 16. The upland forest on the left descends to swamp lowland on the right, and is separated from the lake by a narrow border of sweet gale. Only a few emergent pond lilies appear near the shore in this deep end of the lake.

Fig. 17. Fragrant waterlilies cover the surface of a quiet bay. The lake is bordered by marsh plants in the foreground, sweet gale at the upland forest edge on the left, and heath shrubs blending into swamp forest on the right.

To a great extent, the plants in a water habitat influence the species of animals found there. The plants, in turn, are influenced by a number of physical factors: acidity or alkalinity of the water, turbidity, speed of flow, physical and chemical nature of the bottom, and exposure to sun and wind. Quiet bays and lee shores harbor a greater variety of plants and animals than do swift waters and windward shores. The shores of white water rivers are usually scoured clean of all but woody plants.

The area of emergent plants around a body of water may be narrow or broad, depending upon the slope of the shore and the speed of the current. Plants appear in zones governed by the depth of the water. Thus a river or lake with a steep shore may have virtually no emergent plants, in which case the upland forest may come down almost to the water's edge, separated from it by only a narrow fringe of alder and sweet gale. If the slope is gentle, there may be an area from a few feet to several hundred feet in breadth, with more or less clearly defined plant zones.

Water lilies are the deepest growing plants, floating their fragrant white blossoms on water as much as six to eight feet deep. Their leaves provide sunning places for frogs, and are one of the favored summer foods of moose. Between the lilies and shallow water are the zones of bulrushes, pondweeds, wild rice, and pickerelweed. All these provide food and cover for waterfowl. From shallow water to wetland is the zone of the treeless marsh, where tall cattails conceal the busy thoroughfares of muskrats, and where soras and bitterns hide their nests among the sedges. On the flood plains of rivers, and wet lowland areas around lakes and marshes, are swamp forests of those coniferous and deciduous trees and shrubs which are adapted to the wet environment. This in general is the order of succession from deep water to dry land. It should be understood, however, that not all zones are necessarily present in any one area, nor are they always sharply defined.

The northern bog, known by the Ojibwa name of "muskeg," is a type of water habitat with characteristics that set it apart from other water areas. There is a parallel between the development of a marsh and a bog, but whereas a marsh develops along a flowing river or well-drained lake, a bog forms in water having little or no flow. A bog may occupy a shallow, poorly-drained lake left by the retreating glacier, or a quiet bay in any cold lake where its position cuts it off from the general movement of current through the lake.

In the beginning of a bog's development, the water vegetation is like that of any other cold northern lake, and the plants pass through normal cycles of growth and death. However, since there is little or no drainage to carry away waste products, acids from the partial decomposition of plant matter accumulate in the water. When the acidity reaches a degree intolerable to the original vegatation, it gives way to a specialized bog flora which is able to thrive in a water environment high in acid and low in nutrients.

The characteristic bog association consists of a floating mat of sphagnum moss bound together by the tough roots of sedges and small heaths, backed by a stand of black spruce and tamarack. The small plants crowd upon each other and push out little by little over the water until eventually the mat may completely cover the surface, leaving many feet of open water beneath. Black spruce and tamarack trees venture out from shore where the mat has become somewhat stabilized, and before long young trees, too, are growing on the trembling water-soaked mat without contact with solid ground.

Leatherleaf, bog rosemary, and bog laurel are some of the most abundant heaths on the bog, often entirely hiding the moss beneath their interlacing branches. Cranberry vines creep along the surface

Fig. 18. A typical open bog, or muskeg, showing black spruce trees beginning to invade the floating mat of sphagnum moss, sedges, leatherleaf, and other heath shrubs.

Mark Trail: *By Ed Dodd*

30	General Hospital (CC) 60312		The Ellen DeGeneres Show		Judge Judy	Judge Judy	[illegible]	[illegible]
er	Design Inv	Like a Star	Montel Williams (N) 94770		Maury (CC) PG 80577		Fear Factor (CC) 7867	
	Starting Over (N) PG 15886		EXTRA 1683	Access H.	Millionaire	J'pardy! 3916	News 3428	NBC News
					House, Senate Coverage		Sesame Street Y 96157	
7954	Celebrity Jst	Marketplace	MegaMan	Mucha Luch	Pokmon	Yu-Gi-Oh!	The People's Court 78931	
stice	Cops 98138	Cops 25770	Yes, Dear	Home Imp.	Yes, Dear	King of Hill	Malcolm	'70s Show
og.	Paid Prog.	Paid Prog.	Paid Prog.	Paid Prog.	KARE 11 Today 17225		Pyramid	Shop/Drop
6	Hawaii Five-0 (CC) 38916		Cosby Show	Cosby Show	Little House on the Prairie		Hogan Hero	Dharma/Greg

0	8:00	8:30	9:00	9:30	10:00	10:30	11:00	11:30
eno. (N)	**American Experience:** Ulysses S. Grant. The military career and presidency of Ulysses S. Grant. (Part 2 of 2) (CC) 1515				**Keeping Up Appearances** (CC) 67664	**My Hero** 76312	**Independent Lens:** Sisters of '77. National Women's Conference. (CC) 43119	
Jp (CC)	**Everybody Loves Raymond** (CC) 1022	**Two and a Half Men** (CC) 14 5747	**CSI: Miami:** Addiction. A brutal carjacking turns into murder. (CC) 14 2003		**News** 1514193	**Late Show With David Letterman:** (10:35) Queen Latifah. (N) (CC) PG 9907751		**Late Late Show/Craig Ferguson**
Edi- ?: 93515	**The Bachelor:** (Season premiere) Charlie O'Connell, a 29-year-old jack of all trades, looks for love in a group of 25 beautiful bachelorettes. (N) (CC) PG 73751				**News** (CC) 6574157	**Nightline** (10:35) (CC) 1236867	**The King of Queens** (11:05) 9107157	**Dharma & Greg** (11:35) PG 4427480
mily	24: Day 4: 9:00PM - 10:00PM		News 35515		A Current	Frasier: IQ	Will & Grace	Just Shoot Me

of the moss. Pitcher plants and sundews hold their traps in readiness for the unwary insect. Elusive grass-pinks and pogonias beckon the venturesome bog-trotter to the edge of the quaking mat for a close look at their fragile beauty. And the surface of the mat may be dotted with silky white tufts of fruiting cotton grass.

Although a bog is an aquatic habitat, in reality bog plants are living under very arid conditions. The high acidity and coldness of the water limit the amount of water the plants can take in through their roots. If one examines bog plants, he will find that many have leaves which are waxy, or inrolled at the margins and covered with matted hairs underneath. These adaptations, similar to those found on some desert plants, serve to slow the loss of moisture through transpiration from the leaves. Bog plants' ability to withstand arid conditions may explain why a few of them are found in seemingly alien habitats on sand barrens, or at the top of sandstone cliffs.

Openings

It is fortunate, perhaps, that no matter how intently one studies the hundred little dramas of the woods and meadows, one can never learn all the salient facts about any one of them.

Aldo Leopold

An opening is a clearing in the forest which in most cases is the result of some natural or man-produced catastrophe. Temporary natural openings may be caused by lightning, blowdown, blight, or beaver activity. To these natural causes man has added logging, fire, cuts for right of way, agriculture, and others. Thus an opening may be a small space produced by the death of a few forest trees, or an extensive area created by forest fire or clear-cut logging. Small openings more closely resemble the surrounding forest than large ones.

A temporary opening is the place of pioneering plants, and is made up of an unstable community moving in a succession of growth toward the climax forest. Each stage in this succession tends to destroy the conditions necessary to its own continuance, and to produce those more suitable to the next stage. What an opening will look like at any given time will depend upon the degree of destruction of the original forest, the present stages of succession, and the nature of the surrounding forest.

If the original forest and its supporting soil has been severely disturbed, the opening may be covered for a long time with bracken, fireweed, or sweet fern. In burned areas on sandy soil, jack pine will spring up above the bracken. If the disturbance was less severe, the area may be spread with bunchberry or wild lily-of-the-valley, or it may be bright with lilies, roses, dogbane, asters, and goldenrod. It will soon grow up with sprouts and seedlings of aspen, birch, and pincherry; or, with seedlings of red pine, white pine, balsam fir, spruce, or arbor vitae.

Pioneer plants modify the harsh environment of the opening, creating conditions suitable to the growth of those shrubs and trees which require more moisture and shade for germination. When an opening develops to the brush stage, it is approaching the end of its

Fig. 19. An opening in the recovery stage, showing goldenrod in the foreground and fireweed behind it, with shrubs and immature woodland in the background.

Fig. 20. Bunchberry and a single birch seedling growing in a fissure of a sun-bleached stump in a cutover area.

Fig. 21. Fox pups resting in a hollow log in a man-made opening.

life as a distinct habitat because, before long, the species typical of the climax forest will return and the pioneer species will disappear or assume minor roles in the forest.

Some species of animals and birds are found more abundantly in openings than in any other kind of habitat. Meadow voles, masked shrews, and skunks are most prevalent here. Such birds as the vesper sparrow, American goldfinch, and least flycatcher are seldom seen except in the openings.

The edge between opening and forest shows a greater diversity of plants and animals than either the opening or forest itself. Taking advantage of the protective wall of the forest and the increased light yielded by the opening, fruiting shrubs and trees form a colorful screen around the opening. These in turn give cover and food which neither of the adjacent areas alone could provide. Thus, the brushy areas around openings harbor bear, deer, fox, woodchuck, chipmunks, and a host of birds. Ruffed grouse favor openings with nearby brush and a variety of young trees.

In addition to the kinds of temporary openings discussed above, one will find openings in the forest which are of a more permanent nature. Among these are low grassy swales and fern glades where moisture and other factors tend to maintain a stable community.

Rocky outcrops are a type of opening with characteristics distinct enough to be discussed separately.

Fig. 22. A low, moist glade encircled by ostrich fern; an example of a stable opening in a maple forest.

Rocky Areas

. . . these great rocks say,
The sea has gone, but still I stay.
Let scholars read my wondrous tale,
And poets walk my timeless vale.

Louise Leighton

Rock habitats range from exposed cliffs and barren outcrops to protected streamside areas and moist ravines.

Fig. 23. These pine tree roots penetrating far into a cliff face demonstrate the strength of living tissue.

On exposed cliffs and outcrops, plants usually are found in crevices and duff-filled depressions. The crevices catch and hold rain, and their cool surfaces condense moisture from the air, making it available to plant roots. In such fissures, ferns find favorable conditions for growth. There is hardly a cliff area that does not show the delicate fronds of some species arching from niches. It is also common to see white pine or arbor vitae trees grown to large size with their roots firmly clasped to a cliff-side.

If the rocky area is large, as in some extensive Canadian Shield outcrops, or if it is isolated, as in the case of the numerous rocky islands in the Great Lakes, it may have a characteristic growth of its own. However, if the area is small, biological pressure from the neighboring forest may not allow it to show a marked difference from its surroundings.

One of the most picturesque types of rock habitat is the area around a small waterfall in a cool, rocky ravine. In the shady recesses of moist rock, protected from drying winds and hot sun, is a distinctive association of mosses, liverworts, and ferns. In pockets where a little soil and plant debris affords a better foothold, one may find such flowers as miterwort and violets. The brook at the bottom of the waterfall may be bordered by highbush cranberry or shadbush, and shaded by hemlock and birch. Here at the edge of the pool below the falls a northern waterthrush may be seen delicately stepping and bowing along the rocky margin.

Plants of the Northwoods

Without plants the earth would be a barren waste of rock and lifeless water. There could be no wildlife community without the plant kingdom's largess of food and shelter. To understand the interrelationships in any natural area, therefore, one needs to begin with an understanding of the plants that comprise its base. Plants, more than any other living feature, give an area its distinctive character. Although habitats tend to overlap, and most plants grow in more than one kind of habitat, nevertheless there is a distinctiveness about the plant association in a given area that makes it possible to give names to habitat types. Certain plants are indicators that provide clues to the probable presence of other plants as well as animals.

The identification guide which follows is necessarily concise. In a book of this size it would be impossible to include all the plant species that occur in the Northwoods; therefore, only the most prominent and characteristic native species are described. The text points out important features necessary for identification of the species in this region, and text and illustrations complement each other. In seeking to identify a species, look for combinations of features, and use a magnifying glass for fine details. Examine more than one specimen since any individual plant may be atypical. Sizes and colors described are average; these features may vary with local conditions. (*CAUTION*: Do not pick any plants protected by law, or any that are scarce in a locality.)

Be sure to read family descriptions because characteristics common to all members of a family are not repeated in the species descriptions. Also, for the sake of brevity and simplicity, only those distinguishing family features noticeable in the species occurring in this region are mentioned. If, after examining a plant carefully with reference to both the description and illustration, you are unable to make a positive identification, you may have a hybrid, a local variation, or an uncommon or introduced species not included in this book. However, in many cases the family descriptions may enable you to place a species within a family group.

Drawings have been made accurately to scale from living specimens, and details are reproduced to natural size except where noted.

Nomenclature and plant groupings are based primarily upon *Gray's Manual of Botony*, 8th edition, 1950; and secondarily upon *The New Britton and Brown Illustrated Flora*, 1958.

Refer to the glossary for explanation of unfamiliar terms.

HORSETAIL FAMILY. Primitive relatives of ferns, with stems jointed, fluted, hollow; with or without whorls of branches at joints on upperpart of plant. Seemingly leafless, but with the leaves reduced to toothed sheaths at joints. Spores in cones on fertile stems. Sterile stems of most species average 15-18" tall. Eaten by moose, and to a lesser degree by muskrat.

Common Horsetail. *Equisetum arvense. Fig. 24.* Sterile stems green, rough-textured, with long simple branches; sheaths with 8-12 large dark brown teeth whose tips clasp stem. Fertile stems stout, succulent, flesh color, disappearing after the cones mature in spring. Regular in form, but often presents untidy appearance, for it tends to grow in crowded groups with branches tangled together. Marshes, shores, open woods; in semishade.

Wood Horsetail. *E. sylvaticum. Fig. 25.* Sterile stems green, rough-textured, with branches that fork and refork in lacy pattern; sheaths with light brown teeth fused into 3-4 loose lobes. Fertile stems green or flesh color, with short incipient branches that later develop into normal branches; cones maturing in spring, deciduous. The most beautiful horsetail, of delicate symmetrical form, with arching tips and regularly-spaced whorls of horizontal branches. Usually each graceful plant stands singly in the colony. Marshes, forest edges, and open mossy woods where some sun strikes through the trees; on moist rich soil.

Water Horsetail. *E. fluviatile. Fig. 26.* Sterile and fertile stems alike, green, smooth, to 36" tall, hollow as a thin-walled tube; unbranched, or with few to many branches from upper half of stem; sheaths with 15-20 small, sharp, dark brown teeth. In quiet muddy-bottomed water, swamps; one form in running water.

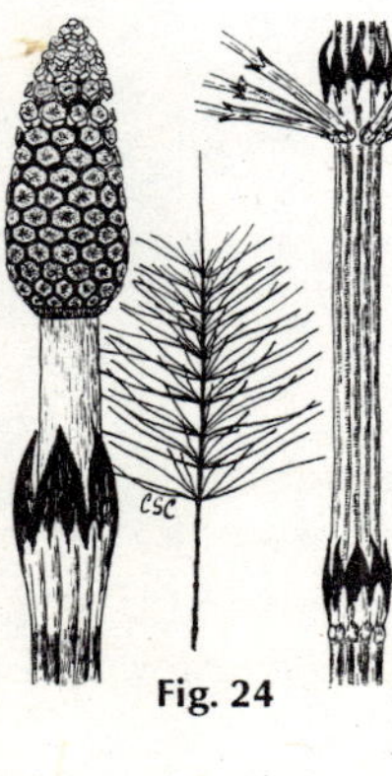

Fig. 24

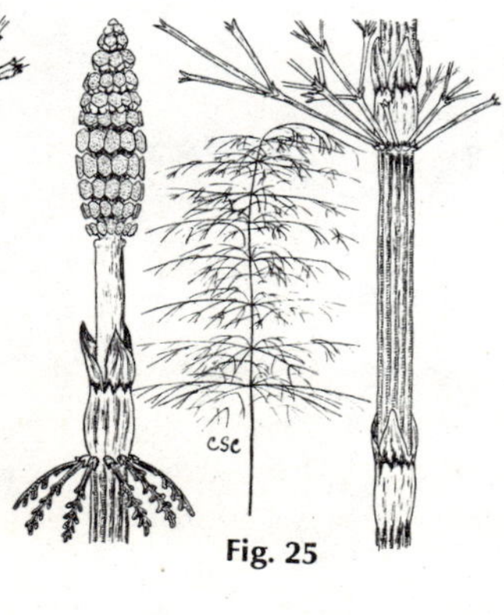

Fig. 25

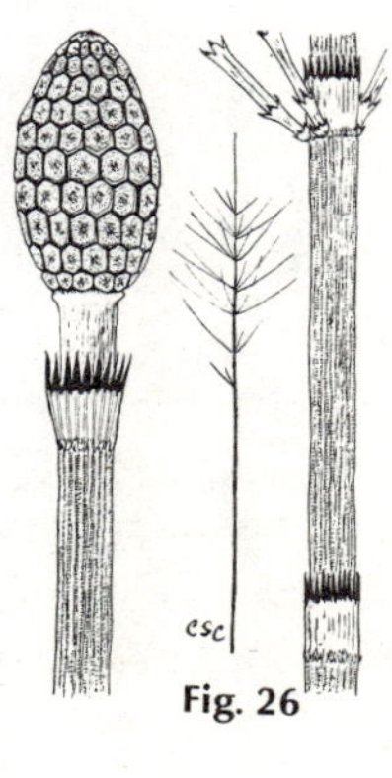

Fig. 26

CLUBMOSS FAMILY. Small evergreen fern relatives, with upright branches 4-12" tall from prostrate stems that trail for many feet on the surface or underground. Whorls of evergreen leaves cover branches. Most species have yellow spore cones at ends of branches.

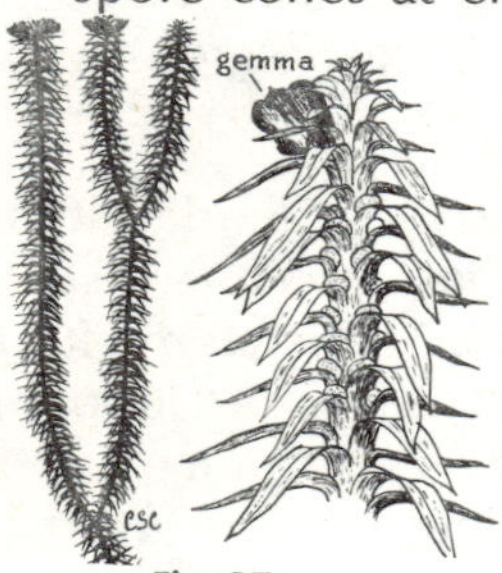

Fig. 27

Shining Clubmoss. *Lycopodium lucidulum. Fig. 27.* Upright branches simple or forked; often grows in cuplike tufts. More leafy looking than other species, its shiny dark green leaves larger, broader, softer to touch. Without cones; with yellow spore cases in axils of upper leaves. May have gemmae near tips. In moist hardwood forests.

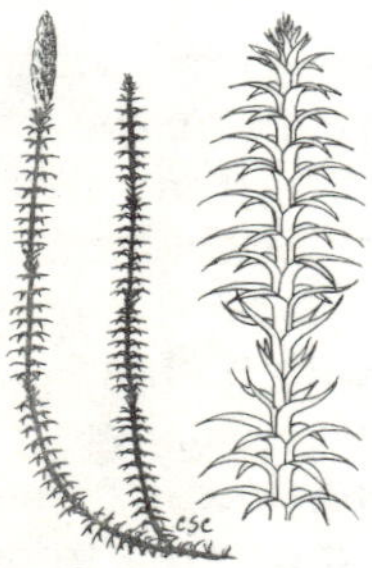

Fig. 28

Bristly Clubmoss. *L. annotinum. Fig. 28.* Upright branches simple or forked; stiff leaves set in neat, precise whorls. Leaves tipped with sharp prickly bristles. Sessile cones. Woods and moist edges.

Running Clubmoss. *L. clavatum. Fig. 29.* Branches forked, arising from surface-running stems in erect clusters, or spreading to form a loose mat. Leaves with long, soft bristle tips. Cones on long peduncles. Dry woods, openings.

Ground Pine. *L. obscurum. Fig. 30.* Plants arise singly from underground stems, like miniature trees, with small spreading leaves in whorls. Sessile cones at apex. Open woods.

Fig. 29

Fig. 30

Fig. 31

Ground Cedar. *L. complanatum. Fig. 31.* Branches flattened, with scalelike leaves similar to arbor vitae. Irregularly treelike, but growing in more crowded colonies than the former. Cones on long peduncles. Woods, forest edges, sandy openings.

ADDER'S-TONGUE FAMILY. Succulent-stemmed primitive ferns. From a common stem there rises one sterile leaf, and one long-stalked fertile branch that bears either an elongated or a paniclelike cluster of spore cases at its apex.

Rattlesnake Fern. *Botrychium virginianum. Fig. 32.* Triangular three-parted leaf, with the subleaflets deeply-cut and toothed; stem smooth and round. Fertile stalk arises in midsummer. Deciduous woods. A northern form with the leaf not so finely cut occurs in coniferous woods and moist openings.

Fig. 32

ROYAL FERN FAMILY. The largest ferns, 2-6′ or more tall. Spores develop from fertile leaflets that contract at maturity into clusters of small globular spore cases.

Royal Fern. *Osmunda regalis. Fig. 33.* Doubly compound leaves with distinctly separated subleaflets. Panicles of spore cases at apex of fertile leaves. Wet habitats.

Interrupted Fern. *O. Claytoniana. Fig. 34.* Compound leaves; leaflets cut almost to midrib into quite uniform rounded lobes; woolly only when young. Fertile fronds "interrupted" by several pairs of fertile leaflets. Edges of moist woods and swamps.

Fig. 33

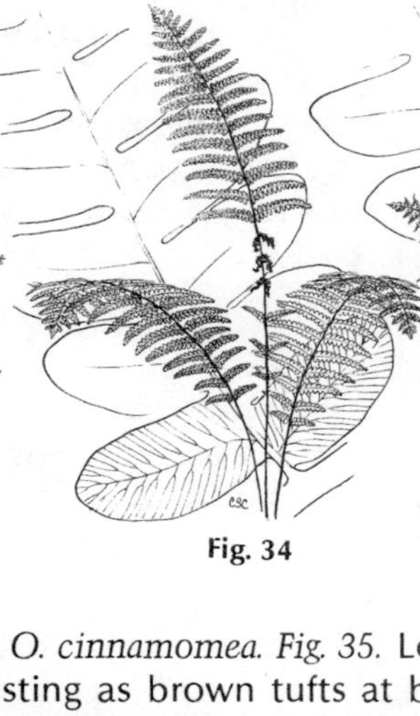

Fig. 34

Fig. 35

Cinnamon Fern. *O. cinnamomea. Fig. 35.* Leaves similar to above, but with wool persisting as brown tufts at base of sterile leaflets. Fertile leaves composed entirely of woolly fertile leaflets that wither early. Edges of wet woods and water areas.

FERN FAMILY. Spore cases clustered into "fruit-dots" (or sori) on the backs of fertile leaves which, except in a few species do not differ greatly from the sterile leaves.

Fig. 36

Rusty Woodsia. *Woodsia ilvensis. Fig. 36.* Small 4-8" leaves hairy on both surfaces, densely hairy and scaly on backs and on the brown stems. Stems jointed near base. In tufts on or near rocks.

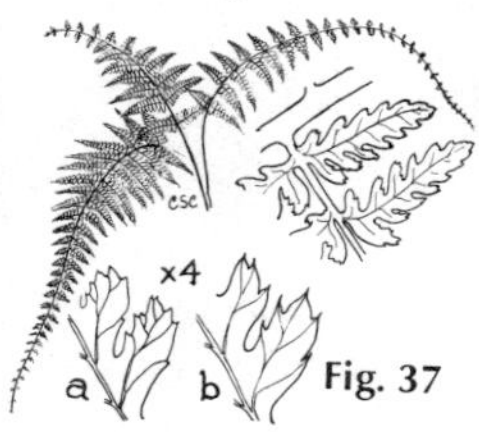

Fig. 37

Bulblet Fern. *Cystopteris bulbifera. Fig. 37.* Lacy-cut delicate fern 1-2' long. Fertile fronds tapered to very long slender tips; often with bulblets on undersides. Sterile fronds shorter, less tapered; lowest pair of leaflets longest. Most veins end in sinuses between teeth (*Fig. 37a*). Ravines, shaded calcareous rocks.

Leaves of the highly variable Fragile Fern, *C. fragilis*, also found on rocks, resemble the sterile leaves of the bulblet fern; but in this species there are no bulblets, the lowest pair of leaflets usually is not longest, and the veins end in the teeth (*Fig. 37b*).

Fig. 38

Ostrich Fern. *Pteretis pensylvanica. Fig. 38.* Beautiful vase-shaped plants 2-5' tall. Sterile leaves plumelike, widest near the top. Leaflets running almost the length of the stem, gradually diminishing to a very narrow base. Veins not forked. Fertile fronds overwintering; leaflets contracted and rolled back over sori. Swamps, bottomland.

Sensitive Fern. *Onoclea sensibilis. Fig. 39.* 1-3' tall. Easily recognized by the long-stemmed, net-veined leaves that rise singly from creeping rootstock. Sori enclosed in beadlike divisions of fertile fronds which persist over winter. Swamps and low openings.

Fig. 39

Fig. 40

Marsh Fern. *Dryopteris Thelypteris. Fig. 40.* 16-30" tall. Leaf blades 7-16" long, on slender stems, rising singly from creeping rootstock.

Leaves slightly hairy. Stem smooth. Sori covered by recurved margins of leaflets (*Fig. 40a*). Low openings.

Oak Fern. *D. disjuncta. Fig. 41.* Delicate three-parted leaves stand almost horizontally on slender stems 3-8" tall, rising singly from creeping rootstock. Moist hardwood forests, shaded rocks.

Fig. 41

Fig. 42

Long Beech Fern. *D. Phegopteris. Fig. 42.* To 1' tall. Leaves rise singly from creeping rootstock; blades tilted back; lowest pair of leaflets tipped forward from rest of blade, others connected by wing at midrib. Moist woods, shady cliffs, ravines.

Spinulose Wood Fern. *D. spinulosa. Fig. 43a.* Large graceful woodland ferns to 30" tall with very lacy-cut evergreen leaves, usually triply compound, but variable in form and degree of cutting. Identify by the spine-tipped teeth, the unequal length of subleaflets on basal leaflets, and the round sori on veins. Moist woods.

Similar Marginal Shield-fern, *D. marginalis*, has leathery leaves less finely cut, no spines on teeth, and the sori on the margins (*Fig. 43b*). Rocky woods and slopes.

Fig. 43

Lady Fern. *Athyrium Filix-femina. Fig. 43c.* Size and habit like wood ferns but distinguished from them by elongated sori. The form most likely to be seen in this region, var. *Michauxii*, has doubly compound leaves without spine-tipped teeth, and subleaflets of equal length. Woods, edges.

Fig. 44

Bracken. *Pteridium aquilinum. Fig. 44.* Large triangular leaves rest almost horizontally on 3' stems, from creeping rootstock. Sori covered by the recurved margins of subleaflets. Sterile openings.

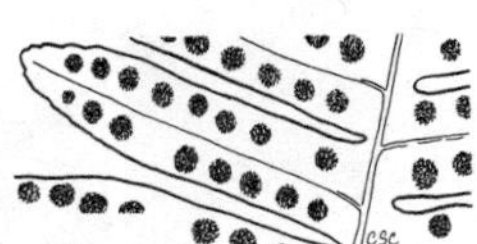

Fig. 45

Rock Polypody. *Polypodium virginianum. Fig. 45.* Evergreen leaves to 10" long. Very large sori. On shaded rocks.

YEW FAMILY. A single species of low evergreen shrub bearing seeds singly in red cuplike fleshy fruits.

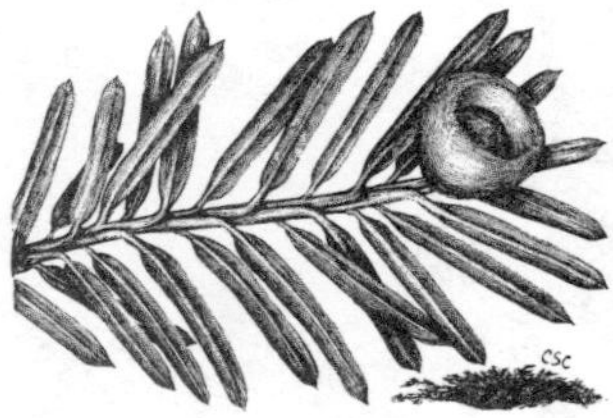
Fig. 46

Ground Hemlock. *Taxus canadensis. Fig. 46.* Leaves flat, yellow-green beneath, with petiole and abrupt pointed tip. Seeds poisonous. Low moist areas, especially climax forest.

PINE FAMILY. Trees, with seeds in woody cones. Leaves alternate or in bundles, mostly evergreen. All are valuable as cover and food for wildlife.

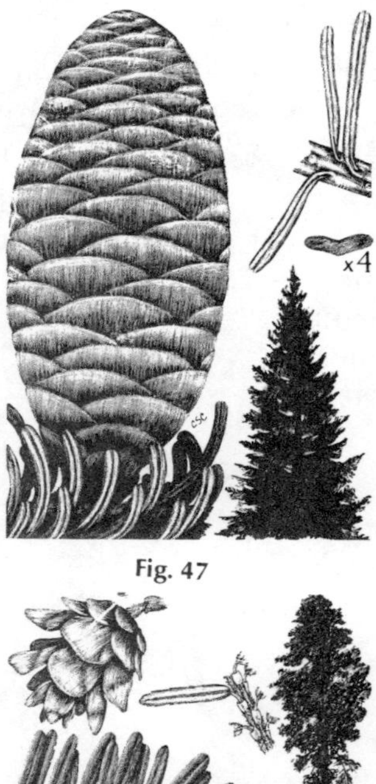

Fig. 47

Balsam Fir. *Abies balsamea. Fig. 47.* Tree to 75′, leaves flattened, whitened beneath, sessile, blunt or notched at tip. Mature cones erect. Bark blistered, not scaly. Woods, shores, and mountains.

Hemlock. *Tsuga canadensis. Figs. 7, 48.* Tree to 90′. Small leaves flattened, whitened beneath, petioled, blunt at tip. Climax tree of moist hardwood forests and rocky slopes. Favored nest site of veery, warblers, northern junco. West to Wisconsin.

Fig. 48

White Spruce. *Picea glauca. Fig. 49.* Tree to 75′. Four-sided leaves curved upward, whitened, sharp-tipped, sessile on peglike projections that persist after leaves drop. Mature cones pendulous. Twigs not pubescent. Bark scaly. Low woods, shores, openings.

Red Spruce. *P. rubens. Fig. 50.* Tree

Fig. 49

Fig. 50

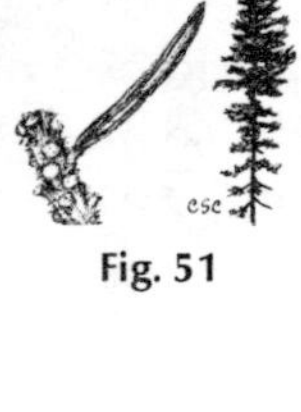
Fig. 51

to 90′. In general similar to white spruce but twigs pubescent, leaves not whitened. Well drained areas; Appalachian Region only.

Black Spruce. *P. mariana. Figs. 2, 51.* Small tree similar to white spruce but less symmetrical, twigs pubescent, cones persistent for several years. Poorly-drained areas, bogs.

Tamarack. *Larix laricina. Fig. 52.* Tree to 60′. The only deciduous conifer in the north. Leaves soft, light green, scattered on young growth, but in tufts on short spurs on older twigs. A soft airy tree, but very hardy, at home in cold swamps and bogs, and on shores.

Fig. 52

White Pine. *Pinus Strobus. Fig. 53.* Tree to 100′. Soft needle leaves five in bundle. Branches in layers; branchlets ascending, tufts of needles reaching upward. Fertile sandy soil, rocks. Pine seeds are principal food of red crossbill.

Red Pine. *P. resinosa. Fig. 54.* Tree to 90′. Long flexible leaves two in a bundle. Branchlets ascending, needles standing out from twig like bristles on an oversized bottle brush. Bark red-tinged, with broad flat plates on older trunks. Dry sandy or rocky soil.

Jack Pine. *P. Banksiana. Figs. 6, 55.* Tree to 60′. Short rigid needles two in a bundle, spreading, curved. Cones curved and ascending, remaining closed many years, persisting on tree 10-15 years. Inhospitable sites such as sand or rock barrens.

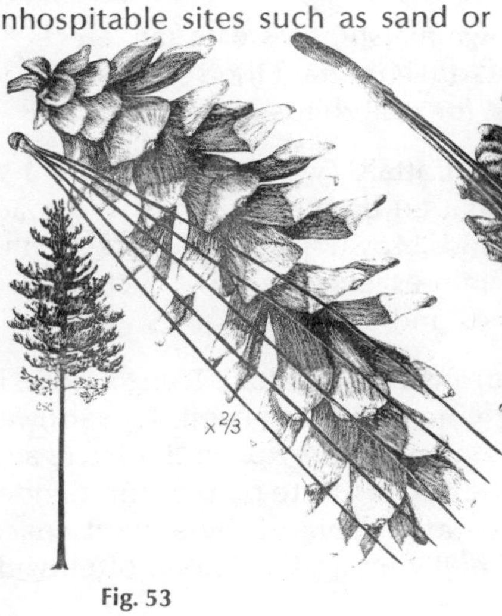

Fig. 53

Fig. 54

Fig. 55

CYPRESS FAMILY. Evergreen trees or shrubs. Seeds in cones or berrylike fruits. Leaves opposite or whorled.

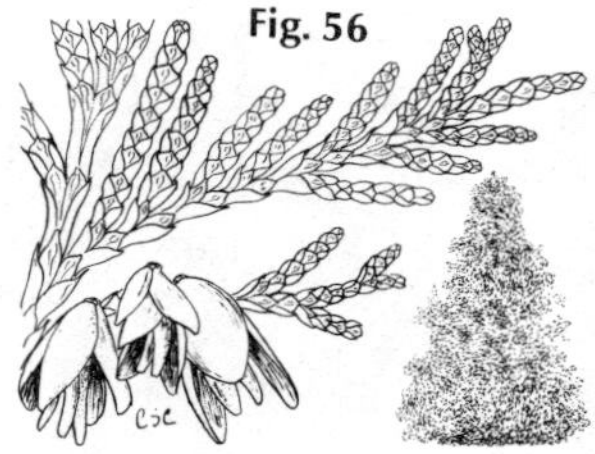
Fig. 56

Fig. 57

Fig. 58

Arbor Vitae. *Thuja occidentalis. Fig. 56.* Tree to 60′. Branchlets in very flat smooth sprays, leaves all tightly appressed. Seeds in small loose cones. Swamps, shores, and rocky islands. Seeds are important food for pine siskin, leaves for deer.

Ground Juniper. *Juniperus communis. Fig. 57.* Shrub 1-5′, forming broad circular patches. Leaves very sharp, spreading, in whorls of three. Fruit blue or black with a bloom, berrylike. Dry sandy or rocky openings, occasionally on dried bogs.

Creeping Juniper. *J. horizontalis. Fig. 58.* Prostrate shrub to 1′ tall, often forming large patches. Leaves sharp-pointed, short and appressed or longer and slightly spreading. Fruit is similar to above. Similar habitats. Plentiful near coast and in Great Lakes area. Both junipers are important wildlife cover, and the fruits are eaten by many birds.

CATTAIL FAMILY. Well known marsh herbs with tall, erect linear leaves. Stalks and roots are important food of muskrat and beaver. Provides cover for waterbirds and fish.

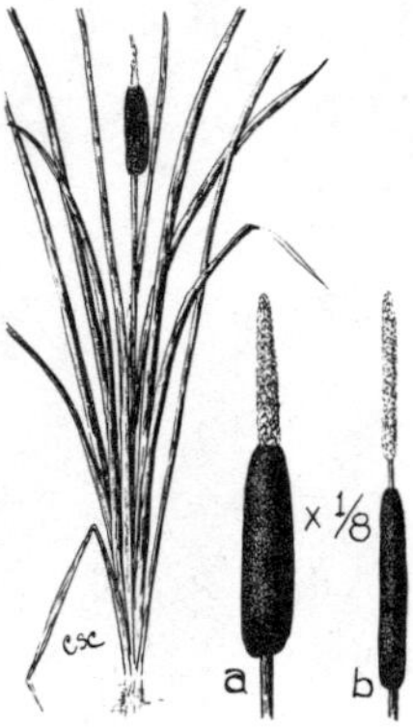

Fig. 59

Common Cattail. *Typha latifolia. Fig. 59.* 3-9′ tall. Leaves flat on both sides, up to 1″ broad. Staminate and brown pistillate parts of the cylindrical inflorescence usually touching (*Fig. 59a*). Marshes and shores.

The Narrow-leaved Cattail, *T. angustifolia*, is similar but more slender in habit. Its narrower leaves are somewhat convex on the back, and the staminate and pistillate parts of the slender inflorescence are separated by a short space (*Fig. 59b*). Chiefly in alkaline water, often with the former species.

BURREED FAMILY. Marsh or water herbs with alternate linear leaves flat or triangular in cross section. Apetalous flowers in globular heads on upperpart of stem. Staminate flowers deciduous; pistillate persistent, forming burlike fruits. Food for muskrat and deer; cover for waterfowl. Mucky-bottomed shallow water.

Green-fruited Burreed. *Sparganium chlorocarpum. Fig. 60.* One of the most common of the nine species in this region.

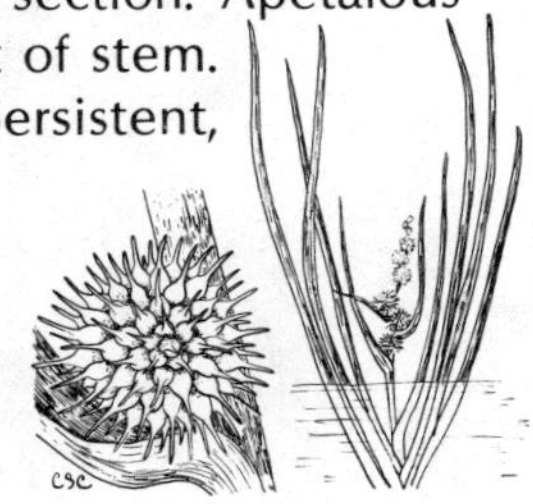

Fig. 60

PONDWEED FAMILY. Common water herbs with jointed leafy stems mostly submersed; some with floating upper leaves and emergent flowers. Ponds, lakes, slow rivers.

Though the genus *Potamogeton* is too complex to treat by species in this book, it is included as a group because it is the dominant plant of many lakes and ponds in the region, and is perhaps more important to aquatic wildlife than any other single group. The submersed parts offer protection to young fish; the seeds, tubers, and whole plants are eaten according to need by fish, water and marsh birds. Without pondweeds, waters would sustain far less wildlife.

Some species with floating leaves and spikes of pink flowers might be confused at first with water smartweed (see p. 55), but the presence of submersed foliage and parallel veins from base to tip of leaf on pondweeds (*Fig. 61*) readily separates them.

Fig. 61

WATER PLANTAIN FAMILY. Aquatic herbs common in the southern part of the region. Flowers on naked stems, usually standing above the basal sheathing leaves; three green sepals, three white or pink-tinged petals.

Arrowhead. *Sagittaria latifolia. Fig. 62.* 4-40″. Leaves are typically arrow-shaped. Flowers and globular fruit heads typically in whorls of three. Petals white; pistils and stamens in separate flowers, on the same or separate plants. Fleshy tubers eaten by waterfowl and muskrat. Marshes and quiet shallow water. Summer.

Fig. 62

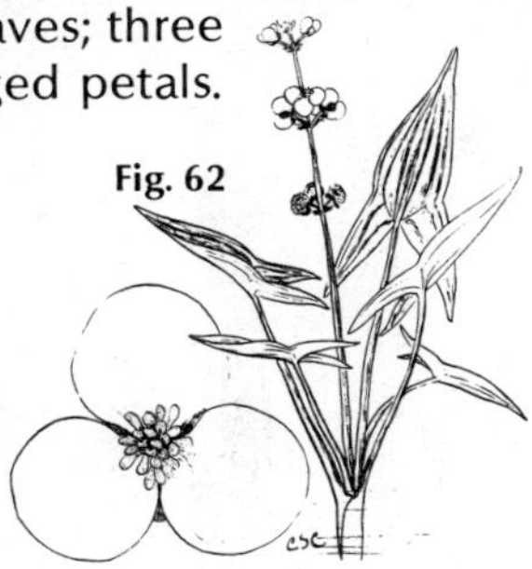

GRASS FAMILY. Familiar plants occurring in all habitats. Cylindric stems usually hollow except at nodes. The leaves 2-ranked, with basal sheaths. Flower parts enclosed between *pairs* of scales on spikelets.

Identification of most of the nearly 200 species in this region requires study of florets under high magnification, so field recognition by the amateur is all but precluded.

Wild Rice. *Zizania aquatica. Fig. 63.* 3-6′. Flowers in a panicle; terminal part composed of stiff upright pistillate florets, lower part of green to reddish staminate florets that hang loosely on very slender pedicels from more or less horizontal branches. Lakes and slow rivers at depth of 1-3′. An easily identified species. Provides food and cover for marsh and water birds. Early summer.

Fig. 63

SEDGE FAMILY. Grasslike plants. As with the grasses, this family is too large and complex to consider in detail in a book of this kind. The beginner may be content to distinguish the two families and learn a few of the forms.

In most sedges the stems are solid or pithy, often triangular. Leaves 3-ranked, with tubular sheaths, blades sometimes reduced or absent. Flower parts in axils of *single* overlapping scales, on spikelets. In all habitats; characteristic of bogs and marshes; plentiful. Important wildlife cover.

The genus *Cyperus*, found mostly south of our region, is shown here to prevent its being confused with certain species of *Scirpus* where ranges overlap. *Cyperus, Fig. 64,* has scales in 2 rows.

Three-way Sedge. *Dulichium arundinaceum. Fig. 65.* 12-36″. Leaves noticeably 3-ranked on hollow cylindric stems. Flower spikes from leaf axils; scales in 2 rows. Mostly southward.

Fig. 64

Fig. 65

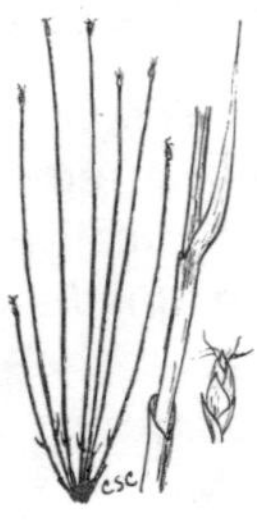

Fig. 66

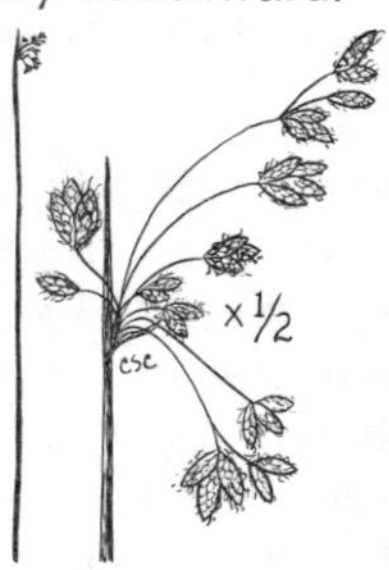

Fig. 67

Fig. 68

Bulrushes, *Scirpus,* have 3 general forms. The first, *Fig. 66,* has solitary terminal spikelets, similar to *Eleocharis,* but in these the topmost leaf sheath bears a short blade. The second, *Fig. 67,* has the inflorescence appearing lateral, with a solitary upright bract growing above it like an extension of the stem, similar to rushes. The third, *Fig. 68*, has a loose, branched terminal inflorescence above several leaflike bracts, similar to *Cyperus,* but in these the spikelet scales are spirally arranged.

Fig. 69

Fig. 70

Fig. 71

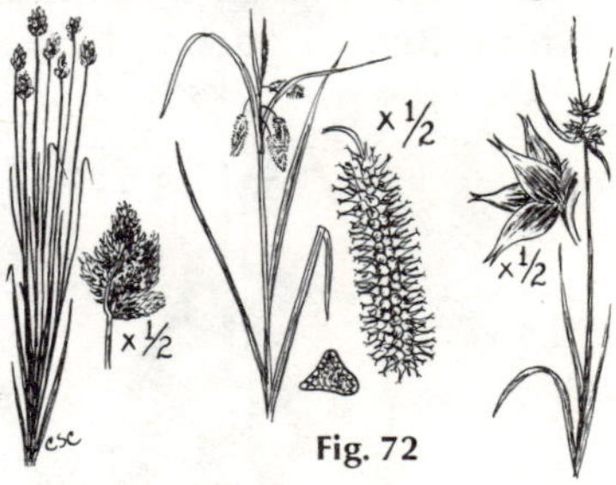

Fig. 72

Spike Rushes. *Eleocharis. Fig. 69.* Solitary terminal spikelet on naked stem. Leaves all reduced to close sheaths at base of stem.

Cottongrasses. *Eriophorum. Fig. 70.* Numerous very long silky bristles surround the fruits, like tufts of cotton.

Beakrushes. *Rhynchospora. Fig. 71.* Spikelets in clusters in axils of upper leaves.

Sedges. *Carex. Fig. 72.* Most difficult of all. In general, stamens and pistils are borne separately, either on different parts of spike or in separate spikes; leaves with a noticeable midrib, stems usually triangular. Over 150 species in this region.

RUSH FAMILY. Herbs resembling bulrushes in habit, but the small stiff flowers and fruits are lilylike in structure. Leaves few and grasslike, or reduced to sheaths.

Rushes. *Juncus. Fig. 73.* 4-36″. Plants smooth; cylindric stems hollow or pithy; inflorescence often appearing lateral, with one or more erect bracts. Water and wet or dry openings.

Fig. 73

Fig. 74

YELLOW-EYED GRASS FAMILY. Represented in this region by a single species, *Xyris montana, Fig. 74.* To 16″. Mats of grasslike basal leaves. Stems topped by solitary heads of yellow 3-petaled flowers. Bogs, shores; Michigan eastward. Summer.

ARUM FAMILY. Herbs with minute flowers crowded on a fleshy spadix surrounded by a large leaflike spathe.

Jack-in-the-pulpit. *Arisaema atrorubens. Fig. 75.* 12-30″. Palmately compound leaves with three leaflets. Spathe green or purple-brown, striped. Shining scarlet berries. Moist woods. Spring.

Wild Calla. *Calla palustris. Fig. 76.* 10-16″. Leaves simple. Spathe white. Berries dark red. Shallow water. Early summer.

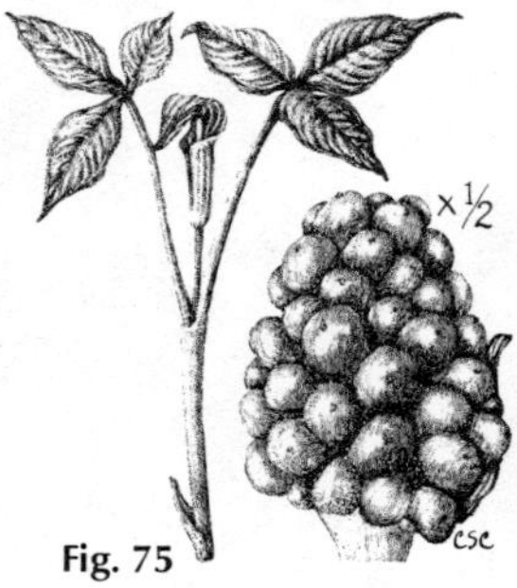

Fig. 75

Fig. 76

Fig. 77

PICKERELWEED FAMILY. Aquatic herbs. 6-parted perianth united into tube at base. Inflorescence above a spathe.

Pickerelweed. *Pontederia cordata. Fig. 77.* 12-36″. One firm arrowhead-shaped leaf on flowering stem. Flowers light violet-blue on a spike; spathe sheathlike. Shallow water. Summer through fall.

LILY FAMILY. Herbs with parallel-veined leaves. Flowers mostly showy; perianth usually of 6 similar divisions.

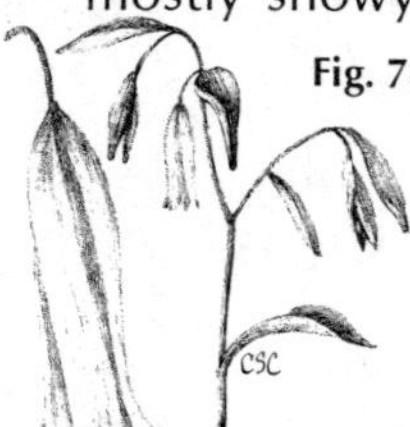

Fig. 78

Bellwort. *Uvularia sessilifolia. Fig. 78.* 6-12″. Leaves with three prominent veins, whitened beneath, tapering at both ends, sessile on smooth forked stems. Flowers pale yellow, pendulous, solitary on slender peduncles from upper leaf axils. Woods. Late spring.

Fig. 79

All three *Līlium* species in this region have showy, spotted orange flowers blooming midsummer; leaves whorled. Open woods, meadows, and roadsides.

Michigan Lily. *L. michiganense. Fig. 79.* 2-6′. Nodding flowers with perianth divisions strongly recurved. Southern Ontario westward.

Canada Lily. *L. canadense. Fig. 80.* 2-6'. Nodding flowers with perianth divisions spreading, not strongly recurved. Occurs more commonly in east.

Fig. 81 Fig. 80

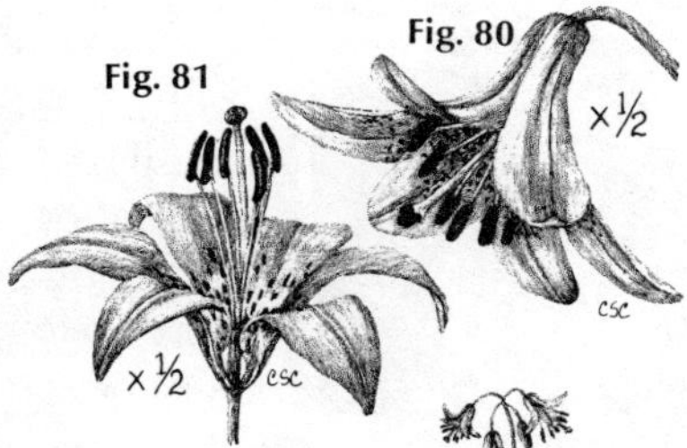

Wood Lily. *L. philadelphicum. Fig. 81.* 8-36". Erect flowers, with perianth divisions spreading. Occurs in sandy soils in the southern part except the Maritime Provinces.

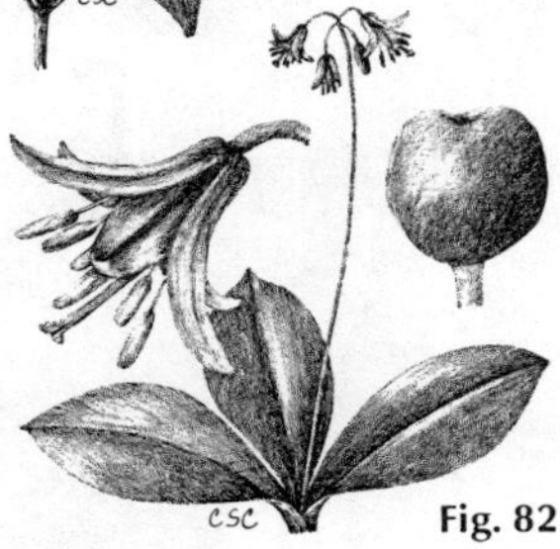

Fig. 82

Clintonia. *Clintonia borealis. Fig. 82.* 10-12". 2-4 smooth light green basal leaves. Flowers pale yellow, nodding in a terminal umbel. Berries Prussian blue. Moist woods. Spring.

Star-flowered False Solomon's Seal. *Smilacina stellata. Fig. 83.* 8-12". Numerous leaves narrow and stiff, alternate, usually folded, sessile or slightly clasping the stem. Flowers white with six-parted corolla and six stamens, in loose raceme. Berries at first green with black stripes, becoming dull dark red. Shores, and in sandy soil in woods, forming colonies. Summer.

Fig. 83 Fig. 84 Fig. 85

Three-leaved False Solomon's Seal. *S. trifolia. Fig. 84.* 2-12". Leaves usually three, narrowed to sessile base. Flowers similar to above. Berries at first brown-speckled, becoming translucent red. Bogs, mossy woods, forming colonies. Early summer.

Wild Lily-of-the-valley. *Maianthemum canadense. Fig. 85.* 2-8". Leaves usually two, nearly sessile, broad and heart-shaped at the base. Flowers white with four-parted corolla and four stamens, in compact raceme. Berries similar to above. Moist woods, openings, rocky areas, forming colonies. Early summer.

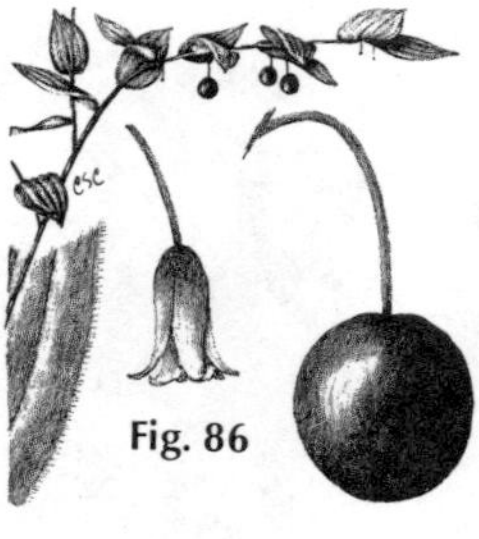

Fig. 86

Twisted-stalk. *Streptopus roseus. Fig. 86*. 8-24″. Leaves sessile on branched or simple pubescent stems; marginal hairs; not whitened beneath. Flowers purple-pink, segments spreading; solitary on slender peduncles, drooping from leaf axils. Fruit a bright red berry. Moist woods. Late spring through early summer.

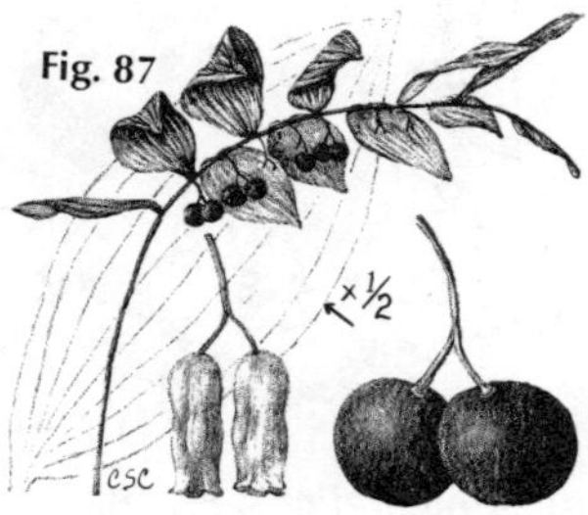

Fig. 87

Solomon's Seal. *Polygonatum pubescens. Fig. 87*. 12-30″. Leaves nearly sessile on simple stems; alternate; the lower surface whitened, finely hairy on veins. Flowers yellow-green, tubular; 1-4 on slender peduncles, drooping from leaf axils. Fruit dark blue berry. Woods, mossy rocks. Late spring through early summer.

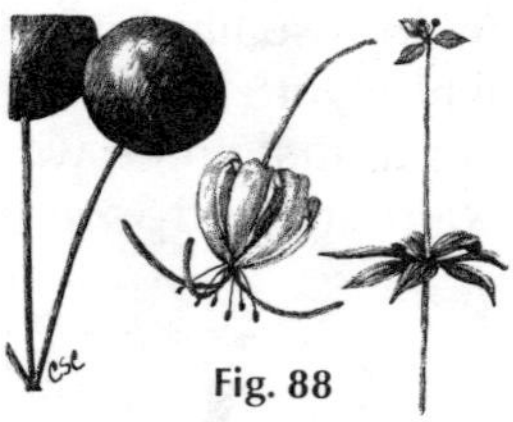

Fig. 88

Indian Cucumber-root. *Medeola virginiana. Fig. 88*. 12-30″. Leaves in two whorls, near middle of stem and at summit. Flowers yellow-green, on slender arching pedicels in a terminal, sessile, few-flowered umbel; pistil with 3 long recurved terracotta styles. Glossy purple berries on red stalks. Rich woods. Spring.

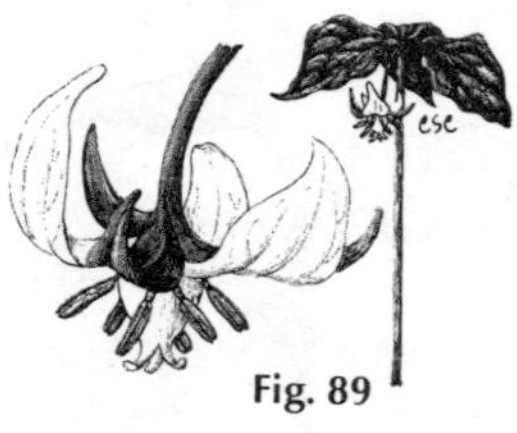

Fig. 89

Nodding Trillium. *Trillium cernuum. Fig. 89*. 8-20″. Leaves three, in a whorl at summit of stem. Flower white, nodding on recurved stalk, often concealed beneath the leaves. Fruit a dark red berry. Moist woods and thickets. Spring.

Fig. 90

IRIS FAMILY. Herbs with flowers from a spathe; mostly blue, showy. Leaves 2-ranked, sword-shaped or grasslike. Fruit a capsule.

Blue Flag. *Iris versicolor. Fig. 90*. 10-30″. Leaves erect, light green. Flowers violet-blue, with a yellow-green (not bright yellow) area at base of sepals. Inner surface of capsule very lustrous. Shallow quiet water, wet meadows. Summer.

ORCHID FAMILY. Herbs with leaves parallel-veined and entire. Flowers asymmetrical, with three sepals and three petals; one petal expanded into a lip that is either flattened or pouchlike. Fruit a capsule.

This family contains some of the most beautiful flowers of the Northwoods, and some of the rarest. Many orchids are characteristic of bogs and mature forests, and some can be found only where their habitat has been undisturbed for centuries. You who use this book are urged to protect them and their habitat wherever you find them, so that others who come after you may experience the delight of discovering them.

The genus *Cypripedium* can be distinguished from all other orchids in this region by the following *combination* of characteristics: one or two (rarely more) terminal flowers; lip a showy inflated sac; leaves two or more, large, prominently ribbed, sheathing the stem; entire plant more or less pubescent.

Small Yellow Lady's Slipper. *C. Calceolus* var. *parviflorum. Fig. 91.* 8-24". Lip yellow, sepals and petals usually madder. Bogs, wet woods, edges of lakes and streams. Spring through early summer. The larger var. *pubescens* occurs southward in moist woodlands.

Fig. 91

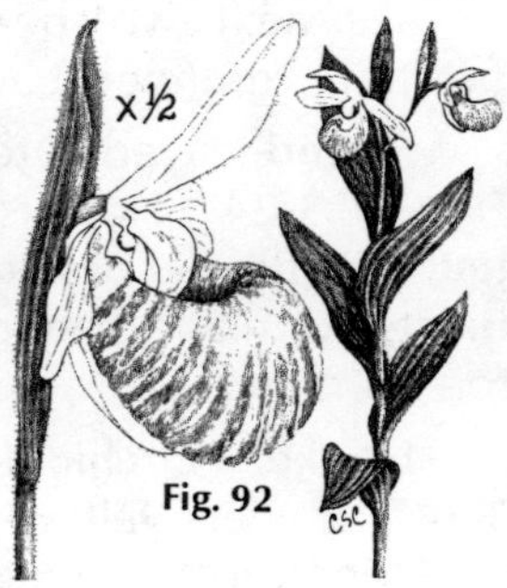

Fig. 92

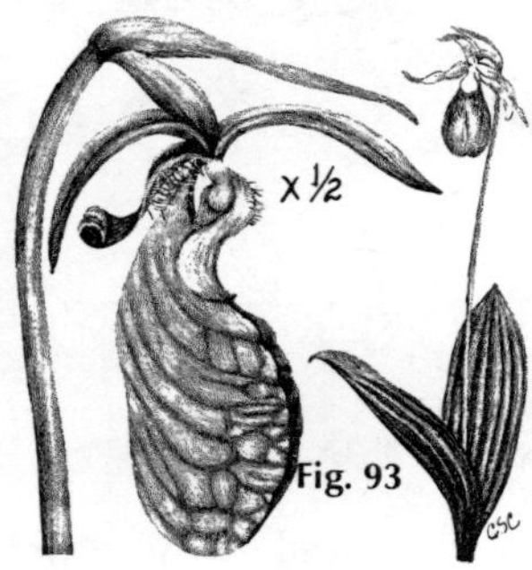

Fig. 93

Showy Lady's Slipper. *C. reginae. Fig. 92.* 14-30". Lip pink with white furrows; sepals and petals white. Neutral or alkaline soil in swamps and mossy uplands. Spring through early summer.

Pink Moccasin Flower. *C. acaule. Fig. 93.* 6-18". Solitary flower; lip pink with prominent crimson veining; sepals green to brown. Two basal leaves. Dry pine woods, or boggy woods among heaths. Spring through early summer.

The rare spring-blooming genus *Calypso*, which has a single terminal flower with a large saccate lip, is a much smaller plant

(3-9″), and differs from *Cypripedium* in the absence of pubescence and in the solitary basal leaf rising from the corm.

With one exception, the genus *Habenaria* differs from other orchid genera in this region in having the lip extended backward into a spur. Flowers on a spike, variable, often inconspicuous.

The exception is the rare genus *Orchis*, which has showy magenta and white flowers, and one or two basal leaves.

The following three species of *Habenaria* have inconspicuous green or white flowers, and leafy stems.

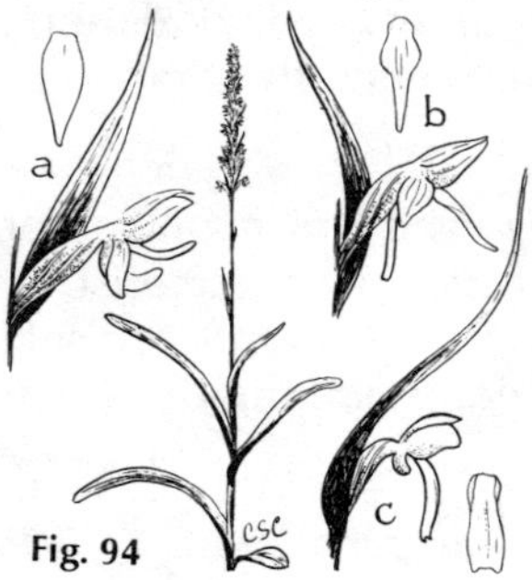

Fig. 94

Northern Green Orchid. *H. hyperborea. Fig. 94a.* 4-30″. Lip lance-shaped. Plant variable in habit. In all habitats in moist to wet soil. Summer.

Tall White Bog Orchid. *H. dilatata. Fig. 94b.* 6-40″. Lip noticeably dilated at base. Similar habitats. Spring through summer.

Long-bracted Green Orchid. *H. viridis* var. *bracteata. Fig. 94c.* 3-24″. Lip toothed at apex. Spur very short. Moist woods, thickets. Spring through summer.

The next two species have a pair of prostrate, rounded basal leaves.

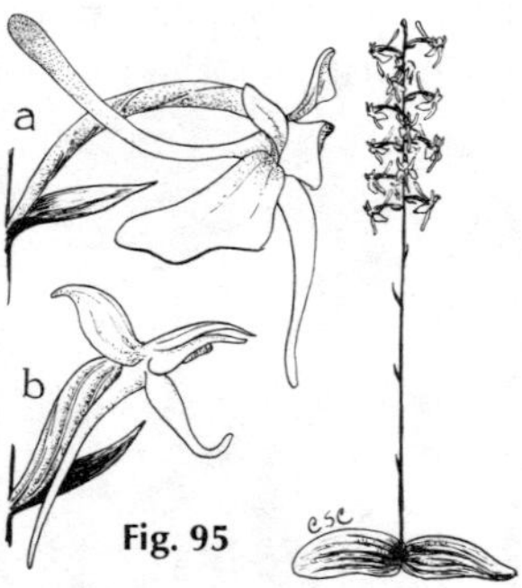

Fig. 95

Round-leaved Orchid. *H. orbiculata. Fig. 95a.* 3-24″. Flowers white with green tint; spur dilated or blunt at tip. Stalk with bracts. A striking plant of moist hardwood forests. Summer.

Hooker's Orchid. *H. Hookeri. Fig. 95b.* 3-14″. Flowers yellow-green; spur taper-pointed. Stalk without bracts. Drier forests. Spring through summer.

The next two species have small greenish flowers, and one leaf.

Fig. 96

Blunt-leaf Orchid. *H. obtusata. Fig. 96a.* 4-12″. Few flowers on a bractless stem. Leaf at base. Moist woods, bogs. Summer.

Green Woodland Orchid. *H. clavellata. Fig. 96b.* 4-16″. Flower twisted so lip and spur are oblique. Leaf partway up the stem. Wetlands, and in water on shores. Early summer.

The next four species have lip variously fringed or divided. Bogs, marshes, glades.

Small Purple Fringed Orchid. *H. psychodes. Fig. 97a.* 8-36″. Lilac pink; lip 3-parted, toothed. Summer.

White Fringed Orchid. *H. blephariglottis. Fig. 97b.* 8-36″. Flowers white, lip fringed, not divided. Summer.

Prairie Orchid. *H. leucophaea. Fig. 97c.* 8-36″. Flowers white, fragrant; lip 3-parted, deeply fringed. Summer.

Ragged Orchid. *H. lacera. Fig. 97d.* 8-30″. Flowers yellow-green to white; lip 3-parted, deeply slashed. Summer.

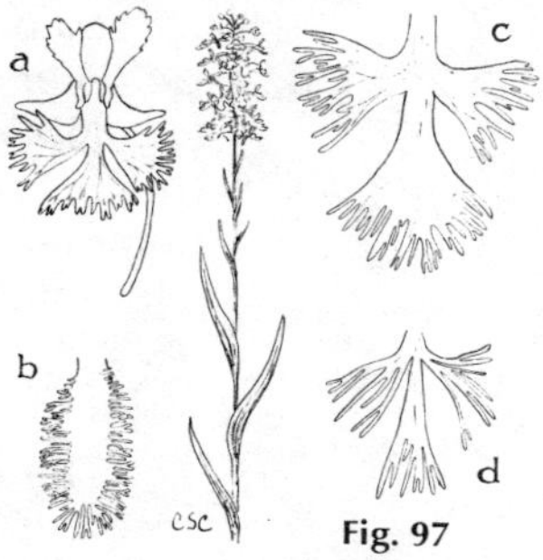

Fig. 97

Rose Pogonia. *Pogonia ophioglossoides. Fig. 98.* 4-16″. Flowers pale crimson-pink, usually single; fringed lip marked with dark crimson, bearing a fleshy yellow beard on median crest. One prominent floral bract. One lance-shaped leaf partway up the stem. Open bogs, often in large colonies. Early summer.

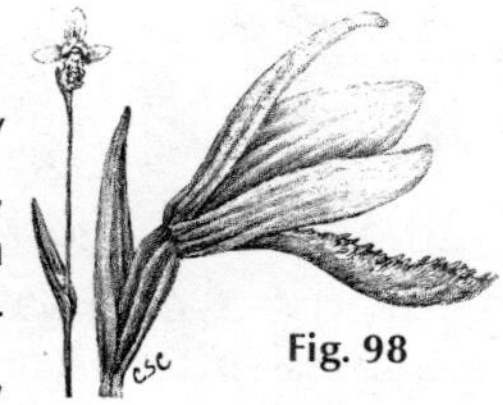
Fig. 98

Grass-pink. *Calopogon pulchellus. Fig. 99.* 6-18″. Flowers magenta-pink, several in a loose raceme, but dropping if not fertilized, so plant may have only 1 or 2 flowers when seen. Lip is in uppermost position, in contrast to lowermost on most orchids; with a yellow beard. One grasslike leaf. Bogs and wet acid openings. Early summer.

Fig. 99

Arethusa. *Arethusa bulbosa. Fig. 100.* 3-12″. Flower bright magenta-pink, usually solitary; ruffled lip marked with deep magenta, and crested with three rows of yellow fringe; two very inconspicuous floral bracts. One linear leaf developing after flower. One of our most beautiful northern orchids, its favored habitat is open sphagnum bogs very near the water's edge. Early summer.

Fig. 100

The genus *Spiranthes* is distinguished by its white flowers in a spiral on a slender spike. Most often found in open moist woods, meadows, and sandy edges of lakes and streams.

Hooded Ladies' Tresses. *S. Romanzoffiana. Fig. 101a.* 3-18″. Sepals and petals form hood over lip. Common in north. Late summer.

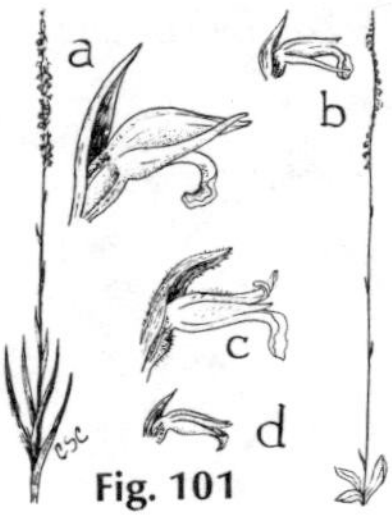

Fig. 101

Three more southern species occur here:

Slender Ladies' Tresses. *S. gracilis. Fig. 101b.* 8-24". Very slender. Lip with green stripe. Summer.

Nodding Ladies' Tresses. *S. cernua. Fig. 101c.* 4-16". Pubescent flowers on a compact spike. Late summer through early fall.

Shining Ladies' Tresses. *S. lucida. Fig. 101d.* 3-12". Shining fleshy leaves. Lip with yellow central stripe. Early summer.

Fig. 102

The genus *Goodyera* is characterized by its rosette of basal leaves (usually net-viened) with a pattern of pale green on dark green.

Dwarf Rattlesnake Plantain. *G. repens* var. *ophioides. Fig. 102.* 4-9". Recognized by its small size and prominently one-sided raceme of white flowers. Moist mossy forests. Summer.

Heart-leaved Twayblade. *Listera cordata. Fig. 103.* 3-10". Inconspicuous plants with small madder purple flowers and pair of heart-shaped leaves midway up stem. Forests and bogs. Early summer.

Plants of the genus *Corallorhiza* are saprophytes lacking green foliage. Stems are succulent, with membranous sheaths.

Early Coralroot. *C. trifida. Fig. 104a.* 2-12". Plants yellow to green. Lip white, sometimes spotted. Forests, bogs. Spring.

Spotted Coralroot. *C. maculata. Fig. 104b.* 6-24". Plants madder to umber. Lip white with purple spots. Forests. Summer.

Striped Coralroot. *C. striata. Fig. 104c.* 6-16". Plants madder. Entire flower whitish-tinged and striped with purple. In dense hardwood forests from Quebec westward. Summer.

Fig. 103

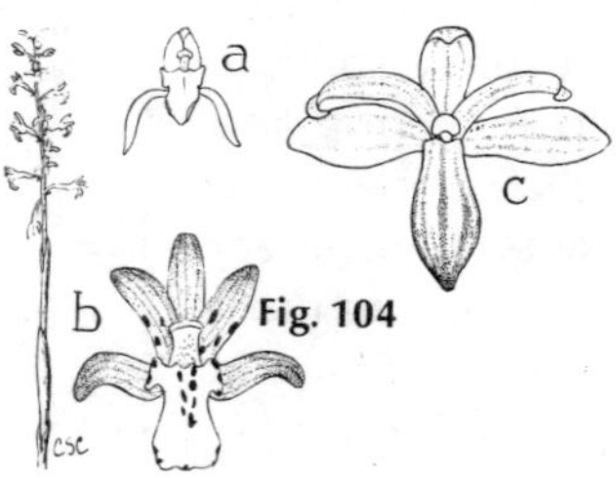

Fig. 104

Fig. 105

Fig. 106

White Adder's-mouth. *Malaxis monophylla* var. *brachypoda. Fig. 105.* 4-9". Flowers greenish, loosely spaced on a wandlike raceme. One sheathing leaf near base. Wet habitats. Early summer.

Yellow Twayblade. *Liparis Loeselii. Fig. 106.* 3-8". Flowers yellow-green in loose raceme; threadlike reflexed petals; broad flat lip. Two shining basal leaves. Cool moist areas. Early summer.

WILLOW FAMILY. Trees or shrubs with simple, unlobed alternate leaves. Flowers in catkins. Seeds bearing tufts of silky hairs. Important food for beaver, hare, deer, moose, and grouse.

Willows. *Salix.* Shrubs or small trees characteristic of wet habitats as far north as the tundra. Leaf buds covered by a single scale. Leaves usually at least twice as long as wide. Many are difficult to identify with certainty, and many are of local distribution. Of the numerous species in this region, the following are common throughout, on shores, in swamps, and wet or dry thickets.

Large Pussy Willow. *S. discolor. Fig. 107.* To 15′. Leaves bright green above, whitened but not pubescent beneath. Twigs smooth, lustrous. Both pussy willows bloom before the leaves.

Small Pussy Willow. *S. humilis. Fig. 108.* To 9′. Leaves dull gray-green, more or less pubescent above; gray, often densely pubescent beneath. Twigs dull or ashy pubescent.

Balsam Willow. *S. pyrifolia. Fig. 109.* To 15′. Leaves with a pungent balsamic fragrance; whitened on the lower surface. Twigs smooth and shining. This and the following two species bloom after the leaves develop.

Fig. 107

Fig. 108

Fig. 109

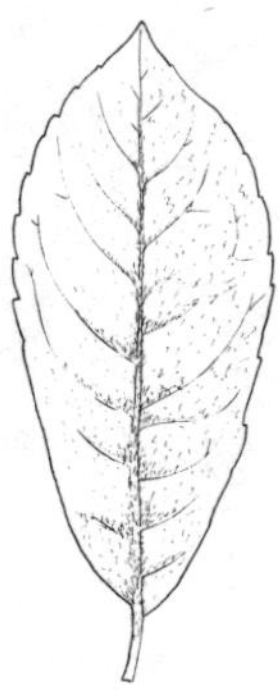
Fig. 110

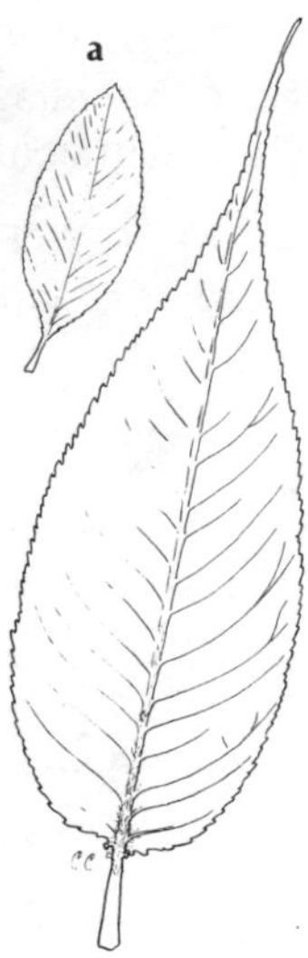

Fig. 111

Long-beaked Willow. *S. Bebbiana. Fig. 110.* To 15′. Leaves dull green above; pale and pubescent beneath, with prominent veins. Twigs woolly; older bark furrowed.

Shining Willow. *S. lucida. Fig. 111.* To 18′. Mature leaves large, lustrous green on both sides, with long tapering tips. Immature leaves very different (*Fig. 111a*). Twigs smooth, shining.

Poplars. *Populus.* Trees with the bark on branches and young trunks smooth ochreous, greenish or nearly-white, marked with horizontal ridges and warts, becoming dark and furrowed on old trunks. Leaves about as wide as long. Buds with several scales.

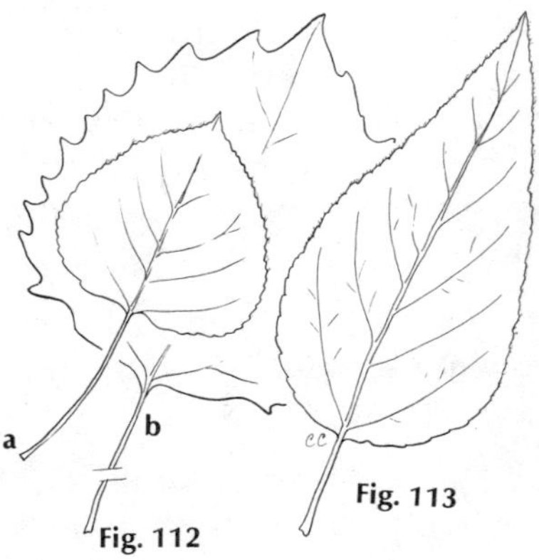

Fig. 112

Fig. 113

Quaking Aspen. *P. tremuloides. Fig. 112a.* To 45′. Bark green to nearly-white. Common in cutover and burned areas, and in all lowland habitats.

Large-toothed Aspen. *P. grandidentata. Fig. 112b.* Similar to preceding species, but note different leaf. Silvery tomentose in spring. Shores and moist sandy soil, in southern part of region.

Balsam Poplar. *P. balsamifera. Fig. 113.* To 70′. Leaves pale beneath; veins umber, giving a bronze tinge to the foliage. Bark ochreous to green-gray. Large pointed buds fragrant with balsam resin. Swamps and shores.

WAX MYRTLE FAMILY. Shrubs. Leaves alternate, spicy fragrant, with resinous dots. Flowers in short catkins.

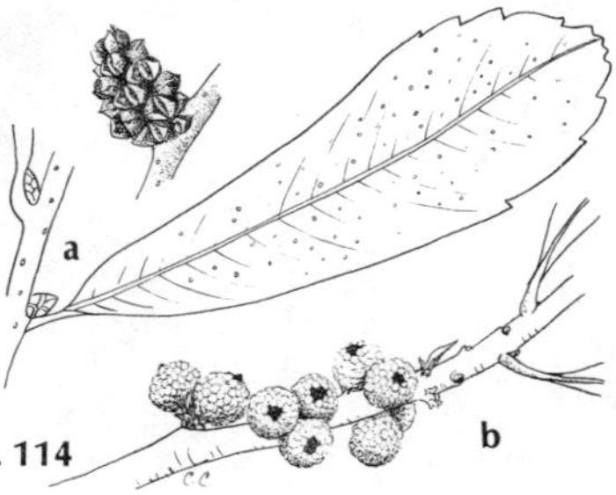

Fig. 114

Sweet Gale. *Myrica Gale. Fig. 114a.* 2-6′. Leaves toothed at the apex. Fruits conelike. Common on shores in shallow water.

Bayberry, *M. pensylvanica*, has similar but larger leaves than sweet gale. Fruits wax-covered, nutlike, solitary or in small clusters below the leaves (*Fig. 114b*). Fruits important food of tree swallow. Dry hills, to marshes and shores, in the east.

Sweet Fern. *Comptonia peregrina. Fig. 115.* 1-2′. Fruits burlike. Characteristic of dry sterile openings and pine barrens in south and west, covering large areas. Sometimes browsed by deer.

Fig. 115

HAZEL FAMILY. Trees or shrubs. Alternate leaves with sharp-toothed margins. Flowers in catkins.

Beaked Hazel. *Corylus cornuta. Fig. 116.* Shrub 3-6′. Edible nut enclosed in a bristly involucre that is prolonged into a tubular beak. Twigs not glandular-pubescent, or scarcely so. Open woods, edges.

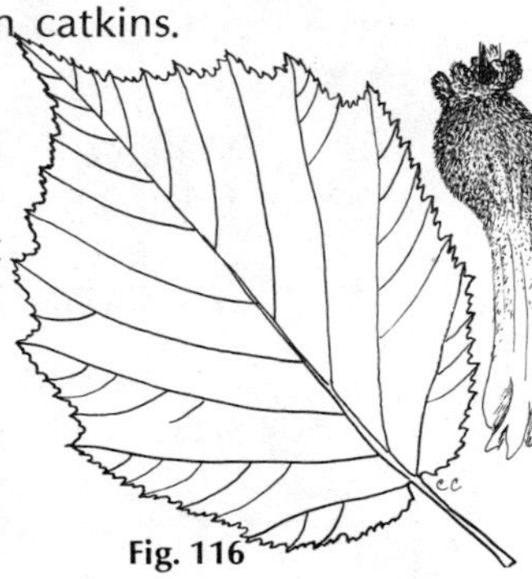
Fig. 116

American Hazel, *C. americana*, occurs south and west in this region, has glandular-pubescent twigs, and nut enclosed in leaflike bracts.

Hazels provide cover and food for wildlife, and illumine the forest understory in autumn with their glowing golden leaves.

Ironwood. *Ostrya virginiana. Fig. 117.* 20-30′. Thin leaves dull above, downy beneath. Bark gray-brown, thin, scaly. Small nuts enclosed in pubescent papery bladders. Upland woods and gravelly slopes. Nuts eaten by mice and squirrels.

Yellow Birch. *Betula lutea. Fig. 118.* 60-80′. Bark shining yellow-gray, detaching in thin curled strips and shreds; twigs wintergreen-flavored. All birches have small winged seeds in conelike catkins. Forests.

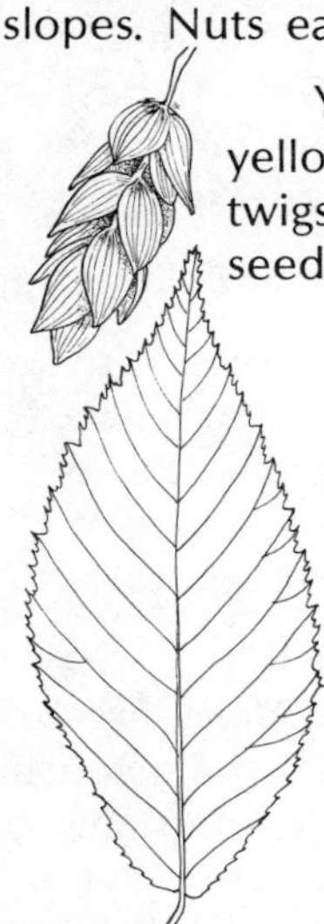
Fig. 117

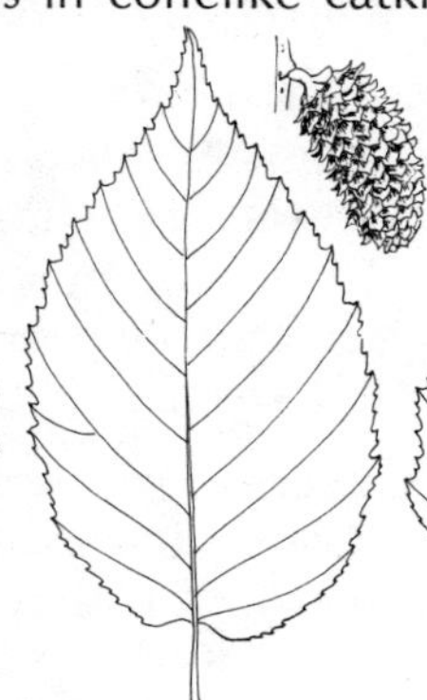
Fig. 118

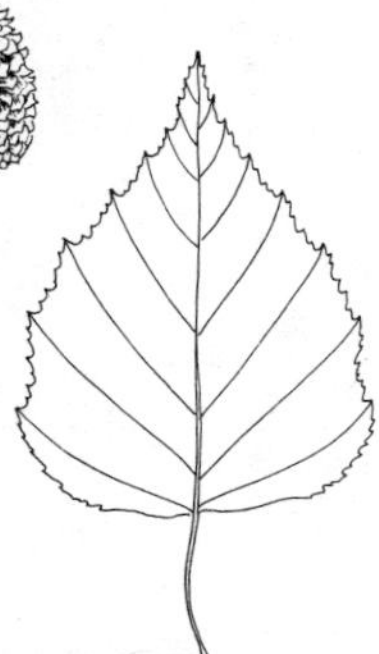
Fig. 119

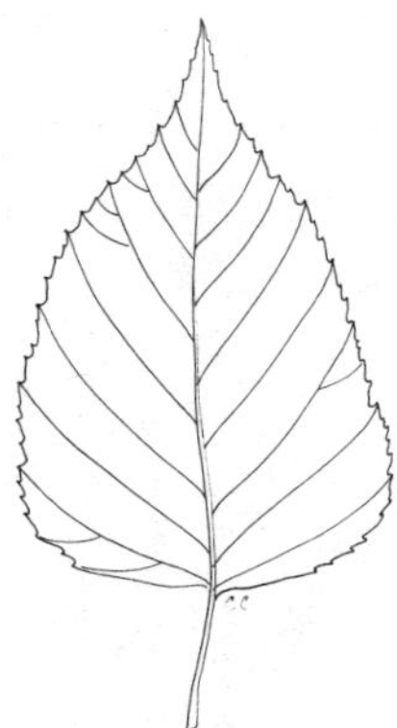
Fig. 120

Gray Birch. *B. populifolia. Fig. 119.* 20-30′. Bark chalky white, not detaching in layers. Burned and sterile areas, edges, abandoned farms; in the east.

Paper Birch. *B. papyrifera. Fig. 120.* 50-75′. Bark satiny-white or pink-tinged, separating into wide papery layers. (Warning: If you peel off the white bark, a permanent unsightly black callous will disfigure the tree.) Common in all habitats.

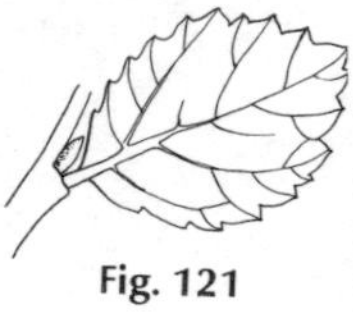

Fig. 121

Swamp Birch. *B. pumila. Fig. 121.* Shrub to 10′. Variable species, plentiful throughout, often forming colonies in bogs and swamps. The smaller Dwarf Birch, *B. glandulosa*, found on mountains in the east, has similar leaves, but glandular twigs.

Fig. 122

All birches provide valuable winter food for wildlife.

Green Alder. *Alnus crispa. Fig. 122.* Shrub to 9′. Leaves green on both sides, sticky if held between thumb and fingertip; margins with fine crowded teeth. Seeds in woody cones. Shores and mountain slopes.

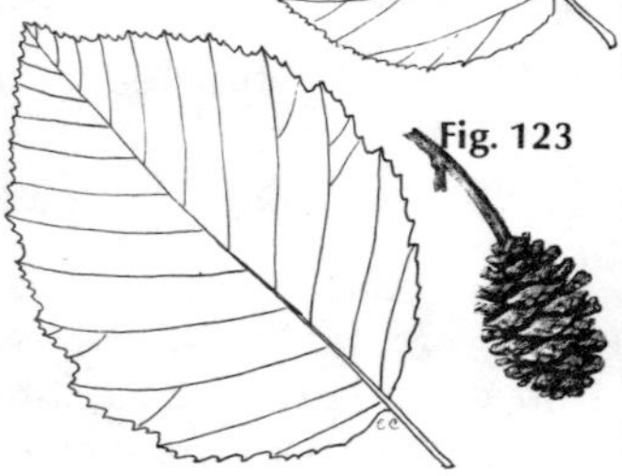

Fig. 123

Speckled Alder. *A. rugosa. Fig. 123.* Shrub or small tree. Leaves usually with lower surface whitened, and with prominent tawny pubescent veins and ladderlike cross veins. Seeds as above. Shores, swamps.

Alders provide good wildlife cover.

Fig. 125

Fig. 124

BEECH FAMILY. Trees with alternate leaves. Staminate flowers in heads or catkins. Fruit a nut. Important food of rodents, raccoon, bear, jays, grackle, and nuthatch.

Beech. *Fagus grandifolia. Fig. 124.* To 75′ or more. Note characteristic leaf margin, and slender buds. Two or more three-sided nuts enclosed in a bristly bur. Bark ashy gray, very smooth. Upland forests, east, from central Wisconsin.

Northern Red Oak. *Quercus rubra*, var. *borealis. Fig. 125.* To 70′. Leaves with bristle-tipped lobes. Acorn cup shallow with close-fitting scales. Hardwood forests and pine barrens.

ELM FAMILY. Trees with simple, alternate leaves unsymmetrical at the base.

Fig. 126

American Elm. *Ulmus americana. Fig. 126.* To 100′. Clusters of small flowers in very early spring before leaves. Fruits in late spring, winged, smooth on face, fringed on margin. Seeds and buds eaten by birds and squirrels. Lowland, streambanks, throughout.

Slippery Elm, *U. rubra*, and Rock Elm, *U. Thomasi*, may be found south and west in this region; the former distinguished by very harsh leaf surface, hairy buds and twigs, and smooth circular fruits; the latter by corky branches and hairy elliptic fruits.

BUCKWHEAT FAMILY. Herbs with simple alternate leaves and sheathing stipules at swollen nodes of stem. Large family, including docks, smartweeds, and knotweeds. Species variable, and hybridization makes identification difficult. Since most are classed as weeds, or are inconspicuous, only the attractive water smartweed is described here.

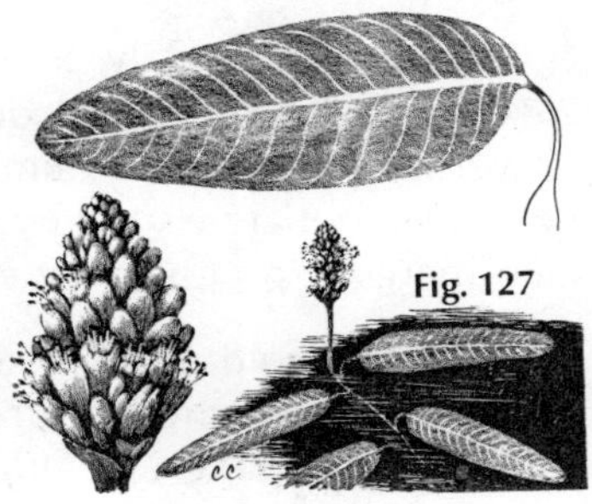

Fig. 127

Water Smartweed. *Polygonum amphibium* var. *stipulaceum. Fig. 127.* Aquatic herb with floating leaves feather-veined. (Note pondweed, p. 41, has floating leaves with longitudinal veins.) Flowers pink, in spikes to 1½″ long. Seeds important food for waterfowl. Summer.

PURSLANE FAMILY. Low herbs with succulent leaves. Flowers with five petals (sometimes lacking), and two sepals. Cross fertilized by bees and butterflies.

Fig. 128

Spring Beauty. *Claytonia caroliniana. Fig. 128.* 6-12″. Leaves 1-4″, oval to broad, lance-shaped. Showy flowers white or pink with darker veins, loosely set on upright racemes. Fruit inconspicuous in pendulous calyx. Plants ephemeral, dying down soon after bloom. Rich open woods. Early spring.

WATER LILY FAMILY. Aquatic perennial herbs with floating leaves and solitary flowers. Fertilized by bees, beetles, and aquatic insects. All parts eaten by various wildlife.

Pond Lily. *Nuphar variegatum. Fig. 129.* Leaves 3-12" long, broadly ovate. Flowers to 3" across, with large, firm, golden-yellow sepals, reddish inside at base; small stamenlike petals; numerous recurving stamens; and large yellow or greenish disklike stigma. Ponds, bays, slow streams throughout. Summer.

Small-leaved Pond Lily, *N. microphyllum*, with leaf blades 1-4" long and flowers about 1½", is less abundant throughout.

N. rubrodiscum, a hybrid of these two, may also occur.

Fig. 129

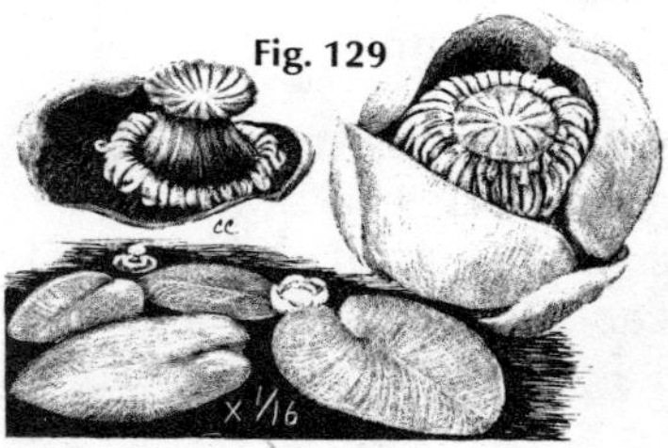

Fig. 130

Fig. 131

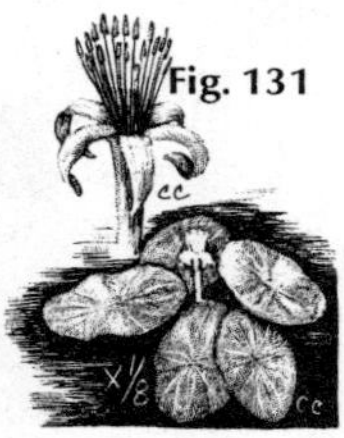

Fragrant Water Lily. *Nymphaea odorata. Fig. 130.* Orbicular leaves 2-10" broad, usually red or purple beneath. Very fragrant white flowers 2-6" across, with luminous golden stamens. Flowers produce no nectar, but are visited by pollen-seeking beetles and bees. Quiet lake margins, ponds, slow streams throughout. Summer.

Water Shield. *Brasenia Schreberi. Fig. 131.* Leaves elliptic, 2-4" long, petiole attached centrally to gelatinous lower surface. Flower dull purple, scarcely 1" high. Bogs, ponds, and slow streams in southern part of region. Summer.

CROWFOOT FAMILY. In this region, herbs or vines with alternate or basal leaves. Regular flowers in which all parts are free and distinct (i.e., not fused); stamens numerous in most species. Generally fertilized by small bees, beelike flies, and butterflies.

Fig. 132

White Water Crowfoot. *Ranunculus trichophyllus. Fig. 132.* Leaves submersed, divided above distinct petioles into many limp threadlike divisions, collapsing out of water. White emergent flowers.

Ponds, slow streams, quiet lakes throughout. Summer.

Another species, *R. subrigidus*, similar in general appearance, has stiffer leaves and shorter petioles.

Creeping Spearwort. *R. reptans. Fig. 133.* Amphibious shore plant, producing roots and a tuft of leaves at each stem node. Leaves threadlike or narrow. Flowers solitary from nodes, bright glossy yellow. Damp shores throughout. Summer.

Fig. 133

In addition to three less common yellow amphibious crowfoots, nine species of terrestrial crowfoots and buttercups may occur here, some rare or inconspicuous, others familiar buttercups of field or lowland, with shiny yellow petals characteristic of this group.

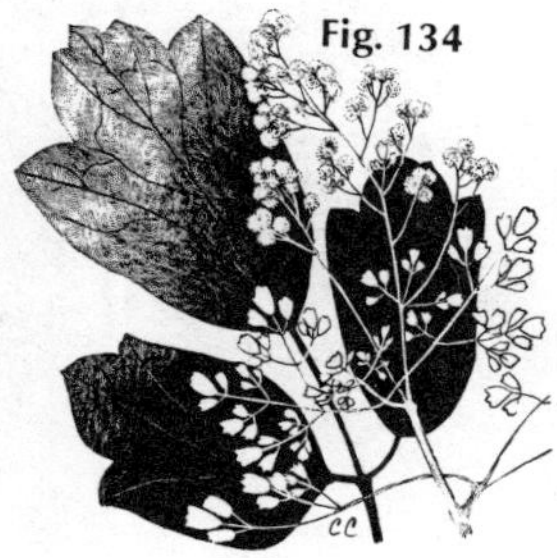
Fig. 134

Tall Meadow Rue. *Thalictrum polygamum. Fig. 134.* Perennial herbs, 2-8′ tall. Alternate, doubly compound leaves mostly three-parted. Flowers without petals, in large compound clusters, conspicuous for many pompons of threadlike stamens and pinkish stipes. Wet meadows and shores throughout. Summer.

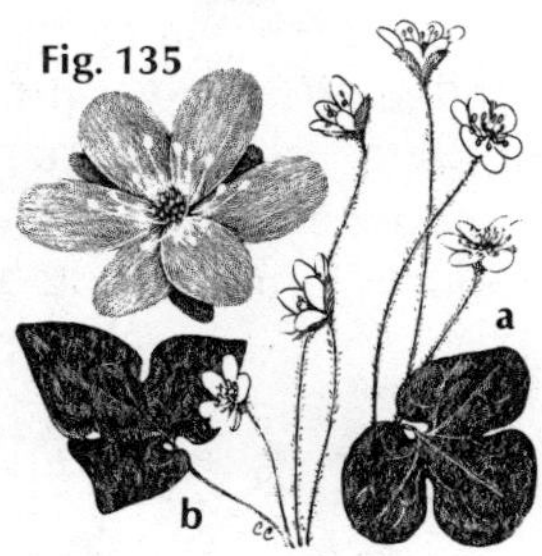

Fig. 135

Hepatica. *Hepatica americana* and *H. acutiloba. Fig. 135.* Perennial herbs 4-6″ tall, with long-petioled three-lobed basal leaves persisting over winter. The former species has leaf lobes rounded *(a)*; the latter, acute *(b)*. Flowers without petals but with attractive purple, pink, or white petallike sepals above three sepallike bracts. Flower stems and young petioles with soft hairs. Dry or moist upland woods. Early spring before the leaves.

Fig. 136

Canada Anemone. *Anemone canadensis. Fig. 136.* Perennial herbs 1-2′ tall. Stem leaves sessile, two to several in a whorl below the flower. Flower showy, with white petallike sepals and golden stamens. Shores, wet meadows. Late spring.

The smaller Wood Anemone, *A. quinquefolia*, with petiolate stem leaves, occurs at woods' edges farther south.

Virgin's-bower. *Clematis virginiana. Fig. 137.* Vine to 9′ long. Opposite, coarse-toothed, 3-parted veiny leaves. Flowers in panicles from leaf axils, white, with four petallike sepals and many white stamens and pistils. Pistils lengthen into plumy heads of fruit. Moist edges in hardwood area. Late summer.

Purple or Mountain Clematis. *C. verticillaris. Fig. 138.* Similar vine to 6′ long. Large solitary flowers with pendulous purple sepals over shorter modified white petallike outer stamens. Rocky woods in west, and down the Appalachians. Late spring.

Fig. 137

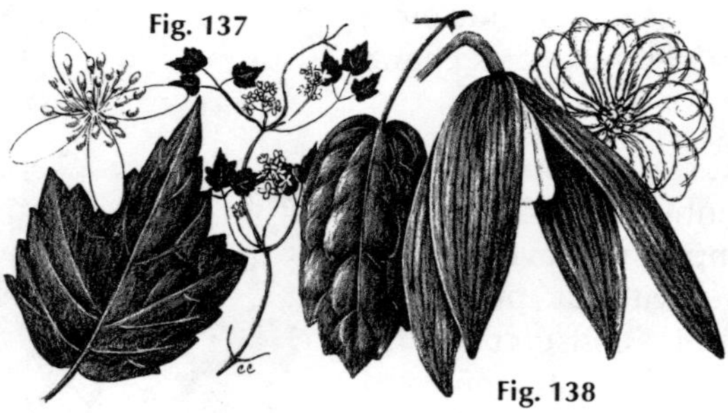

Fig. 138

Fig. 139

Marsh Marigold. *Caltha palustris. Fig. 139.* Perennial herb 8-24″ tall, with broad soft-textured leaves and hollow stems. Flowers with 5-9 glossy golden petallike sepals. Fertilized mainly by the beautiful yellow syrphid flies. Marshes, wet meadows, roadside ditches, shores, throughout. Very early spring.

Fig. 140

Goldthread. *Coptis groenlandica. Fig. 140.* Perennial herb 3-6″ tall, named for its golden threadlike roots. Leaves basal on long petioles, shiny, 3-parted, evergreen. Flower white, solitary, with 5-7 deciduous petallike sepals; and equal number of cup-tipped yellow nectaries which are modified petals; and 3-5 distinct green pistils. Fertilized by fungus gnats and beetles. Moist mossy woods and bogs, throughout. Late spring through early summer.

Wild Columbine. *Aquilegia canadensis. Fig. 141.* A familiar perennial wildflower 1-3′ tall, with alternate compound leaves.

Nodding flowers on long stems from leaf axils; petals yellow shading to scarlet on spurs. Flower stems later turn up to hold fruits erect. Pollinated by moths and butterflies. Woods' edges and moist openings, southern part. Late spring through early summer.

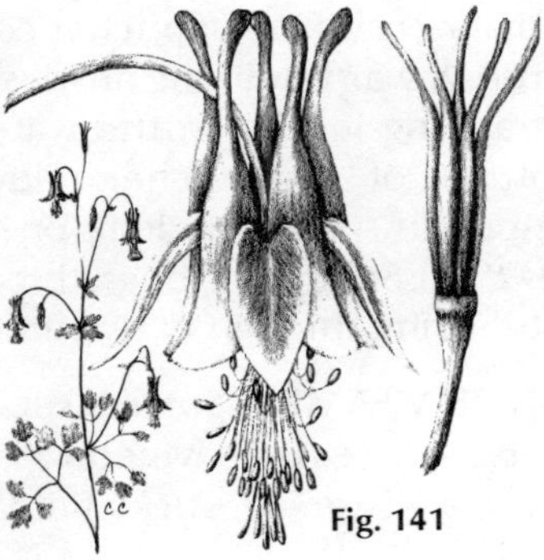

Fig. 141

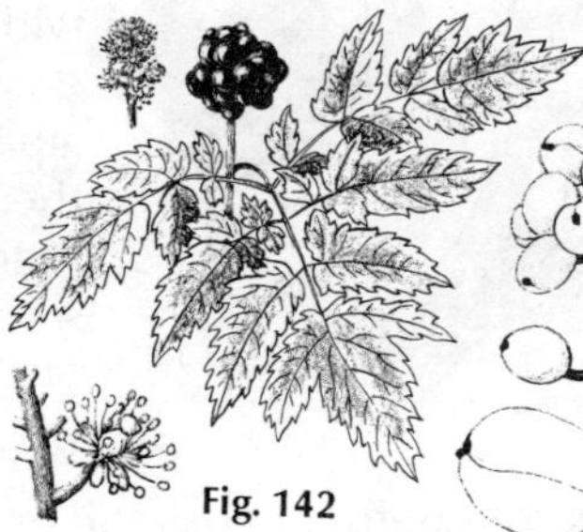

Fig. 142

Fig. 143

Red Baneberry. *Actea rubra. Fig. 142.* Perennial herb 1-2′ tall. Leaves doubly or triply compound, sharp-toothed. Flowers in a terminal cluster, entirely white, with 4-10 narrow petals and many stamens. Fruit a dense cluster of bright red shining berries; poisonous. Woods and thickets, throughout. Late spring; fruit late summer.

White Baneberry. *A. alba. Fig. 143.* Very similar to above, but with leaflets more sharply-toothed and deeply-cut. Fruit, on thick (usually red) stems, is white with a dark purple spot on each berry. Similar habitats and seasons as red baneberry, but more southerly.

FUMITORY FAMILY. Sometimes classed as a subfamily of the Poppy Family. Herbs with alternate, finely-dissected compound leaves, and bilateral compressed flowers with the corolla closed at the base and (with one exception) drawn back into a spur.

Fig. 144

Pale Corydalis. *Corydalis sempervirens. Fig. 144.* Biennial, 8-24″ tall. Leaves pale green, delicate, usually 3-parted. Flowers in a raceme, pale crimson or magenta-pink, with yellow tips. Rocky areas and clearings, throughout. Summer.

The yellow-flowered Golden Corydalis, *C. aurea*, also occurs in rocky areas and open woods west of the Maritimes.

PITCHER PLANT FAMILY. Insectivorous bog plants with pitcher-shaped hollow leaves.

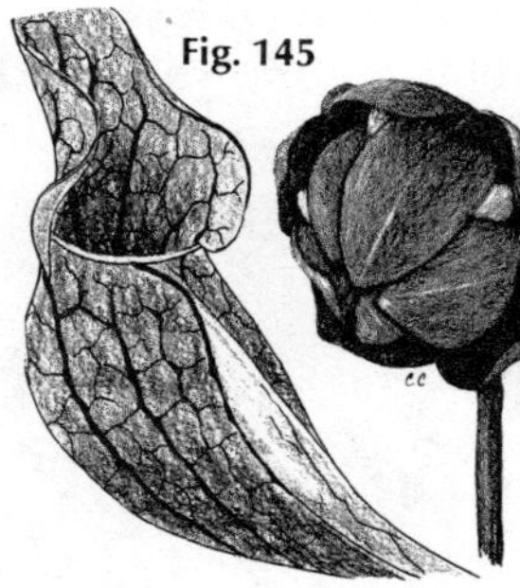
Fig. 145

Pitcher Plant. *Sarracenia purpurea. Fig. 145.* Clustered leaves 4-10″ long, veined with red; inner surface of pitcher covered with downward-pointing bristles that aid in trapping insects in the water in the bottom of the pitcher. Flowers reddish-purple, solitary, nodding on stout stems 1-2′ tall. Sphagnum bogs, throughout. Late spring through early summer.

SUNDEW FAMILY. Small insectivorous herbs of bogs and peaty acid soil. Leaves covered with red gland-tipped hairs that secrete a glistening, sticky fluid.

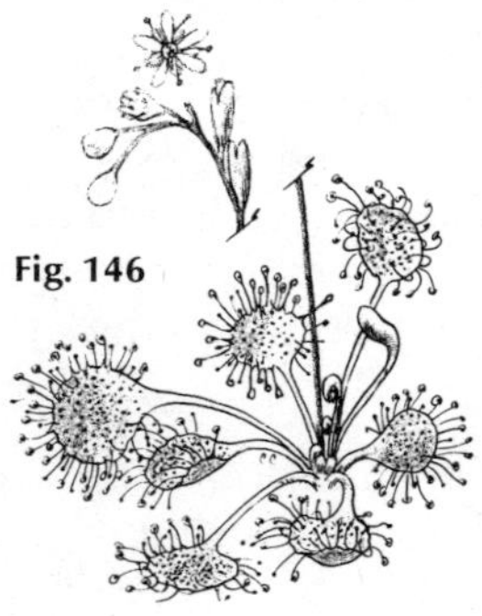
Fig. 146

Round-leaved Sundew. *Drosera rotundifolia. Fig. 146.* Leaves in a basal tuft. The glistening glands attract and trap insects; then the hairs and finally the leaf blade itself folds over the insect until it is digested. Flowers on slender stems 2-12″ tall, white in a one-sided raceme, opening one at a time and only in the sun. Throughout. Summer.

Three other species are less common.

SAXIFRAGE FAMILY. Shrubs or perennial herbs with alternate or opposite leaves, usually without stipules. The flowers variable, mostly 5-parted, perfect, and regular.

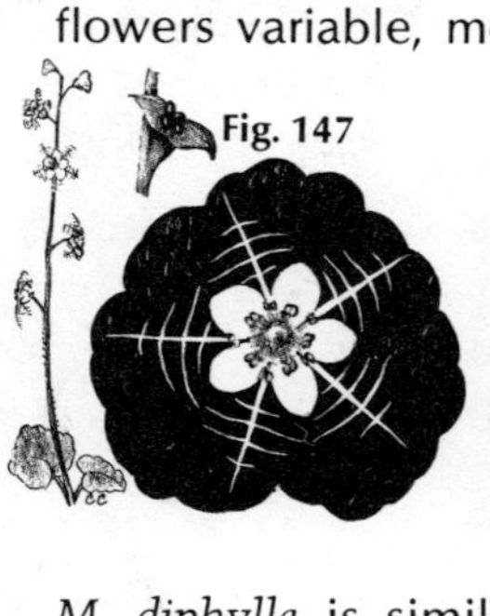
Fig. 147

Miterwort. *Mitella nuda. Fig. 147.* Small herb 4-8″ tall. Leaves basal, from creeping stolons, bright green with stiff hairs; there may also be one very small leaf low on the flower stem. Flowers pale greenish-yellow with fringed petals, on a loosely-flowered spike. Cool mossy woods and swamps throughout. Summer.

M. diphylla is similar to above, but is 8-12″ tall, with white flowers smaller and more closely set on spike; and with two small opposite leaves about halfway up the flowering stem. South and west in rich rocky woods. Spring.

The white feathery spikes of Foamflower, *Tiarella cordifolia*, 6-12″ tall, may be seen in rich woods south and east. Its large lobed maplelike basal leaves are sharp-toothed, hairy, and occasionally mottled. Spring through early summer.

Ribes, gooseberries and currants, are low shrubs with lobed leaves, occurring in moist woods, swamps, and openings. Since they are alternate hosts of the introduced blister rust of white pine, they have been the object of eradication programs, hence are not as abundant in pine areas as they once were. Fruit in summer.

Gooseberries have stiff spines at the leaf nodes (sometimes with bristles on internodes of young stems); flower stalks with 1-5 flowers; stem of individual flower not jointed beneath the ovary, this stem persistent on the edible berry.

Smooth Gooseberry. *R. hirtellum. Fig. 148a.* Ovary and fruit smooth, canes rarely bristly except on very young stems. Leaves without glands. Throughout.

Northern G., *R. oxycanthoides,* also has smooth fruit, but has bristly canes, and leaves with glands. West from Northern Michigan.

Prickly G., *R. cynosbati, Fig. 148b,* has smooth internodes, but ovary and fruit with long stiff prickles. South and west.

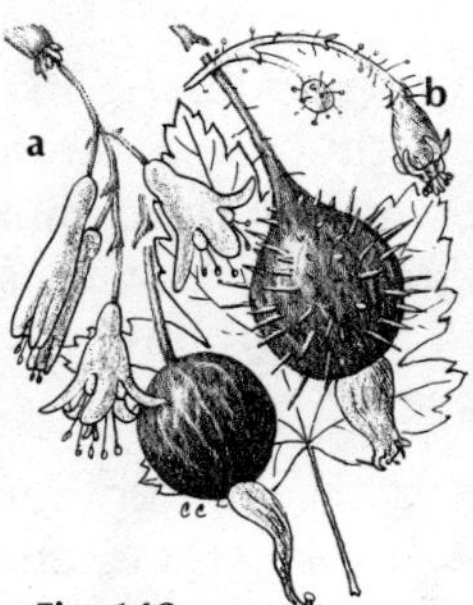

Fig. 148

Fig. 149

Currants have thornless canes (except *R. lacustre*); flowers in racemes of many flowers; stem of individual flower jointed beneath the ovary, the edible berry dropping free at this joint.

Bristly Black Currant. *R. lacustre. Fig. 149a.* Canes with bristles and prickles. Flower stems and black fruits with gland-tipped bristles; bruised shrub has skunklike odor. Throughout.

Skunk Currant. *R. glandulosum. Fig. 149b.* Leaves without resinous dots. Flowers whitish to rosy; flowering stems and red to yellow fruits covered with gland-tipped hairs. Bruised shrub has skunklike odor. Throughout.

Red Currant. *R. triste. Fig. 149c.* Reclining shrub with flowers on old wood, below current year's shoots. Leaves without resinous dots. Flowers smoky to purplish, on glandular stems. Smooth fruits small and hard. Throughout.

R. hudsonianum. Ovaries, fruit, and lower surface of leaves with resin dots. Flowers white, fruit black. West from Quebec.

Wild Black Currant. *R. americanum. Fig. 149d.* Leaves and fruit with resinous dots; flowers yellowish, fruit black. Throughout except easternmost Maritime Provinces.

ROSE FAMILY. Trees, shrubs, or herbs; leaves alternate, mostly with stipules; flowers regular, 5-parted with many stamens and 1-many pistils; rich in pollen and nectar, cross-pollinated mainly by bees.

Fig. 150

Ninebark. *Physocarpus opulifolius. Fig. 150.* Shrub to 9′. White flowers in hemispherical clusters, resembling large bridal wreath. Fruit in clusters of purple-tinged brown pods that persist into winter. Rocky areas and river banks, west from Quebec. Spring.

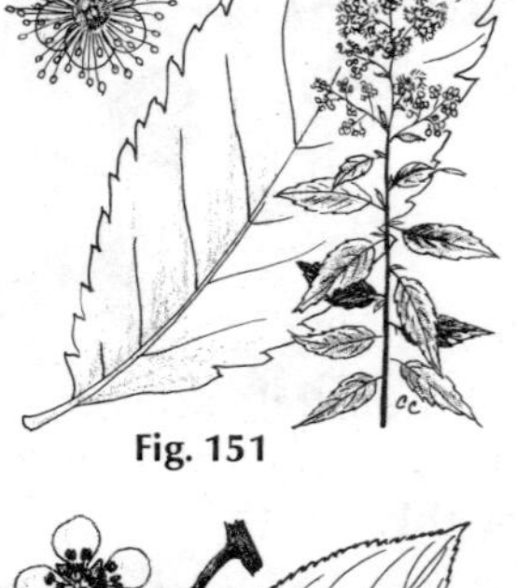

Fig. 151

Meadowsweet. *Spirea latifolia. Fig. 151.* Shrub to 5′. Leaves with coarse teeth; stems red-brown. Flowers white to pink with pink stamens, in long ovoid clusters. Visited by butterflies. Low ground east from Michigan. Summer.

S. alba is similar, with fine-toothed slender leaves, yellow-brown stems, and white flowers. Vermont westward.

Hardhack, *S. tomentosa,* has spirelike clusters of pink flowers, and woolly leaves. Throughout southern half.

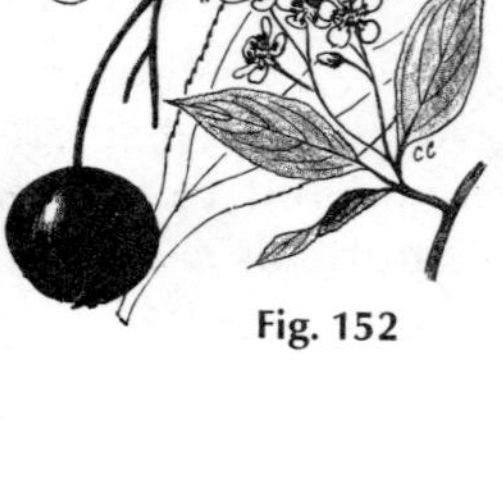

Fig. 152

Black Chokeberry. *Pyrus melanocarpa. Fig. 152.* Shrub 2-4′. Leaves with dark glands along upper surface of the midrib. Flowers in loose clusters, white with dark red anthers. Fruit black, persistent, seldom used by wildlife.Throughout in open areas. Spring; fruit in late summer.

The similar Purple Chokeberry, *P. floribunda,* with purple-black fruit, occurs east from Ontario.

Mountain Ash. *Pyrus decora. Fig. 153.* Shrub or small tree to 30′. Leaves pinnately compound. Flowers white in large flat-topped clusters. Bright red fruit provides food for birds, especially grosbeaks, waxwings, and grouse. Throughout in moist woods, edges, and rocky outcrops. Spring; fruit in late summer through fall.

P. americana has longer leaflets with flowers and fruits smaller than *P. decora.*

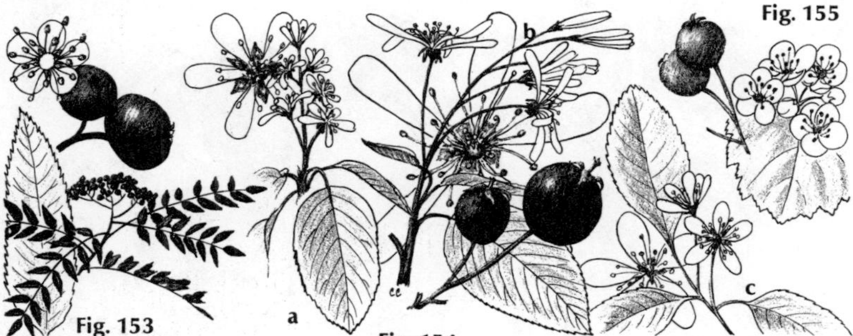

Fig. 153 Fig. 154 Fig. 155

Shadbush. *Amelanchier.* Shrubs or small trees. Showy white flowers in early spring. Purple-to-black, edible fruits in summer; very popular food for a great number of birds and mammals. Twigs browsed by moose and deer. Up to a dozen species occur here in open habitats. Recognizable as a group, but difficult to distinguish as species. The following illustrate variety of habit.

A. stolonifera. Fig. 154a. Colonial shrub 1-5′ tall, spreading by stolons. Small flowers in erect racemes.

A. laevis. Fig. 154b. Shrub or tree to 30′, with branches erect and close together. Large flowers in lax racemes.

A. Bartramiana. Fig. 154c. Slender shrub 2-6′ tall, with stems in tufts, often forming clumps. Flowers solitary or few at ends of twigs. Northern species of boggy areas and mountain slopes.

Hawthorns. *Crataegus.* A large group of picturesque shrubs or small trees, usually with flexuous, thorny branchlets; difficult to distinguish as species, but readily recognized as a genus. Leaves usually lobed and toothed. Flowers in clusters; white, with anthers yellow, red, or white; late spring. Fruits orange or bright red, rarely yellow or purple-red. One or another species throughout, but most common south and east. Golden-fruited Hawthorn, *C. chrysocarpa, Fig. 155,* is widespread, and shows typical form.

Shrubby Cinquefoil. *Potentilla fruticosa. Fig. 156.* Twiggy shrub to 30"; outer bark shredding. Leaves crowded, pinnate, with 5-7 leaflets; whitened and silky-haired beneath. Flowers yellow, at ends of branches. Openings, throughout. Summer.

Three-toothed Cinquefoil. *P. tridentata. Fig. 157.* Low perennial, woody at base, to 10". Smooth leathery leaves with three leaflets, toothed at tips. White flowers rising above the leaves. Rocks, gravelly or peaty soil, throughout. Late spring through fall.

Fig. 156

Fig. 157

Fig. 158

Fig. 159

Marsh Five-finger. *P. palustris. Fig. 158.* Herb to 24". Leaves pinnate, 5-7-parted, sharp-toothed. Flowers reddish-purple. Bogs and shores, usually in water, throughout. Summer.

Silverweed. *P. anserina. Fig. 159.* Low creeping herb with stolons 1-3' long. Leaves pinnate, many-parted, sharp-toothed, covered with shiny silver hairs beneath. Flowers yellow, solitary. Sandy shores and banks, throughout. Summer.

Fig. 160
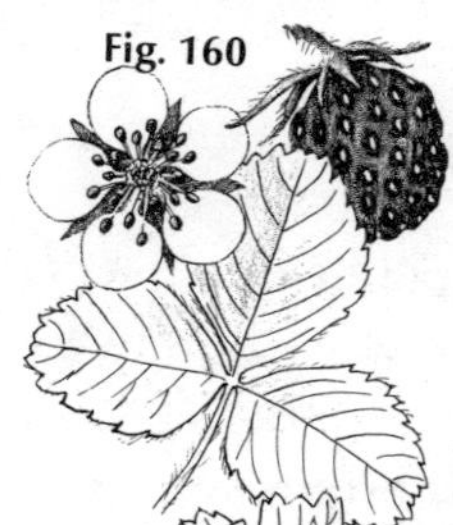

Strawberry. *Fragaria virginiana. Fig. 160.* 3-6" tall. Long-petioled, 3-parted silky basal leaves. Flowers white, several on a stalk, followed quickly by juicy red fruit. Seeds set in pits on surface of globular fruit. Leaves and fruit eaten by upland gamebirds; fruit eaten by man, many songbirds and small mammals. Throughout in fields and edges. Most fruitful in sandy acid soil. Spring through summer. The less common *F. vesca*, of non-acid soil, has conical fruit, seeds not in pits.

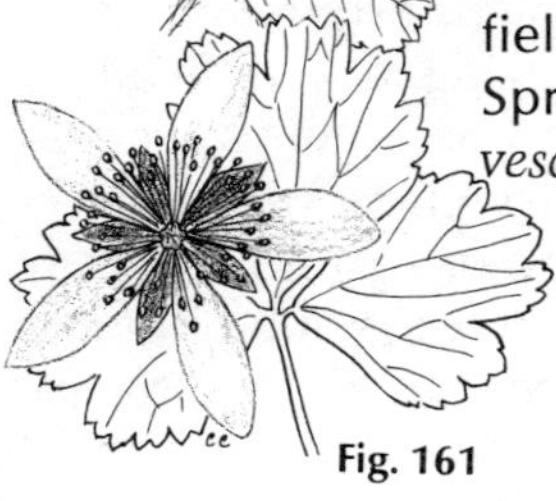
Fig. 161

Barren Strawberry. *Waldsteinia fragarioides. Fig. 161.* 4-7" tall. Similar in habit to above, but with glossy leaves and yellow flowers. Small dry fruits not used by wildlife. New Brunswick westward. Woods and edges. Late spring.

Erect Avens. *Geum aleppicum* var. *strictum. Fig. 162.* Hairy herb to 4′. Leaves pinnate, variable; large and more numerous toward base of plant, small and fewer at top. Flowers deep yellow. Fruits in burlike heads. Swamps and moist openings. Summer.

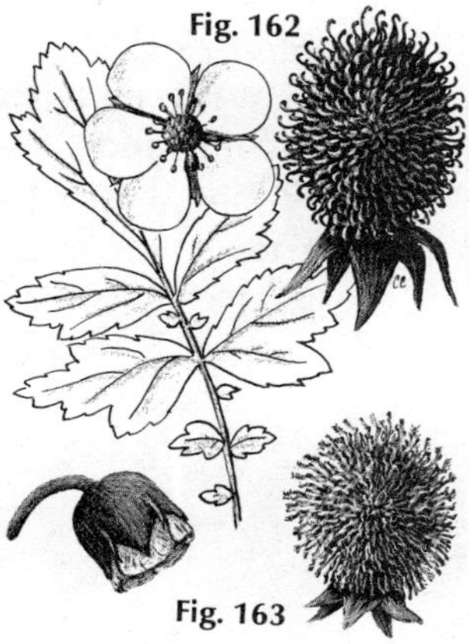

Fig. 162

Water Avens. *G. rivale. Fig. 163.* To 3′. Similar in habit to above, but with nodding cup-shaped smoky purple flowers. Plume-tipped fruits in heads. Bogs, wet meadows, peaty areas throughout. Summer.

Fig. 163

Brambles, *Rubus,* a large genus familiar for the edible fruit. The dozens of species in this region can be divided into two major groups: 1) cloudberry and raspberries, whose fruit falls free of the convex receptacle; and 2) blackberries (very numerous, but mostly southern or local) whose fruit adheres to the receptacle. All are very important in providing wildlife food and cover. Common representative species are described here.

Cloudberry. *R. Chamaemorus. Fig. 164.* Creeping herb 4-12″ tall. Leaves leathery, lobed. Flowers white, solitary at ends of unbranched thornless stems. Fruit pink, becoming yellow when ripe; juicy and soft, dropping quickly. Mountain slopes and bogs throughout northern half. Summer.

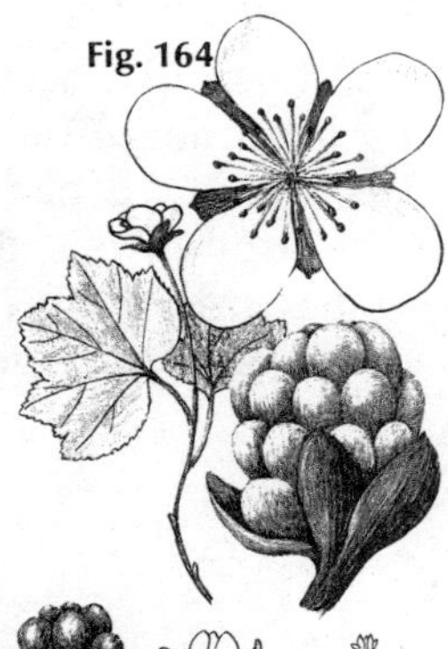

Fig. 164

Dwarf Raspberry. *R. pubescens. Fig. 165.* Delicate trailing herb to 16″ tall, thornless, with whiplike shoots that take root. Leaves 3-5-parted. Flowers white to pink, 1-few on each branch. Berry composed of few large juicy red drupelets. In damp woods throughout.

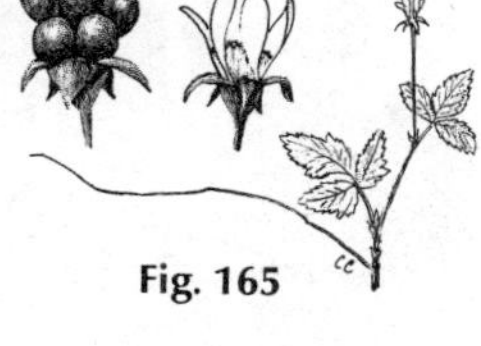

Fig. 165

There are two thimbleberries in this region. Both are shrubs 3-6′ tall, with shallow red berries, and very large maplelike leaves on thornless branches. They grow in dense stands in shady openings across the southern half of the Northwoods Region.

R. parviflorus, Fig. 166, has white flowers and large succulent fruit. Ontario westward; early summer. *R. odoratus* has magenta flowers, young branches and flowering stems densely glandular, with smaller, drier fruit than *R. parviflorus.* Michigan eastward; all summer.

Fig. 166

Fig. 167

Fig. 168

Red Raspberry. *R. idaeus* vars. *Fig. 167.* Woody biennial, canes 3-4′ long, armed with sharp prickles. Leaves pinnate, 3-5-parted, downy beneath. Petals white or greenish. Thickets and edges throughout; all summer.

Common Blackberry. *R. allegheniensis. Fig. 168.* Woody biennial, canes ascending, 3-9′ long, armed with strong roselike thorns. Leaves mostly 5-parted; leaflets all from a single point (a characteristic of blackberries); velvety beneath. Flowers white, in elongate clusters. Fruit black when ripe. Dry openings and thickets, southern half. Late spring through early summer.

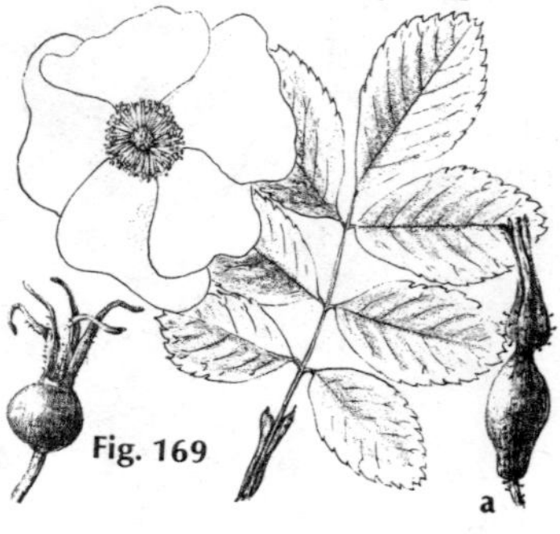

Fig. 169

a

Wild Rose. *Rosa blanda. Fig. 169.* Shrub 1½-5′, with prickles few and scattered, or low on the stems. Leaves with 5-7 coarse-toothed leaflets. Flowers pink. Fruit scarlet, nearly globose, and topped by erect or spreading sepals. Openings, rocky slopes and shores, in southern half. Summer.

R. acicularis, Fig. 169a, has prickles on entire stem, and glands on sepals. Abundant north.

Canada Plum. *Prunus nigra. Fig. 170.* Small tree to 25′. Leaves simple, with rounded gland-tipped teeth, and two red glands on petiole near blade. Flowers white becoming rosy with age, covering tree in early spring; calyx red, hairy above, glandular on margin. Fruit orange-red with very slight bloom; delicious when fully ripe. Thickets and edges, southern half.

Fig. 170

Fig. 171

Fig. 172

Three species of Sandcherries (*P. pumila, P. susquehanae,* and *P. depressa*) occur locally south and west. These are low shrubs with ½″ purple-to-black fruit, growing on sandy shores and dunes, often with juniper.

Pincherry. *P. pensylvanica. Fig. 171.* Shrub or small tree to 25′, of slender and delicate mien, with lustrous red-brown bark. Leaves simple, membranous, shining, with glands on petiole near blade. Flowers white, in profuse loose clusters. Fruit light red, with thin juicy flesh; a particular favorite of birds. Woods, openings and burns, throughout. Very early spring.

Chokecherry. *P. virginiana. Fig. 172.* Shrub or small tree to 12′. Leaves simple. Flowers white or creamy, in a dense raceme 2-4″ long. Fruit deep red to purple-black, astringent. Thickets, edges, and shores throughout. Spring.

PEA FAMILY. Flowers and fruits resembling the garden pea.

Beach Pea. *Lathyrus japonicus. Fig. 173.* Creeping perennial with trailing stems to 4′ long. Pinnate leaves ending in tendrils; large arrow-head shaped stipules. Flowers several on stem, purple to violet-pink. Great Lakes and other gravelly shores. All summer.

Fig. 173

Vetchling, *L. palustris,* is similar but has

Fig. 174

narrow leaves, and occurs throughout in marshes, thickets, moist woods, and shores.

WOOD SORREL FAMILY. Small herbs with sour juice. Flowers 5-parted, leaves 3-parted, somewhat cloverlike.

Common Wood Sorrel. *Oxalis montana. Fig. 174.* Creeping perennial 3-4" tall. Flowers white with lilac veins and a bright yellow spot at the base of each notched petal. Moist mossy woods throughout. Summer.

GERANIUM FAMILY. Herbs with palmately divided opposite leaves, 5-parted flowers and elongate beaked fruits.

Cranesbill. *Geranium Bicknellii. Fig. 175.* Stems 6-24", upright or prostrate with many ascending branches, covered with plain or glandular hairs. Leaves deeply 5-parted. Flowers pale magenta. Seeds eaten by chipmunks and birds. Openings and disturbed soils throughout, except the Appalachians. Late summer.

Fig. 175

a

Herb Robert, *G. Robertiana, Fig. 175a,* is similar to cranesbill except it has 3-5 separate leaflets, darker flowers usually in pairs, and deciduous seed cases. Cold ravines, shores, and woods throughout. All summer.

MILKWORT FAMILY. Small herbs with alternate, simple leaves. Flowers bisymmetrical, with 5 sepals (of which 2 are enlarged to petallike wings), and 3 petals more or less united. Fruit a 2-parted capsule.

Fig. 176

Fringed Polygala. *Polygala paucifolia. Fig. 176.* 3-6". Leaves few, at top of stem; bright green, glossy, persistent in winter. Flowers few, magenta-pink, the lower petal pouchlike (sometimes white) tipped with a tuft of fringe. Moist rich woods in southern half. Late spring through early summer.

CASHEW FAMILY. Trees or shrubs with milky or resinous sap. Leaves alternate. Small 5-parted flowers in clusters.

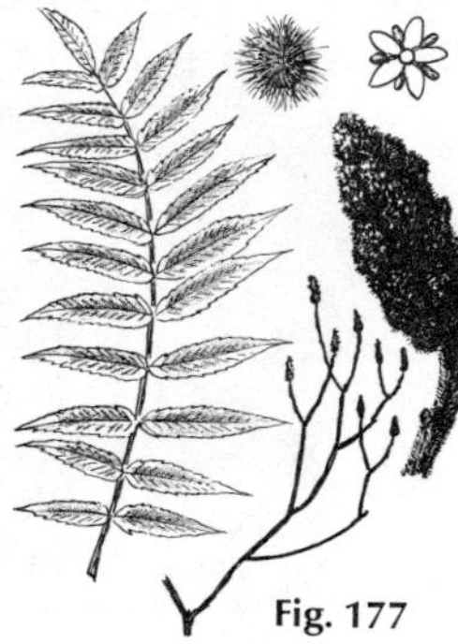
Fig. 177

Staghorn Sumac. *Rhus typhina. Fig. 177.* Shrub or small tree to 15′, with downy twigs and a bold open habit. Pinnate leaves to 2′ long, with 11-31 smooth leaflets, brilliant red in fall. Staminate and pistillate flowers in separate clusters; greenish. Fruits velvety with red acidic hairs; persisting over winter. Dry rocky soil in southern half. Early summer.

HOLLY FAMILY. Shrubs or small trees with simple alternate leaves. Tiny flowers in leaf axils; staminate and pistillate often on separate plants. Small red or yellow pulpy fruits.

Fig. 178

Black Alder. *Ilex verticillata. Fig. 178.* To 12′. Leaves with prominant, slightly hairy veins. Flowers greenish-white. Fruit bright scarlet, persisting into winter. Edges of moist woods and swamps, southern half. Summer.

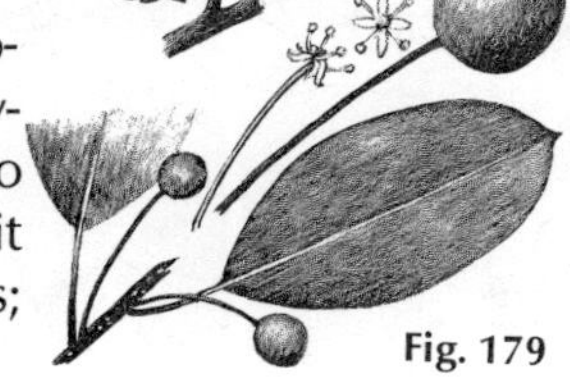
Fig. 179

Mountain Holly. *Nemopanthus mucronatus. Fig. 179.* To 12′. Leaves dull yellow-green, smooth, narrowed abruptly to needle tip. Flowers yellowish, the fruit dull red. Edges of swamps, bogs, streams; southern half. Late spring.

TOUCH-ME-NOT FAMILY. Succulent annuals. The flower bisymmetrical with a spurred sac. Fruit a capsule.

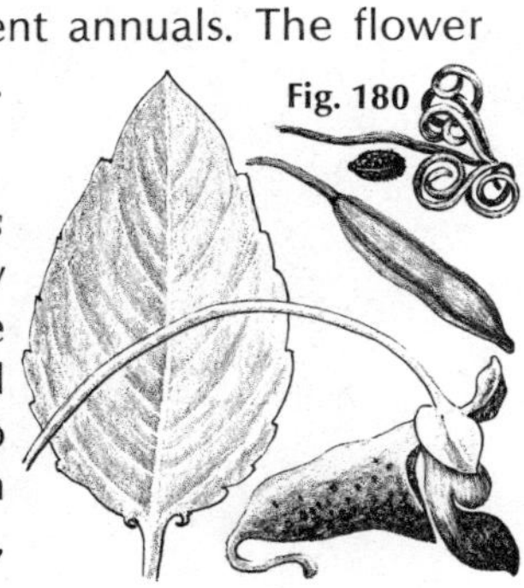
Fig. 180

Spotted Touch-me-not. *Impatiens capensis. Fig. 180.* 1½-4′. Flowers yellow to orange, with dark red spots. Capsule with 5 elastic valves which, if touched when ripe, coil forcibly like springs to eject the seeds (hence the common name). Springy wet soil and swamps, throughout. All summer.

MAPLE FAMILY. Trees or tall shrubs with sweet watery sap. Leaves opposite, palmately veined and lobed. Winged fruit united in pairs. Important food for many birds and mammals.

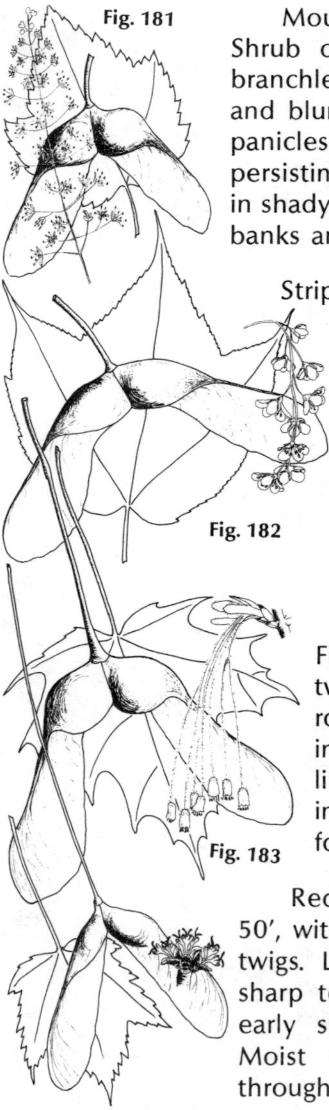

Fig. 181

Fig. 182

Fig. 183

Fig. 184 **All maple leaves and flowers x½**

Mountain Maple. *Acer spicatum. Fig. 181.* Shrub or tree to 25′, with red pubescent branchlets. Leaves downy beneath; teeth large and blunt. Flowers yellow-green in ascending panicles to 5″ long; early summer. Fruit red, persisting into winter. Common understory tree in shady, moist or rocky woods, edges, streambanks and mountainsides throughout.

Striped Maple. *A. pensylvanicum. Fig. 182.* Small tree to 20′; bark smooth with green or reddish vertical stripes; favored by moose. Leaves with 3 taper-pointed lobes, and fine sharp teeth. Flowers yellow-green, bell-shaped, in drooping racemes to 6″ long; late spring. Fruits mature in fall. Cool rocky or sandy woods, southern half from Michigan eastward.

Sugar Maple. *A. saccharum. Fig. 183.* Fine-branched tree to 80′, with brown twigs. Leaves with pointed lobes and rounded sinuses. Flowers yellow-green, in pendulous clusters, on hairy thread-like pedicels; late spring. Fruits mature in summer. Typical of upland hardwood forests throughout.

Red Maple. *A. rubrum. Fig. 184.* Tree to 50′, with smooth light gray branches and red twigs. Leaves with sharp-pointed lobes and sharp teeth. Flowers red, in dense clusters; early spring. Fruits mature early summer. Moist woods, swamps, and streambanks throughout.

BUCKTHORN FAMILY. Small trees or shrubs with simple, alternate leaves.

Alder-leaved Buckthorn. *Rhamnus alnifolia. Fig. 185.* Small erect shrub to 3′ tall. Leaves shiny, with prominent veins. Small greenish flowers, without petals, 1-3 in axils of upper leaves, as leaves are expanding. Black berrylike fruits. Swamps throughout. Summer.

Fig. 185

LINDEN FAMILY. Mostly tropical trees and shrubs, with but one native species in this region.

Fig. 186 **all x½**

Basswood. *Tilia americana. Fig. 186.* Large straight-trunked tree to 70′, with smooth branches and smooth red winter buds. Alternate simple leaves, oblique at base. Flowers pale yellow, very fragrant and a source of fine honey; in pendulous clusters, each peduncle attached to a large bract that serves as a parachute for the clusters of gray fruit. Hardwood areas from New Brunswick west and south. Early summer; fruit in fall persists into winter.

VIOLET FAMILY. Represented in this region by the single genus *Viola.* Familiar spring-flowering herbs with irregular 5-parted flowers. The lower petal has a nectar spur extending back behind the base of the lower sepals. *(Fig. 187a, b.)* In some species the petals have fleshy hairs called "beards" at their base. All produce inconspicuous self-fertile buds in summer which never open into bloom, but which develop seed capsules. *(Fig. 187c.)*

The number of species is greatest in the hardwood forest zone, where identification is complicated by the intermingling of northern and southern species, as well as by their tendency to hybridize, and to produce albino forms.

The 16 species described below can be divided into two main groups by their habit of growth, and these two groups subdivided by characteristics outlined in the accompanying tables. Refer to the tables and illustrations for details of flower, leaf, fruit, and rhizome.

Leaves are all shown ½ their maximum size at summer maturity. Refer to the descriptions for habitat, range, and any significant features not explained in the tables.

The first main group appears stemless, with leaf and flower stalks all arising at ground level directly from the rhizome (underground stem). In this group are four species with fleshy rhizomes resembling tiny tubers ⅛″-⅜″ thick. *(Fig. 188a.)* Two others have somewhat stiff scaly rhizomes about ⅛″ thick. *(Fig. 188b.)* And four others have slender cordlike rhizomes less than ⅛″ thick, and very slender shoots called stolons growing horizontally from the base of the plants. *(Fig. 188c.)*

Table 1, part 1

STEMLESS, fleshy rhizomes ⅛ - ⅜″ thick	Flower color	Petals bearded	Size of leaf blade
Blue Marsh Violet Fig. 189a	Violet, darker toward center	Lateral	To 4″
Northern Bog Violet Fig. 189b	Violet, darker toward center	Lateral and lower	¾ - 2½″
Northern Blue Violet Fig. 189c	Violet, white at center	All, slightly	2 - 4″
Round-leaved Yellow Violet Fig. 189d	Yellow, with brown veins	Lateral	1½ - 4¾″

When making identification, one can usually determine the size and form of these features by gently drawing the humus away from the base of the plant without disturbing the roots.

Blue Marsh Violet. *Viola cucullata. Fig. 189a.* 5-10″ tall. Flowers usually taller than leaves. Lower petal usually shorter than laterals; dense beard with club-tipped hairs. Swamps, bogs, and wet openings throughout.

Northern Bog Violet. *V. nephrophylla. Fig. 189b.* Similar to above, but smaller. Beard not club-tipped. Similar habitats and range.

Northern Blue Violet. *V. septentrionalis. Fig. 189c.* Entire plant slightly hairy; petioles sometimes reddish at base. Thin woods and openings throughout.

Round-leaved Yellow Violet. *V. rotundifolia. Fig. 189d.* 2-5″ tall. The only yellow "stemless" violet. Blooms with, or before, earliest leaves. Leaves spreading prostrate on ground. Two or more capsules at intervals on stolonlike stems. Woods in southern parts and the Appalachians.

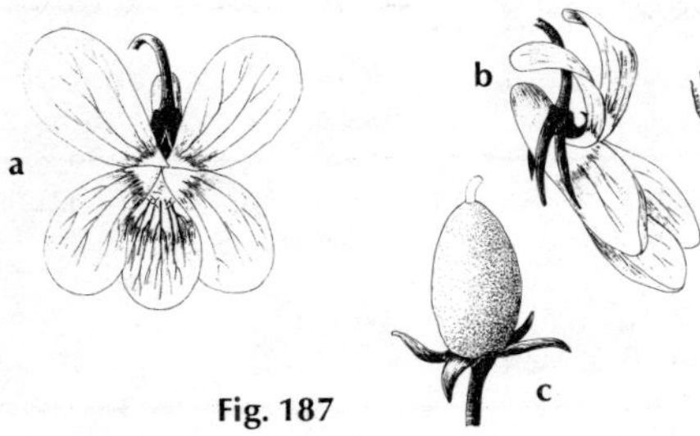

Fig. 187

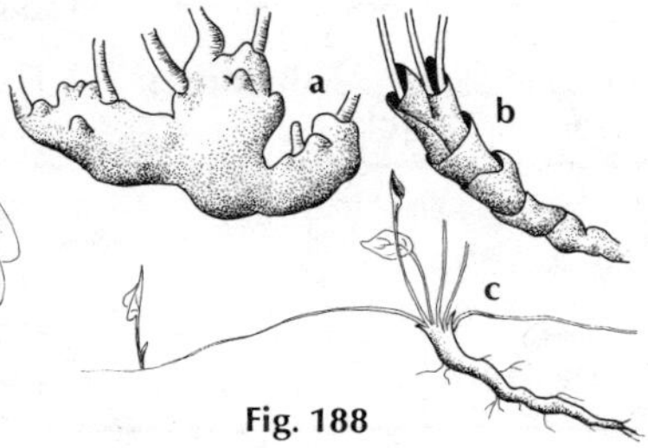

Fig. 188

Table 1, part 2

Leaf shape	Mature leaf texture, color	Capsule	Ripe seed color
Heart-shaped, acute tip	Smooth	Green	Black
Heart-shaped, obtuse tip	Smooth	Green	Olive-brown
Heart-shaped, broad obtuse	Slightly hairy, thin, pale green	Purplish	Dark brown
Oval to round	Smooth, somewhat leathery	Purple-dotted	Ivory

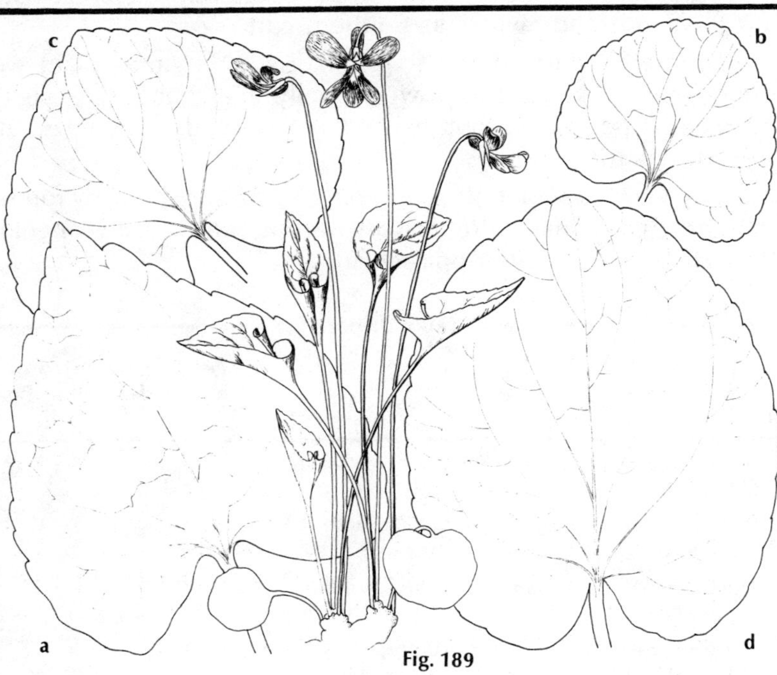

Fig. 189

Table 2, part 1

STEMLESS, scaly rhizomes about ⅛″ thick	Flower color	Petals bearded	Size of leaf blade
Great-spurred Violet Fig. 190a	Violet	None	½ - 1¾″
Kidney-leaved Violet Fig. 190b	White, with purplish veins	None	½ - 3″

Great-spurred Violet. *V. Selkirkii. Fig. 190a.* Delicate rosettelike plant 2-4″ tall. Spur as long as blade of lower petal. Woods and cool rocky slopes throughout, except the Appalachians.

Kidney-leaved Violet. *V. renifolia. Fig. 190b.* Low, lax plant, white-hairy when young. Cool woods, arbor vitae swamps, and rocky slopes; mostly north; scattered elsewhere except Appalachians.

Alpine Marsh Violet. *V. palustris. Fig. 191a.* Small creeping plant with stiff leafy stolons. Flowers fragrant. Subalpine slopes of northern mountains.

Sweet White Violet. *V. blanda. Fig. 191b.* Small creeping plant with leafy stolons. Leaf and flower stalks reddish. Very fragrant flowers usually taller than leaves; upper petals reflexed and twisted at tip. Woods and ravines in southern part.

Northern White Violet. *V. pallens. Fig. 191c.* Small plant with sinuous threadlike stolons. Flowers usually taller than leaves; slightly fragrant; upper petals not twisted. Wet woods, openings, and streamsides throughout.

Large-leaved Violet. *V. incognita. Fig. 191d.* Spreading by runners to form dense mats. Wet or dry woods, edges, and openings throughout, except the Appalachians.

Table 3, part 1

STEMLESS, cordlike rhizomes less than ⅛″ thick, slender stolons	Flower color	Petals bearded	Size of leaf blade
Alpine Marsh Violet Fig. 191a	Violet or white, with lilac spur	None or lateral	¾ - 1½″
Sweet White Violet Fig. 191b	White, with purplish veins	None	1 - 3″
Northern White Violet Fig. 191c	White, with purplish veins	None	½ - 3″
Large-leaved Violet Fig. 191d	White, on hairy stalks	Lateral	1 - 4″

Table 2, part 2

Leaf shape	Mature leaf texture, color	Capsule	Ripe seed color
Heart-shaped to oval, closed sinus	Appressed hairs on upper surface, thin	Purple-dotted	Buff
Rounded to kidney-shaped	Hairy or smooth	Purple	Brown

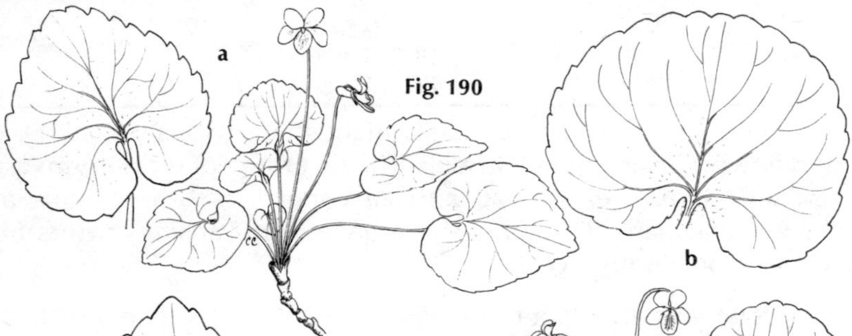

Fig. 190

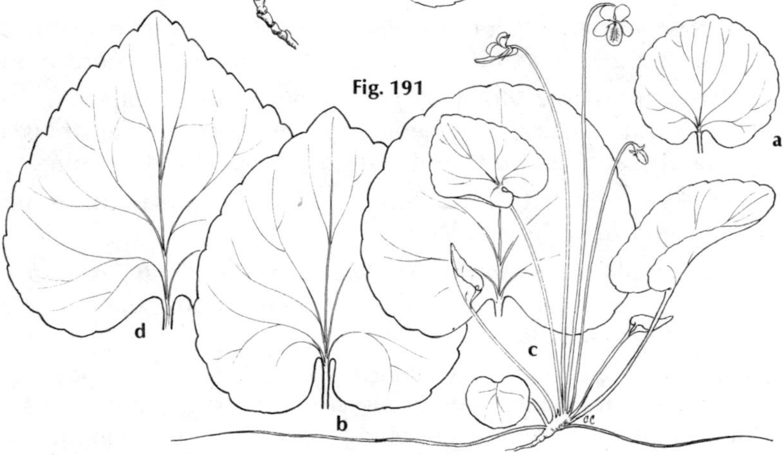

Fig. 191

Table 3, part 2

Leaf shape	Mature leaf texture, color	Capsule	Ripe seed color
Rounded	Smooth, thin	Green	Buff or grayish
Heart-shaped, acute tip	Scattered hairs above, firm and satiny	Purplish	Dark brown
Heart-shaped to kidney-shaped	Smooth, thin, not satiny, pale green	Green	Black
Heart-shaped	Hairy beneath, thin, somewhat wrinkled	Purplish	Buff to olive

Table 4, part 1

LEAFY-STEMMED, O-few basal leaves, 1-few stems	Flower color	Petals bearded	Size of leaf blade
Downy Yellow Violet Fig. 192a	Yellow, with purple veins	Lateral	1½ - 4½″
Smooth Yellow Violet Fig. 192b	Yellow, with purple veins	Lateral	1½ - 4″
Tall White Violet Fig. 192c	White to lilac, purple veins, yellow eye	Lateral	2 - 4″

The second main group has upright stems with alternate leaves and flowers arising from leaf axils. The first three of these forms have few stems from each root, and all occur in southern parts and the Appalachians. The other three have stems arising in tufts from rosettes of basal leaves.

Downy Yellow Violet. *V. pubescens. Fig. 192a.* Stout, hairy plant to 16″, with 1-2 stems and 0-1 basal leaf. Stipules toothed. Woods.

Smooth Yellow Violet. *V. pensylvanica,* var. *leiocarpa. Fig. 192b.* Not as stout or hairy as preceding species, with several stems and 1-3 basal leaves. Stipules not toothed. Woods and openings.

Tall White Violet. *V. canadensis. Fig. 192c.* Several purplish stems, and several basal leaves. Woods.

Dog Violet. *V. conspersa. Fig. 193a.* Plants 2-10″ tall, from rosette of basal leaves that soon shrivel. Damp woods, openings, and lowlands throughout.

Hooked-spur Violet. *V. adunca. Fig. 193b.* Similar to dog violet, but smaller and hairy; numerous stems prostrate and spreading when mature. Dry woods, openings, and rocks throughout.

Long-spurred Violet. *V. rostrata. Fig. 193c.* Slender spur ⅜″-¾″ long. Woods in southern parts and the Appalachians.

Table 5, part 1

LEAFY-STEMMED, many basal leaves, many stems	Flower color	Petals bearded	Size of leaf blade
Dog Violet Fig. 193a	Pale violet, white center	Lateral	¾ - 1½″
Hooked-spur Violet Fig. 193b	Violet	Lateral	½ - 1¼″
Long-spurred Violet Fig. 193c	Violet, darker toward center	None	¾ - 1½″

Table 4, part 2

Leaf shape	Mature leaf texture, color	Capsule	Ripe seed color
Broad heart-shaped	Hairy, prominent veins, pale green	Green, white-woolly	Pale brown
Broad heart-shaped	Scarcely hairy, dark green	Green, mostly smooth	Light brown
Heart-shaped, narrow tip	Smooth to scarcely hairy, thin	Green	Brown

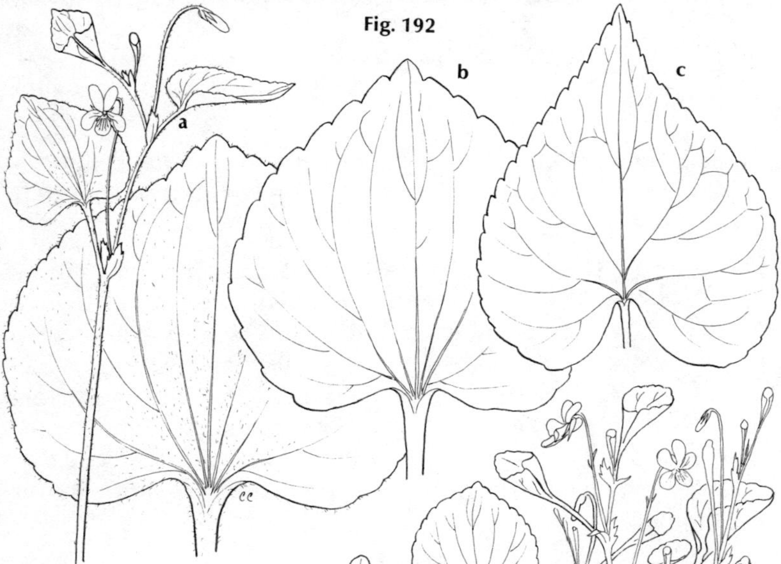

Fig. 192

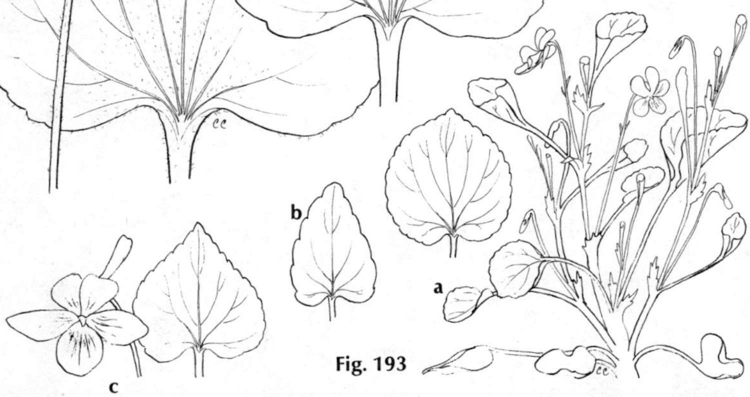

Fig. 193

Table 5, part 2

Leaf shape	Mature leaf texture, color	Capsule	Ripe seed color
Rounded	Nearly smooth	Tan	Buff to brown
Heart-shaped	Minutely hairy or smooth, leathery		Dark brown
Heart-shaped, tapering tip	Smooth		Light yellow-brown

ST. JOHNSWORT FAMILY. One small shrub, the rest herbs, with simple opposite leaves. Most have yellow 5-parted flowers, with many stamens, clustered at the top of stems. A few are showy, but most here have small flowers. Fruit a capsule. Mainly wet habitats throughout.

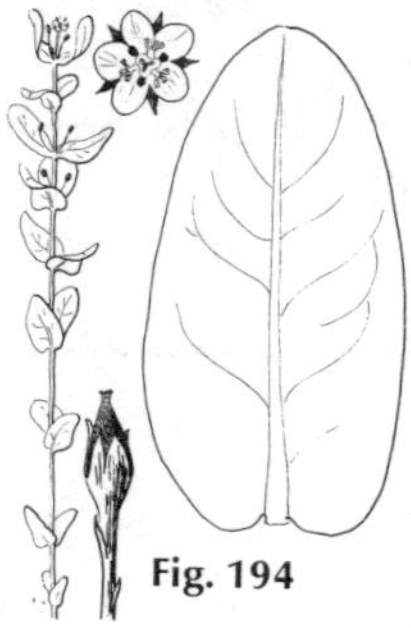

Fig. 194

Marsh St. Johnswort. *Hypericum virginicum*, var. *Fraseri (Triadenum Fraseri). Fig. 194.* Herb 1-2′. Stem and lower leaves reddish, smooth. Flowers pale pink to red, stamens united into bundles separated by 3 orange glands. Fruits reddish. Shores, bogs, and swamps throughout. Summer.

ROCKROSE FAMILY. Herbs or small shrubs with simple, alternate or opposite leaves, and 3- or 5-parted yellow or red flowers.

a

Fig. 195

Beach Heath. *Hudsonia tomentosa. Fig. 195.* Low sub-shrub 3-8″ high, forming dense broad mats in sand. Leaves tiny, scalelike and crowded, nearly hidden by tangled woolly hairs. Numerous yellow flowers on very short stems, solitary at ends of branches. Dunes, sandy beaches, sand plains; central Quebec west and south across Great Lakes area, and on coast from Gaspé southward. Late spring through early summer.

Golden Heather, *H. ericoides, Fig. 195a,* has awl-shaped leaves that are longer, more loosely arranged, and not so densely woolly as beach heath. Flowers on longer stems. Sands, disturbed soil, acid rocks; coast and inland on mountains, south to New England.

OLEASTER FAMILY. Shrubs or small trees represented in this region by the following single species.

Fig. 196

Soapberry. *Shepherdia canadensis. Fig. 196.* Shrub 3-9′. Young leaves and twigs cinnamon, scurfy. Opposite leaves, felted beneath with dense, silvery, radiate hairs, and brown scurf. Flowers 4-parted, yellowish, solitary or in small clusters on previous year's wood; male and female on separate plants. Pulpy, inedible, yellow-to-red fruit. Sandy or rocky limestone areas throughout. Flowers in spring, fruits in summer.

EVENING PRIMROSE FAMILY. Herbs with simple alternate or opposite leaves. Flowers, mostly showy, are 4-parted and borne at the top of the ovary.

Fireweed. *Epilobium angustifolium. Fig. 197.* Perennial to 6′, with alternate leaves. Magenta flowers open a few at a time over a long period, from bottom to top of elongating inflorescence, so that later in the season all stages of bud, flower, and fruit may be seen at one time. Very slender pods split apart to release masses of seeds floating on silky tufts. Seeds are eaten by chipmunks. Fireweed is a prime honey plant and a favored feeding and resting place for bumblebees. This plant beautifies waste places and hastens the healing of cutover, burned, and abused land. Throughout.

Fig. 197

Many other species occur northward in boggy and mossy wet habitats typical of the northern conifer region. Though most are smaller and differ in detail, they can be recognized as *Epilobium* by the general characteristics described in the above species.

Evening Primrose. *Oenothera biennis. Fig. 198.* One of three species in this region, representative of a very difficult and variable genus. A stout biennial to 5′ tall, with alternate leaves. The fragrant yellow flowers open late in the day, one or a few at a time, in the same manner as *Epilobium*, and each flower lasts but one day. Visited by many kinds of increasingly scarce hawkmoths. Roadsides and openings throughout.

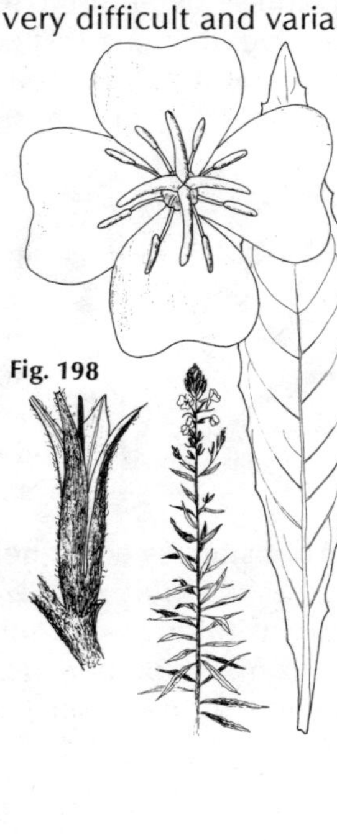
Fig. 198

The similar but smaller *O. parviflora* may be seen on sandy or gravelly shores and slopes in the north.

Sundrops, *O. perennis,* is a slender, more delicate day-blooming perennial of dry or moist openings. The tip of the inflorescence droops in bud, but straightens as the flowers open one by one. Throughout.

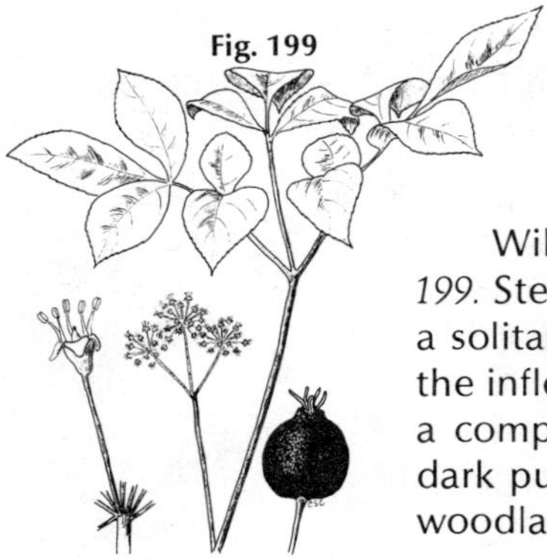
Fig. 199

GINSENG FAMILY. Herbs with compound leaves, small 5-parted flowers in umbels, and berrylike fruits.

Wild Sarsaparilla. *Aralia nudicaulis. Fig. 199.* Stem very short, at ground level, holding a solitary umbrellalike leaf 8-20″ tall above the inflorescence. Flowers greenish-white in a compound umbel on a naked stalk. The dark purple fruit is relished by birds. Shady woodlands throughout. Spring.

Bristly Sarsaparilla, *A. hispida,* to 3′, is a branched plant with spiny stems, and bears few umbels loosely at the ends of the leafy branches. Openings and rocky open woods. Summer.

Spikenard, *A. racemosa,* to 6′, is a branched plant with large leaves and many umbels in large, loose panicles at the end of the leafy stems. Rich woods. Summer.

PARSLEY FAMILY. A large group of herbs with distinctive family characteristics, some of the most poisonous as well as some of the most useful plants. Leaves are compound, alternate, with sheathing bases. Flowers are 5-parted, often minute; petals attached to the perimeter of a swollen disk above the ovary; florets in umbels, usually compound, forming a flat, domed, or spherical inflorescence. Fruits are two-seeded dry capsules.

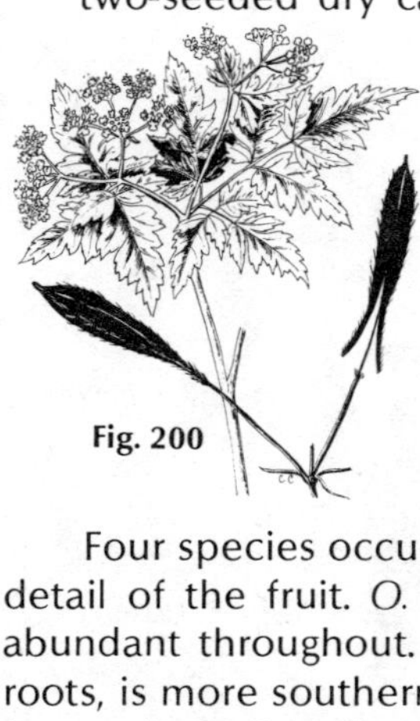
Fig. 200

Sweet Cicely. *Osmorhiza* sp. *Fig. 200.* Graceful aromatic woodland perennials, 1-3′ tall, with bright green leaves divided and subdivided in 3′s. Leaves thin-textured, more or less hairy, with the blades held horizontally below clusters of tiny-flowered white umbels. Distinctive slender fruits dark brown to black, with upward-pointing spines.

Four species occur here, difficult to separate except by minute detail of the fruit. *O. Claytoni,* with soft-hairy stems, is the most abundant throughout. Aniseroot, *O. longistylis,* with sweet-scented roots, is more southern. *O. obtusa,* and *O. chilensis,* are plants of the far north. Spring through early summer.

Water Hemlock. *Cicuta.* Perennial herbs of wet habitats, summer blooming. Two forms are common in this region, both containing a *most violent poison* in their clustered fleshy roots.

C. bulbifera. Fig. 201. A delicate plant with weak stems to 3′ long. Leaves doubly or triply pinnate, leaflets narrow and sparsely-toothed. Umbels of tiny white flowers, sometimes absent. Fruits rarely mature, the plant propagated instead by small bulblets borne in upper leaf axils.

Spotted Cowbane. *C. maculata. Fig. 202.* A stout plant to 6′ tall with smooth hollow stems, the lower part often spotted or streaked with purple. Leaves large, doubly or triply pinnate with many long-ovate coarsely-toothed leaflets. White flowers numerous in flattish umbels, somewhat like Queen Anne's lace. Small fruits nearly globular, with dark furrows between ribs.

Caution: The deadly Poison Hemlock, *Conium maculatum,* introduced from Europe, is now established as a weed in uncultivated but less wet habitats. It may be encountered from southern Quebec southward. Poison hemlock has lacy parsleylike leaves, showy white umbels, spotted stems, and parsniplike roots. It should be recognized so it can be avoided. All parts are poisonous, particularly the leaves and seeds.

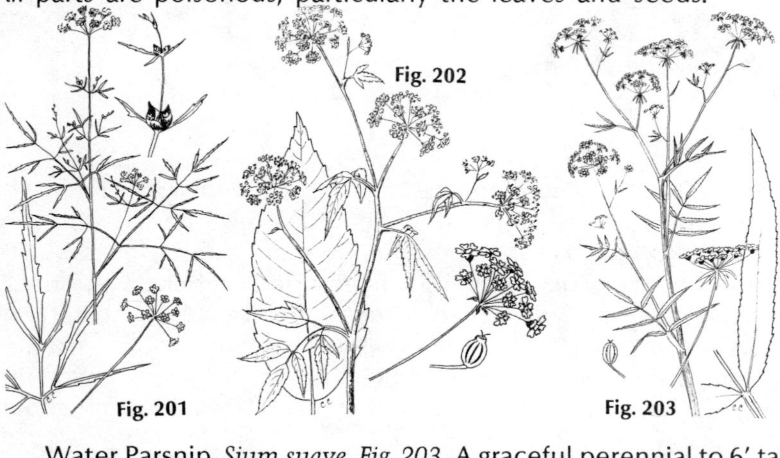

Fig. 202

Fig. 201

Fig. 203

Water Parsnip. *Sium suave. Fig. 203.* A graceful perennial to 6′ tall. Easily distinguished from the extremely poisonous species above by its corrugated stems and once-pinnate leaves with slim saw-toothed leaflets. White flowers in flat-topped umbels above a whorl of slender bracts. Tiny fruits oval with corky ridges. Toxicity suspected but not documented. Wet meadows, swamps, shores, often in shallow water. Summer.

Angelica. *Angelica atropurpurea. Fig. 204.* An imposing perennial to 8′ tall, very conspicuous for its size, form, and thick smooth purple stems. Lower leaves very large, doubly pinnate with many leaflets; upper leaves reduced to a few leaflets, or none, above large bulging sheaths. Creamy flowers in great globular umbels. Fruits elliptic with longitudinal ridges. As soon as seeds ripen, the plant dies back leaving only a skeleton standing. Rich lowlands throughout. Late spring through summer.

Fig. 204

Fig. 205

Cow Parsnip. *Heracleum maximum. Fig. 205.* Robust perennial to 8′ tall, with stout, hairy, grooved stems. Leaves 3-parted with very large sheaths; bold leaflets resembling giant maple leaves. White flowers in spectacular domed or flat-topped umbels, with deeply notched petals and distinctive eccentric florets at the perimeter of the outer umbels. Fruits flattened, somewhat heart-shaped, marked by four dark longitudinal lines above the middle. Like angelica, the plant dies back early, but seeds hold longer. Lowlands throughout. Summer.

DOGWOOD FAMILY. Shrubs, trees or woody herbs. Leaves opposite, with one exception; simple, with smooth or wavy margins; lateral veins prominent, arching toward the tip. Flowers small, in convex clusters, or bunched at the center of a whorl of petallike bracts. Fruits fleshy, red, blue, or white; important wildlife food, especially for birds.

BUNCHBERRY

Bunchberry. *Cornus canadensis. Fig. 206.* Low, somewhat woody perennial 4-12" tall, forming colonies. Leaves opposite, crowded in a whorl at the top of the stem. Flowers with four showy white bracts surrounding a tight cluster of creamy florets, held on a short stalk above the leaf whorl. Fruits bright red. Moist mossy woods or sandy pine barrens; throughout. Spring.

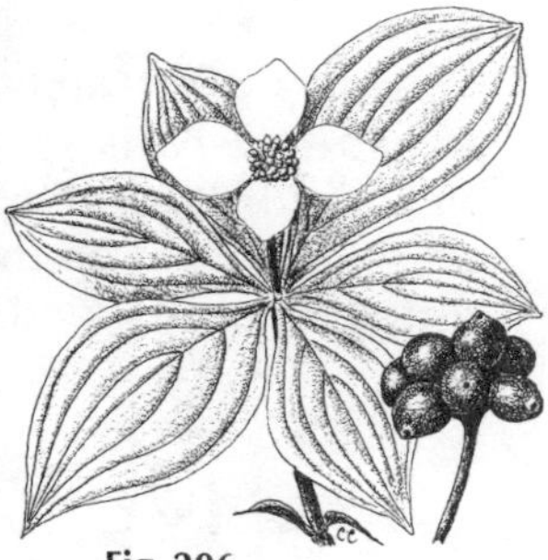

Fig. 206

C. suecica is similar but smaller, with purple floret clusters. This boreal species of wet wood and rocky habitat may be found north and east in our region.

Red Osier. *C. stolonifera. Fig. 207.* Shrub 3-9' tall, forming thickets. Twigs and stems red to maroon. Leaves opposite, long-ovate, and tapering to the tip; whitened beneath. Flowers with 4-petaled white florets in flat or convex clusters to 2" across. Fruit white, sometimes blue-tinged. Swamps, shores, and marsh edges; throughout. Spring through summer.

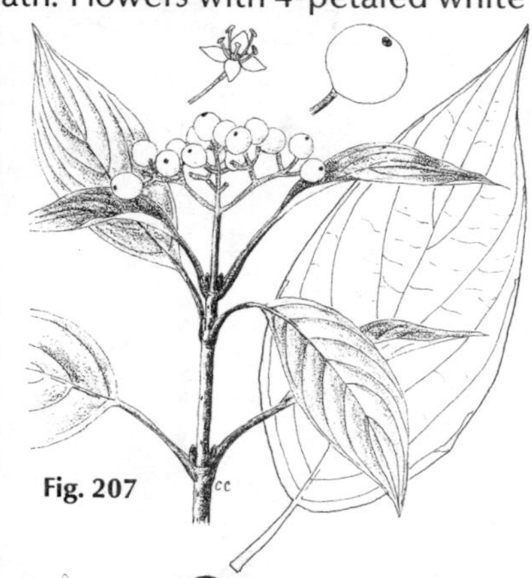

Fig. 207

Pagoda Dogwood. *C. alternifolia. Fig. 208.* Shrub or small tree to 25' tall, with a horizontal branching habit; twigs and young branches green. Leaves alternate, broad-ovate, crowded at the ends of twigs below the flower clusters. Flowers same as red osier. Dark blue fruit on bright red stems. Woods and thickets throughout. Spring.

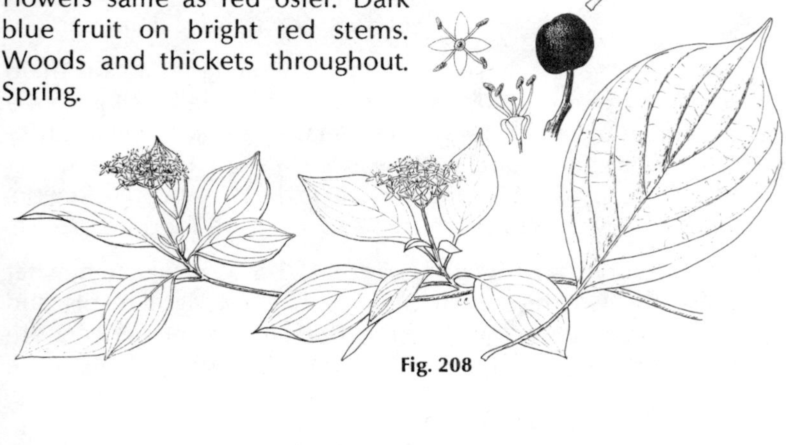

Fig. 208

WINTERGREEN FAMILY. Small perennial woodland herbs, spreading by creeping subterranean shoots. Leaves arranged in whorls or rosettes. Flowers nodding, white or pink, distinctly 5-petaled. The brown 5-lobed globular seed capsules remain on the plants well into winter. Flowers are visited by many kinds of bees, flies, and butterflies.

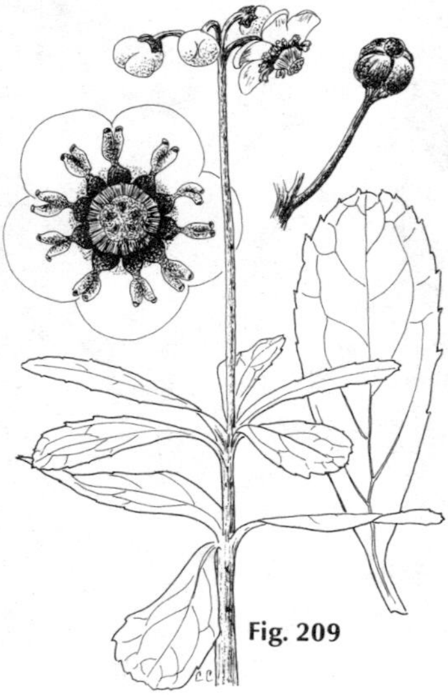

Fig. 209

Prince's Pine. *Chimaphila umbellata,* var. *cisatlantica. Fig. 209.* 4-12". Stems woody at base. Leaves evergreen, thick and shiny, wedge-shaped. Flowers creamy or pink, waxy, in a loose cluster; the rounded convex petals draw backward to expose a green dome-shaped ovary and circle of purple anthers. Arched pedicels become erect as the capsules develop. Dry woods, usually under conifers; throughout. Summer.

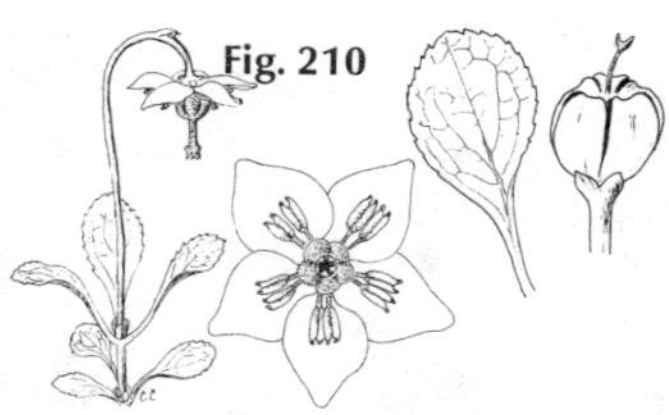

Fig. 210

One-flowered Wintergreen. *Moneses uniflora. Fig. 210.* Dainty plant 2-6" high, often in groups. Leaves thin, dark green, and veiny. Flower solitary, fragrant, waxy, white or rosy, relatively large, hanging at the end of a curved stalk; petals open wide around a green globular ovary and circle of yellow anthers. Stalk becomes erect as capsule develops. Cool mossy woods under conifers; throughout. Summer.

Shinleaves, *Pyrola* sp., have a distinctive mien that makes them easy to recognize as a group. All have a solitary stalk rising from a basal cluster of alternate leaves, terminated by an elongated inflorescence of nodding cupped blossoms. These are followed by flattened globular capsules. Six species occur in the Northwoods Region, all blooming early to mid-summer. Seeds provide food for grouse.

One-sided Pyrola. *P. secunda. Fig. 211.* 3-8". Leaves somewhat leathery, shiny. Greenish-white flowers have straight pistils and skirts of stamens projecting beyond the petals. The flowers are arranged on one side of the stalk, which often bends below the inflorescence so that the flowers hang like a string of bells under the arched tip. Stalk becomes erect as capsules develop. Woods or bogs throughout.

Shinleaf. *P. elliptica. Fig. 212.* 6-12". Leaves thin, not shiny, the blades broadly ovate with a narrow base extending down the sides of the petiole. The fragrant flowers are white, lightly veined with green, waxy, and spirally arranged around the stalk in a loose cluster; petals cupped over a cluster of yellow upturned stamens and a long pistil upcurved at the tip. In general appearance this species is typical of the genus. Very common in dry or moist woods throughout.

Fig. 211

Fig. 212

Greenish Pyrola, *P. virens*, 4-10", has thick dull-surfaced leaves, the small roundish blades often shorter than the petioles. Flowers similar to above, but more prominently veined with green, slightly fragrant. Common in dry woods under conifers; throughout.

Pink Pyrola, *P. asarifolia,* 6-12", has broad leathery leaves, more or less shiny above, often tinged reddish beneath. Flowers crimson or pink, with thin veiny petals. Calcareous woods or swamps throughout.

Small Pyrola, *P. minor,* 2-6", is a diminutive plant with thin dull leaves. Flowers white, nearly globular, with straight pistil barely visible beyond the petals. Cool woods in the north.

Fig. 213

Round-leaved Pyrola, *P. rotundifolia,* 6-12", has leathery, shiny, evergreen leaves, the blades decurrent on the sides of the petiole. Flowers white or pink-tinged, with thick petals, very fragrant. Woods, sandy openings, or bogs; rather rare.

Indian Pipe. *Monotropa uniflora. Fig. 213.* 4-12". Unique in the family, this waxy white succulent plant grows as a saprophyte on forest humus. Leaves reduced to translucent scales close against the thick stem which bends at its summit to hold the nodding white flower. The plant becomes marked with black as it begins to fade. It then dries dark brown or black, and stiff brown capsules stand erect through the winter. Woods throughout. All summer.

HEATH FAMILY. Small woody plants growing (with a few exceptions) in cold bogs, acid sandy barrens, or peaty soils in woods and openings. They are as much a distinguishing feature of the Northwoods as the pines, spruces, and mosses that accompany them. Many have cylindric or urn-shaped waxy flowers; most have small firm leaves, often rolled under along the margins, some woolly, powdery or waxy beneath; some are aromatic. These characteristics of flower, foliage, and habitat, taken singly or in combination, give them an indefinable quality that enables one to say at a glance: This is a heath.

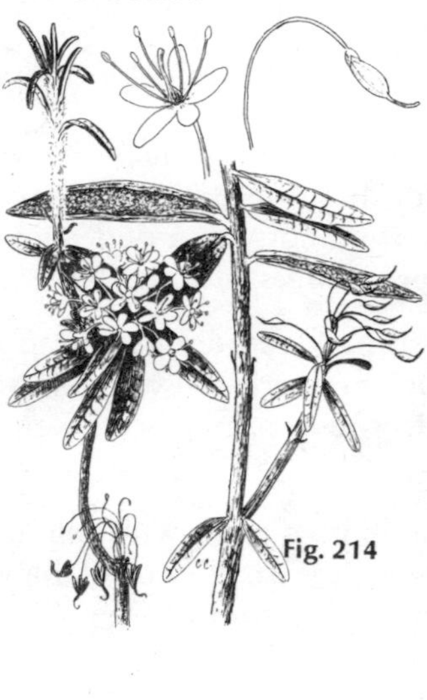

Fig. 214

Labrador Tea. *Ledum groenlandicum. Fig. 214.* To 3'. Young shoots white-woolly, becoming brown. Leaves alternate, evergreen, aromatic; thick and leathery with inrolled margins, prominently indented veins above and dense wool beneath, which is at first white, becoming rusty. Flowers, in a rounded terminal cluster, white, with 5 petals and prominent stamens. Brown ellipsoid capsules on long arching stalks, clustered at the end of the growth of the previous year; persistent. Bogs, peaty shores; throughout. Spring through early summer.

Rhodora. *Rhododendron canadense. Fig. 215.* To 3′. Leaves alternate, deciduous; margins slightly inrolled. Flowers before the leaves; pink to rosy-purple, with a 3-lobed upper petal and 2 slender lower petals, in terminal clusters. Oblong capsules on short stalks, clustered at the end of previous year's growth; persistent. Bogs, acid barrens, wet woods and moist hillsides; eastern half, south to New England. Spring.

Fig. 215

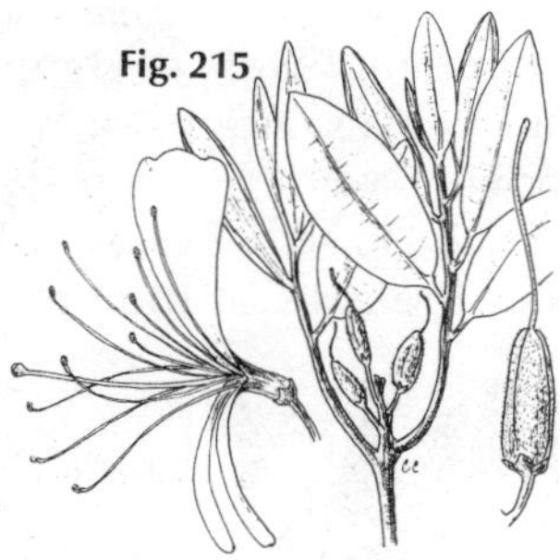

Laurels, *Kalmia* sp. Evergreen shrubs. Each 10-angled flower bud opens into a 5-lobed shallow bowl with 10 tiny pockets which clasp the anthers of 10 stamens arched back from the pistil, holding them under delicate tension until sprung by a visiting insect.

Bog Laurel. *K. polifolia. Fig. 216.* To 3′. Sparsely branched, with 2-edged twigs. Leaves opposite, leathery, with inrolled margins; lustrous above, whitened beneath, with a prominent midrib. Flowers pink, in a small terminal cluster. Capsules reddish, becoming brown. Bogs throughout. Spring through early summer.

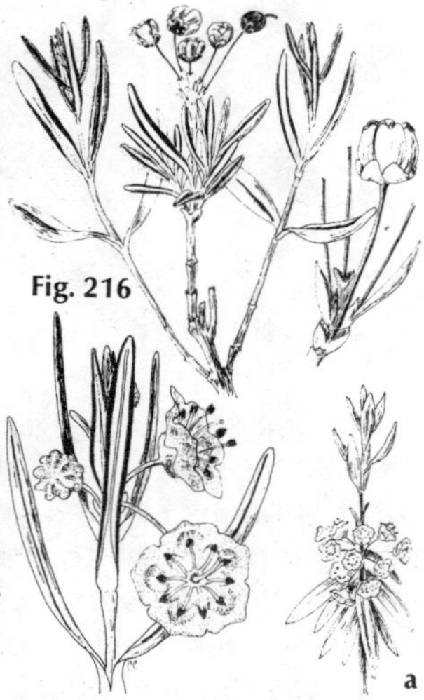

Fig. 216

a

Lambkill. *K. angustifolia,* has smaller deep pink to crimson flowers in dense clusters intermingled with the leaves, the new season's shoots and leaves extending above them; new leaves ascending, older leaves drooping. *Fig. 216a.* Dry or moist sandy acid soil in many kinds of habitats. Eastward from Michigan.

Fig. 217

Bog Rosemary. *Andromeda glaucophylla. Fig. 217.* To 2½′. Slender stems ascending from prostrate bases. Leaves alternate, erect, otherwise resembling bog laurel. Flowers pink-tinged, like delicate globular urns hanging in a cluster from the tips of twigs. Capsules erect. Bogs, pond edges; throughout. Spring through early summer.

Leatherleaf. *Chamaedaphne calyculata,* var. *angustifolia. Fig. 218.* To 3′ or more. Twiggy evergreen, stems bent at an obtuse angle near the top. Leaves alternate, ascending; lustrous with leathery texture above, covered with rusty scales beneath; upper leaves gradually reduced in size. Flowers white with rusty calyx, urn-shaped, hanging from the axils of the erect upper leaves. Fruit a globular capsule. Abundant, nearly universal in open bogs; throughout. Early spring.

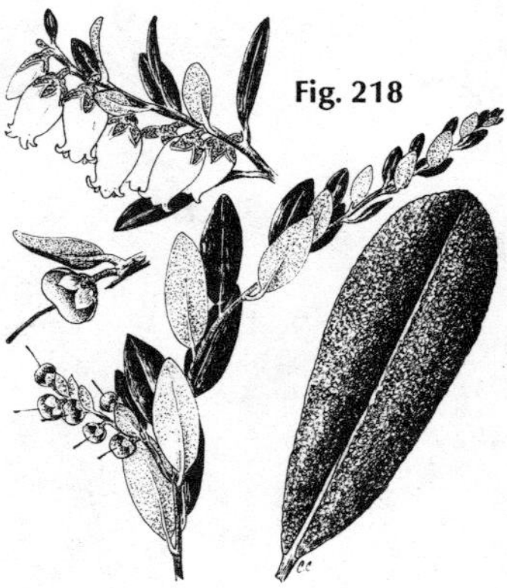

Fig. 218

Fig. 219

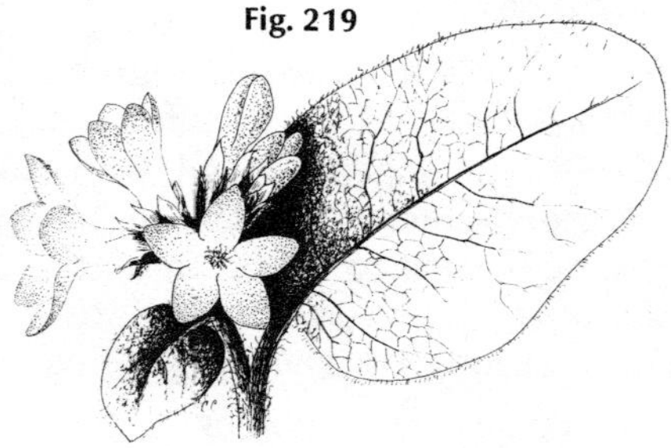

Trailing Arbutus. *Epigaea repens. Fig. 219.* Prostrate evergreen with semi-woody rough-hairy stems. Leaves alternate, net-veined, the midrib sunken; clothed with stiff hairs, particularly when young. Flowers pink or white, tubular with 5 spreading lobes, in small compact clusters; very fragrant. Fruit a flattened globular capsule. Sandy or rocky acid soil in woods and edges, often under evergreens; throughout. Early spring.

Fig. 220

Aromatic Wintergreen. *Gaultheria procumbens. Fig. 220.* Creeping evergreen with erect semi-woody stems 2-6″ high. Leaves alternate, clustered at top of stem; thick, smooth and shining, tender and reddish-tinged when young, stiff and deep green at maturity. Flowers white, waxy, hanging below the leaves. Fruit a satiny red, somewhat mealy berry, persisting and improving over winter. Entire plant wintergreen flavored. Leaves and fruit eaten by deer, bear, grouse, and people. Acid soil in woods, especially under evergreens; throughout. Summer.

Creeping Snowberry. *G. hispidula. Fig. 221.* Small trailing evergreen with threadlike semi-woody stems 3-12″ long, often

Fig. 221

forming mats. Leaves alternate, very small and firm, barely inrolled; smooth and shiny green above, somewhat rusty-hairy beneath. Flowers tiny greenish-white 4-lobed open bells, solitary, nodding from leaf axils. Fruit a white fleshy berry, slightly acidic and delicious; persisting and improving over winter. Fruit and leaves wintergreen flavored. In deep wet moss in conifer forests and bogs; throughout, most abundant northeast. Spring.

Fig. 222

Bearberry. *Arctostaphylos Uva-ursi. Fig. 222.* Trailing evergreen with flexible prostrate branches and short upright flowering twigs, forming mats. Leaves alternate, thick and leathery, glossy above, smooth below. Flowers white or pink, urn-shaped, hanging in small clusters from the tips of twigs. Fruit a dull red mealy berry, of poor flavor; persisting over winter and providing food for grouse. Twigs and leaves browsed by deer. Exposed rocky and sandy areas; throughout. Spring.

Alpine Bearberry, *A. alpina,* with black juicy fruits, occurs on bare rock south to the alpine heights of the New England mountains.

Fig. 223

Black Huckleberry. *Gaylussacia baccata. Fig. 223.* Twiggy shrub to 3′. Young twigs slightly hairy, reddish. Leaves alternate, deciduous, covered on both surfaces with shining yellow resin dots, sticky to the touch. Flowers pale pink to carmine-pink, slenderly ovoid; covered, like the leaves, with resin dots; profuse, hanging in clusters along the twigs of the previous year. Fruit a smooth blue-black berry containing 10 hard seeds; abundant, spicy-sweet and juicy; highly edible. Sandy or rocky open woods, openings; throughout. Late spring through early summer.

A northern variety of Dwarf Huckleberry, *G. dumosa*, a smaller shrub with less tasty glandular-hairy fruit, may be found in bogs near the Atlantic coast.

Low Sweet Blueberry. *Vaccinium angustifolium. Fig. 224.* Dwarf twiggy bush 2-14" high, forming large patches. Leaves alternate, deciduous, usually smooth on both surfaces, with very fine-toothed margins. Flowers white, sometimes pink-tinged, ovoid-cylindrical bells closely clustered at tips of twigs. Fruit a smooth blue berry with a heavy bloom, containing many soft seeds and very sweet. Highly prized by bear, and used by chipmunks and white-footed mice. Entire plant browsed by deer. Very abundant in sandy openings, barrens, old burns, and dry rocky woods; throughout. Early summer.

Fig. 224

Velvet-leaf Blueberry, *V. myrtilloides,* is slightly larger than *V. angustifolium;* soft-hairy, with greenish-white flowers, and bright blue acidic berries. Moist woods and shady rocky areas; throughout.

Bilberries are pink-flowered far northern *Vaccinium* species closely allied to blueberries, but flowers and fruits are 1-3 drooping from leaf axils. Not common here, but any of 4 species might be seen in rocky or peaty open habitats south to the Lake Superior shore, and the mountains of New York and New England. Summer.

Small Cranberry. *Vaccinium Oxycoccos. Fig. 225.* Very slender trailing evergreen with threadlike ascending branches. Leaves very small, with acute tips, the margins strongly inrolled; glossy green above, conspicuously whitened beneath. Flowers like tiny pink shooting stars, with 4 recurved narrow petals; 1-4, borne singly on threadlike pedicels at the end of a leafy branch. Berries ripen to deep shiny red, and persist over winter. Bogs and sphagnous shores; throughout. Summer, fruit from August.

Fig. 225

Large Cranberry. *V. macrocarpon. Fig. 226.* Similar to *V. Oxycoccos,* but with longer and stouter branches. Leaves barely incurved, with rounded tips, only slightly whitened beneath. Flowers 1-10, from axils of bractlike leaves midway up a leafy branch. Fruit larger (the commercial species), persisting through winter. Bogs throughout. Fruit from September.

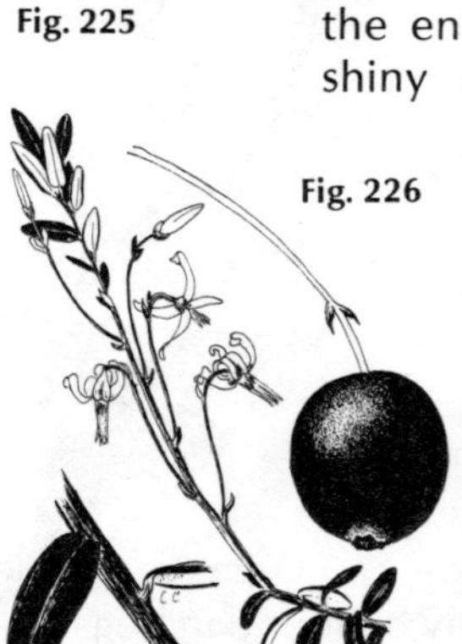

Fig. 226

Mountain Cranberry. *V. Vitis-Idaea. Fig. 227.* Creeping sub-Arctic evergreen only a few inches high, forming broad tight mats. Leaves small, shining green above, leathery with inrolled margins, dotted with pointed black glands beneath. Flowers white-to-pink 4-lobed open bells in small terminal clusters. Fruit a bright red, acidic berry, persisting on plants throughout the year. Important food for birds, especially during migration; and sought by bear in spring. Habitats and range similar to bilberries. Summer.

Fig. 227

PRIMROSE FAMILY. Herbs with simple leaves and perfect radial flowers, petals united at the base, stamens opposite the petals and attached to them.

Swamp Candles. *Lysimachia terrestris. Fig. 228.* Smooth, leafy-stemmed, 1-2′ high. Leaves opposite, tapered at both ends and with black dots on both surfaces. Small leafy shoots grow from axils of each pair of mid-stem leaves. Flowers 5-parted, yellow with pale red streaks on petals; stamens on a collar encircled by a red ring at base of petals; each flower on a slender pedicel from the axil of a bract, in a showy terminal raceme. Fruit a small ovoid capsule. Low moist ground and shores; throughout. Summer.

x½

Fig. 228

a

Tufted Loosestrife, *L. thyrsiflora, Fig. 228a,* has smaller (than *L. terrestris*) 6-parted yellow flowers with prominent stamens, crowded in ovoid racemes on slender stalks, ascending from the axils of leaves lower down on the stem. Similar moist habitats; throughout.

x¼

Fig. 229

Starflower. *Trientalis borealis. Fig. 229.* Easily recognized by the wiry upright stem 4-10″ high surmounted by a whorl of thin lance-shaped leaves and one or more starry white flowers on very slender pedicels. The flowers are usually 7-parted, with sharp-pointed petals. Fruit a globular capsule above the persistent linear calyx segments. Woods throughout. Spring.

OLIVE FAMILY. Represented in this region by a single genus, *Fraxinus*, the ash trees. Leaves are opposite, pinnate; flowers are mostly unisexual.

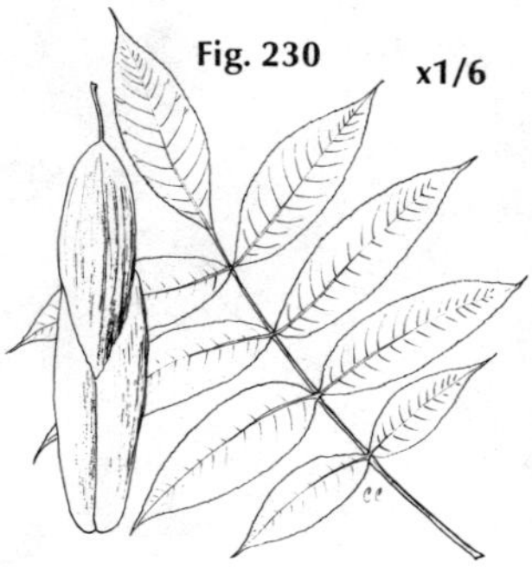

Fig. 230 x1/6

Black Ash. *F. nigra. Fig. 230.* Slender tree to 75′ with ascending branches, smooth gray bark, and nearly black buds. Leaves dark green with 7-11 toothed, sessile leaflets. Flowers are clusters of purple anthers and purple-tipped pistils, without petals or calyx, usually in separate panicles, sometimes on separate trees; open before the leaves. Fruit an oblong brown samara with a wide flattened seed, and a wing notched at the tip; in long pendulous panicles. Most northern of the ashes. Cold swamps and wet shores; throughout.

GENTIAN FAMILY. Smooth herbs with simple untoothed leaves. Flowers 4-7 parted; the petals are united into a tube for part or most of their length; stamens alternate with petal lobes and attached to the tube.

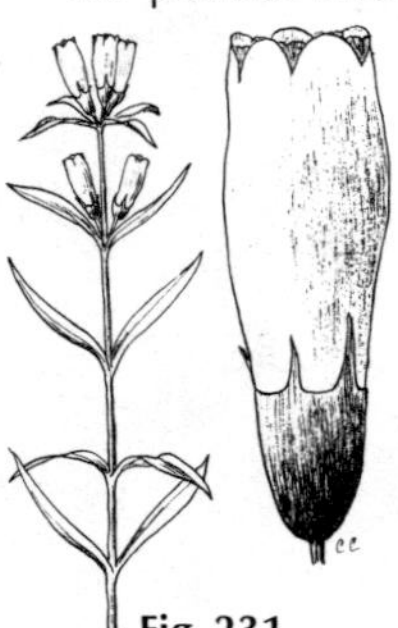

Fig. 231

Closed Gentian. *Gentiana linearis. Fig. 231.* To 2′. Leaves opposite, sessile, narrow, and pointed. Flowers violet-blue, club-shaped, slightly open at the top, stamens enclosed in tube; 5 short, rounded lobes with 5 shorter membranous folds in the sinuses; blooms few in a terminal cluster and in axils of upper leaves. Fruit an ellipsoid capsule bearing innumerable winged seeds. Bogs, wet meadows, Laurentian rocks; throughout. Late summer through fall.

Fig. 232

Buckbean. *Menyanthes trifoliata. Fig. 232.* Smooth perennial 4-12″ high, with leaves and flower stalk rising from the end of a creeping rootstock. Leaf stalk has 3 leaflets, and a membranous basal sheath. Flowers starry white, the 5 lobes clothed with a white fleshy beard, in a raceme on a bright green naked stalk. Fruit a many-seeded globular capsule. Common in bogs, marshes, and shallow water; throughout. Spring through early summer.

DOGBANE FAMILY. Herbs with tough, fibrous stems and milky sap. Representd here by the genus *Apocynum*.

Spreading Dogbane. *A. androsaemifolium. Fig. 233.* 1-4′. A neat plant, easy to recognize because of its spreading habit, leaves hanging in pairs along the branches inclined toward horizontal, clusters of fragrant pink bell-shaped flowers, and paired linear pods filled with silky-tufted seeds. Fields, edges, and upland woods; throughout. Summer.

Indian Hemp, *A. sibericum*, is more upright in habit, has white flowers in ascending clusters, and ascending branches and leaves. Shores; throughout.

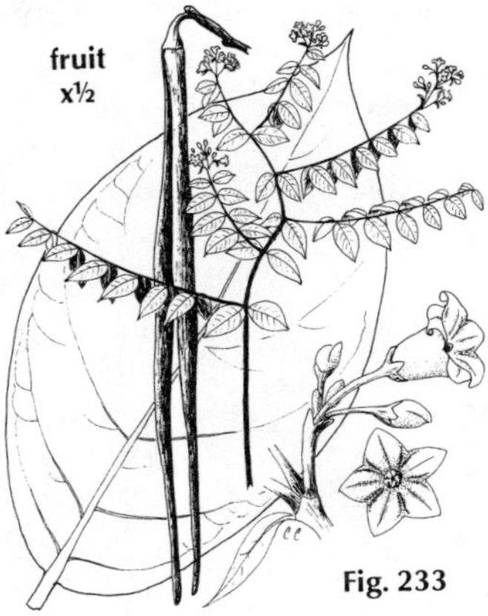

Fig. 233

MINT FAMILY. Herbs, mostly aromatic, with square stems, opposite leaves, and mostly bilabiate flowers. Fruits composed of 4 small nutlets nested in the persistent calyx.

Common Skullcap. *Scutellaria epilobiifolia. Fig. 234.* Perennial 1-3′ high. Recurved hairs on stem angles and lower surface of veiny, nearly-sessile leaves. Flowers strongly bilabiate, with violet hood, fading to white on tube and lower lip; single in the axils of upper leaves, but turned so as to stand in pairs on one side of stem; calyx has a prominent bulge resembling a helmet when the calyx closes over maturing fruit. Shores and wet areas; throughout. Summer.

Fig. 234

Mad-dog Skullcap, *S. lateriflora,* occurs in similar habitats but is less abundant. Flowers in one-sided racemes from leaf axils.

Heal-all. *Prunella vulgaris. Fig. 235.* Perennial with stems 4-24″ long, erect or decumbent. Leaves usually hairy. Flowers strongly bilabiate, with violet hood and paler (to white) 3-lobed, fringed lower lip; close-set in the axils of broad bracts in a 4-sided head. Fruit an elongated brown spike of hairy calyxes

Fig. 235

flattened above the nutlets. In woodland habitats the plants may grow in circular prostrate tufts up to a foot across with or without flowering stems. Roadsides, fields, and open woods; throughout. Summer.

Fig. 236

Wild Basil. *Satureja vulgaris. Fig. 236.* Perennial 8-24", spreading by stolons. Leaves soft-hairy, on short petioles. Flowers strongly bilabiate, deep pink, the lower lip 3-lobed; calyx green with 13 purple ribs, hairy; in dense hemispherical clusters. Fruits in large bristly-hairy clusters encircling the stem. Upland woods and thickets; throughout. Summer.

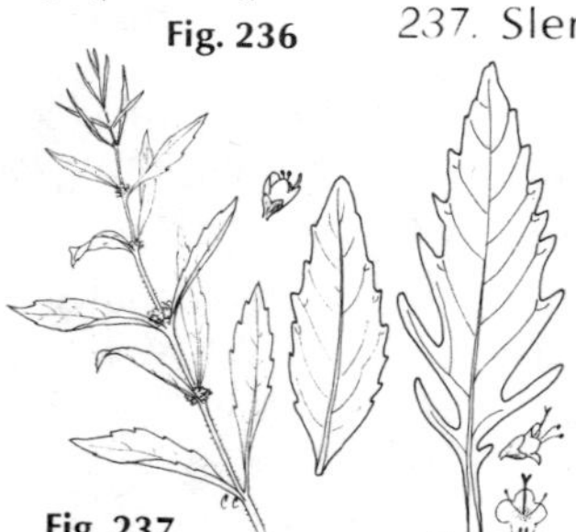

Fig. 237 a

Northern Bugleweed. *Lycopus uniflorus. Fig. 237.* Slender perennial with finely hairy stems 4-32" long. Leaves light green, with coarse teeth, acute base, and very short petiole. Flowers scarcely bilabiate, white, very small, bell-shaped with 4 nearly equal lobes; in small dense whorls in leaf axils on upper half of stem. Moist open ground; throughout; abundant in conifer forest. Summer.

Cut-leaved Bugleweed, *L. americanus. Fig. 237a.* is similar in habit, but the leaves are more deeply toothed, those lower on the stem distinctively cut into lobes which become progressively narrower toward the petiole.

Fig. 238 x½

American Mint. *Mentha arvensis. Fig. 238.* Strongly aromatic hairy perennial, 6-24", spreading by stolons. Stems simple or branched, leaves veiny. Flowers scarcely bilabiate, pink, white, or violet, stamens and pistil prominent; in crowded whorls in leaf axils on upper half of stem. Damp openings and shores; throughout. Summer.

FIGWORT FAMILY. Herbs, most with opposite (a few with alternate) leaves, and tubular bell-shaped or bilabiate flowers, often showy, of various colors.

Turtlehead. *Chelone glabra. Fig. 239.* Stiff perennial, 1-3′. Leaves opposite, nearly sessile, linear to lance-shaped, toothed, to 6″ long. Flowers white to faintly pink; bilabiate, inflated, with a broad keeled upper lip and 3-lobed lower lip, the middle lobe shorter and bearded; in dense terminal spikes. Fruit a globular brown capsule that splits into two sections. Main food plant of the Baltimore butterfly. Shores and wet thickets; throughout. Summer.

Fig. 239

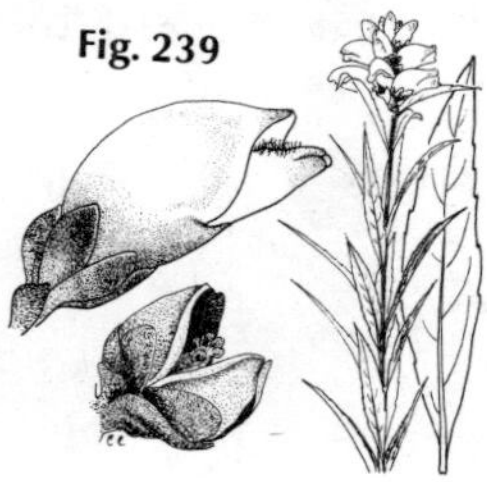

Speedwells. *Veronica* sp. Perennials with opposite leaves; axillary or terminal racemes of small blue flowers marked with dark lines, 4-lobed—the upper lobe widest, the lower narrowest—and with only 2 stamens. Fruits are small compressed 2-celled capsules, often very flat and heart-shaped.

Common Speedwell. *V. officinalis. Fig. 240a.* To 1′. Hairy plant forming mats of trailing stems with ascending tips. Upland fields and open woods; east from Wisconsin. Spring.

American Brooklime. *V. americana. Fig. 240b.* 8-24″. Smooth succulent, decumbent plant, with arching many-flowered racemes from leaf axils. Brooksides, swamps; throughout; common northward. Spring through summer.

Marsh Speedwell. *V. scutellata. Fig. 240c.* To 2′. Smooth slender plant with flowers widely spaced on delicate racemes from leaf axils. Wet habitats; throughout; abundant northward. Spring through summer.

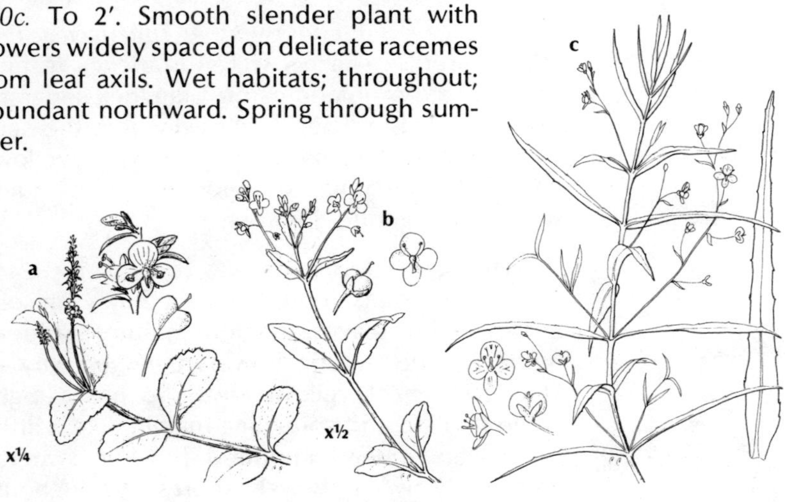

Fig. 240

BLADDERWORT FAMILY. Small carnivorous herbs growing in water or wet habitats, with 1 or more spurred flowers on leafless stalks. Fruit a capsule.

Fig. 241 x½

Butterwort. *Pinguicula vulgaris. Fig. 241.* A solitary 5-lobed violet flower stands on a 2-6″ stalk above a rosette of soft fleshy leaves with inrolled edges. The sticky surface of the leaves serves to trap small insects. Wet rocks, wet meadows, bogs; north of Wisconsin and northern New England.

Bladderworts. *Utricularia.* Named for the small bladders on underwater branches which trap minute water creatures. Flowers yellow or violet, strongly bilabiate, the upper lip erect, the lower lip somewhat 3-lobed with a prominent bulge, or palate, in the middle, and a nectar spur at the base.

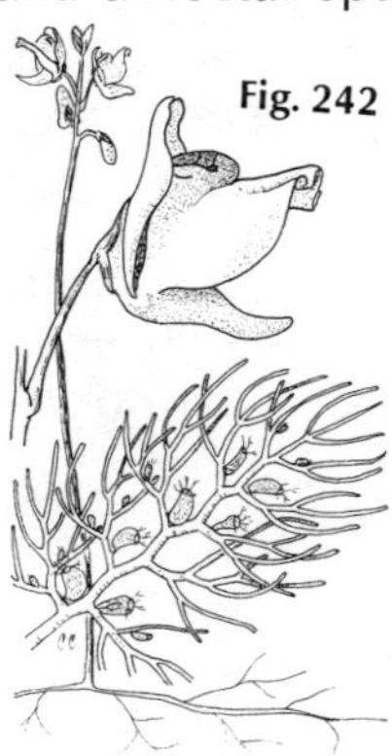
Fig. 242

Common Bladderwort. *U. vulgaris. Fig. 242.* Largest of the bladderworts. Floating stems to 3′ or longer, with plumelike branches of finely divided foliage set with many conspicuous bladders. Few to many flowers in racemes on stout emergent stalks; yellow; lower lip broad with a stout curved spur and a large, bright yellow palate with reddish markings. Common in quiet water; throughout. Summer.

Flat-leaved Bladderwort. *U. intermedia. Fig. 243.* Rooted in shallow water, branches resting on the bottom; bladders on branches separate from foliage branches. Leaves divided, the segments flat and spine-toothed. Flowers yellow, not often appearing. Common in shallow quiet water; throughout. Summer.

Fig. 243

Horned Bladderwort. *U. cornuta. Fig. 244.* Terrestrial; stems rooted in wet moss or soil; linear, simple leaves and few minute bladders hidden in substratum. Flowers 1-few on wiry 4-10″ stalks; light yellow; lower lip has a high, arched palate and spreading margin, like a little bonnet, and a slender pointed spur; very sweetly fragrant. Bogs and wet shores; throughout. Summer.

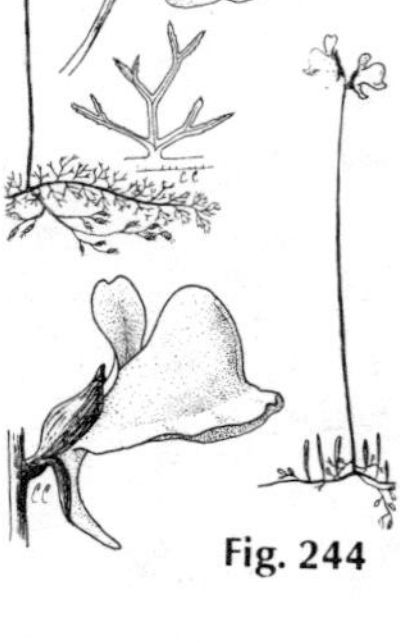
Fig. 244

MADDER FAMILY. A very large family, mostly tropical. Those in this northern region are herbs with simple opposite or whorled leaves, and 3- or 4-lobed flowers.

Bedstraw. *Galium*. At least 13 species in this region, all perennials with long weak 4-sided stems, and leaves in whorls of 4-6. Most are rough to the touch due to bristles on stem angles and leaf margins. They grow as reclining or prostrate nets of tangled branches. All have tiny 3- or 4-lobed white flowers (sometimes tinged with green or pink) that bloom in summer and develop into twin globular fruits. These are eaten by grouse, ducks, and muskrat.

Sweet-scented Bedstraw. *G. triflorum. Fig. 245.* Stems to 3′ long, nearly smooth. Leaves in 6′s. Flowers greenish-white. Fruits bristly. Plants fragrant when dry. Woods, rocky thickets; throughout.

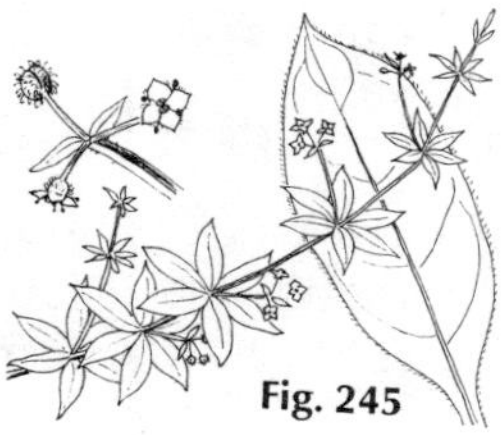

Fig. 245

Marsh Bedstraw. *G. palustre. Fig. 246a.* Stems 8-30″ long, slightly bristly. Leaves in 6′s. Flowers white or pinkish, profuse in loose terminal clusters. Fruits smooth. Wet meadows, water edges; common eastward.

Rough Bedstraw. *G. asprellum. Fig. 246b.* A rough-prickly plant to 6′. Flowers and fruits numerous, but minute. Damp places throughout; abundant eastward.

Fig. 246

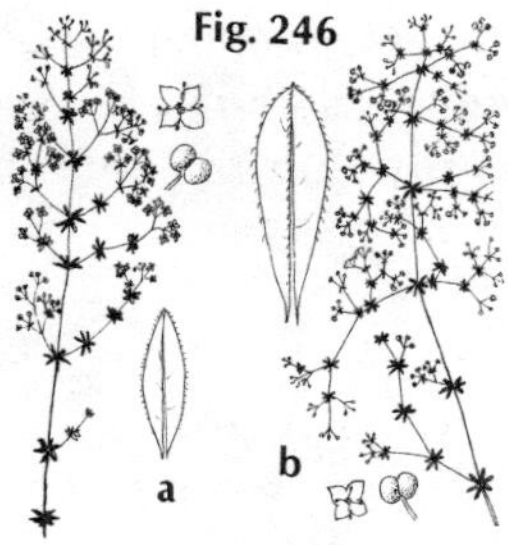

Partridgeberry. *Mitchella repens. Fig. 247.* Trailing semi-herbaceous evergreen with stems to 12″, rooting at the nodes and forming mats. Leaves opposite, firm and glossy, with prominent veins. Flowers in pairs, joined at the base; normally 4-lobed, waxy, white, and velvety-hairy on the upper surface of the lobes, smooth and pink-tinged beneath; fragrant; the stamens and pistils mature in separate flowers. Fruits bright red double berries that persist through winter; edible but without flavor; occasionally eaten by grouse and fox. Dry or moist woods; southern half of region. Early summer.

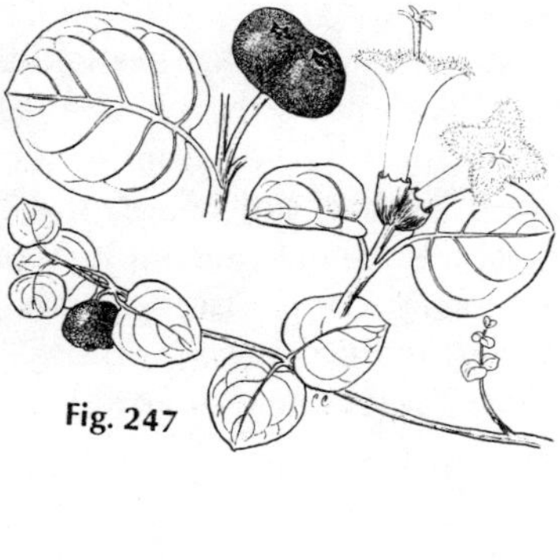

Fig. 247

HONEYSUCKLE FAMILY. Shrubs and one creeping evergreen with opposite, mostly simple, leaves.

Fig. 248

Bush Honeysuckle. *Diervilla Lonicera. Fig. 248.* Shrub 2-4′. Leaves taper-pointed, fine-toothed, smooth or hairy beneath. Flowers usually 3 in terminal clusters and in upper leaf axils; pale yellow becoming dark yellow to red; 5-lobed, funnel-shaped, hairy inside; the calyx tube elongate, narrow at summit, with 5 linear lobes which persist on the beaked capsule. Dry rocky woods and openings; throughout. Summer.

Honeysuckles. *Lonicera.* Small-to-medium shrubs with simple, untoothed leaves. Flowers in pairs on common peduncles from leaf axils. Fruits fleshy berries, quickly eaten by birds.

Fly Honeysuckle. *L. canadensis. Fig. 249.* 2-5′. Loosely branched, twigs smooth. Leaves smooth, thin, broad at base, fringed with hairs. Flowers greenish-yellow, funnel-shaped with 5 short lobes, the tube swollen on one side at the base, the 2 ovaries divergent; nodding on long peduncle. Berries red, in pairs. Woods throughout. Spring.

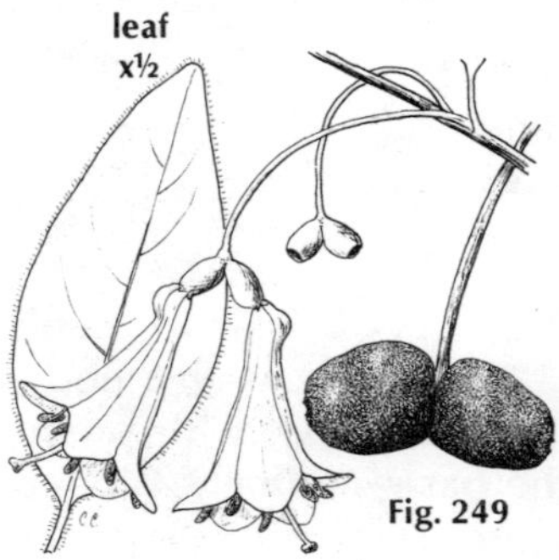

Fig. 249

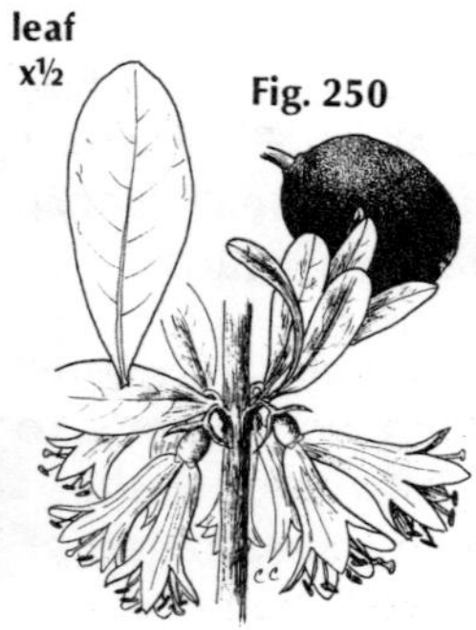

Fig. 250

Fig. 251

Mountain Fly Honeysuckle. *L. villosa. Fig. 250.* 1-3′. Erect, twigs normally densely hairy. Leaves thick, soft hairy, usually broader above the middle, nearly sessile. Flowers pale yellow, funnel-shaped, with 5 long lobes; the ovaries united above a pair of linear bracts; on a short peduncle. Flowers and leaves crowded. Fruit a 2-eyed, dark blue berry with a pale blue bloom; resembling blueberries, eminently edible. Peaty or rocky barrens, bogs, cold woods; mostly north. Spring.

Swamp Fly Honeysuckle. *L. oblongifolia. Fig. 251.* 2-5′. Erect, minutely hairy branches. Leaves downy beneath, oblong, narrowed to a short petiole. Flowers yellowish, fragrant, hairy outside, sometimes streaked with purple inside; deeply 2-lipped, the lower slender and reflexed, the upper broad and erect, 4-lobed; ovaries united or in pairs; on a long peduncle. Berries orange-to-purplish, united or paired. Bogs, swamps, wet woods; throughout except far north and east. Late spring.

Fig. 252

Twinflower. *Linnaea borealis,* var. *americana. Fig. 252.* Dainty, slightly-hairy evergreen with brown, scarcely-woody stems trailing over woodland duff, sending up numerous erect yellow-green leafy branches 1-4″ high. Leaves shiny, rather thick, with a few broad teeth at hairy apex. Flowers pink, funnel-shaped, with 5 pale lobes, fragrant, a pair nodding on slender pedicels on a long glandular-hairy stalk at the end of a leafy branch. Fruits glandular, enclosing a single seed. Dry or moist woods; throughout. Summer.

Viburnum. A genus of medium-to-large shrubs with showy many-flowered clusters of 5-lobed white blossoms and red, purple, or black fruits, each with a single large flattened stone. Incidental food for birds and small mammals. Most are edible.

leaf x½

Fig. 253

Hobblebush. *V. alnifolium. Fig. 253.* Straggling shrub with wide-spreading branches, to 6′ or more. Named for the tendency of the flexible, drooping branches to root at the tips, making hoops to trip the unwary. Leaves 4-8″ long, fine-toothed, deeply veined above with a corrugated look; the veins beneath scurfy with the same kind of rusty hairs that cover young twigs and petioles. Flower cluster flat, 3-5″ across, with outer ring of large sterile florets, often pink-tinged; pedicels sessile. Fruits bright red, maturing to deep purple; raisin sweet when ripe. Cool rich woods, especially in hilly areas; southern half from Michigan eastward. Spring.

Witherod. *V. cassinoides. Fig. 254.* Somewhat straggling to upright shrub, to 6′ or more, with scurfy, slim yellow buds. Leaves 1-5″ long, fine-toothed, thick and smooth; lateral veins do not run to the margin, but end in a network of small veins. Flower clusters flat, 2-4″ across, florets all alike; pedicels on a short peduncle. Fruits blue-black at maturity, with a heavy bloom; sweet with rather dry thin pulp. Moist fertile edges, thickets; especially abundant in swamps and lowlands; throughout, except Minnesota and Wisconsin. Early summer.

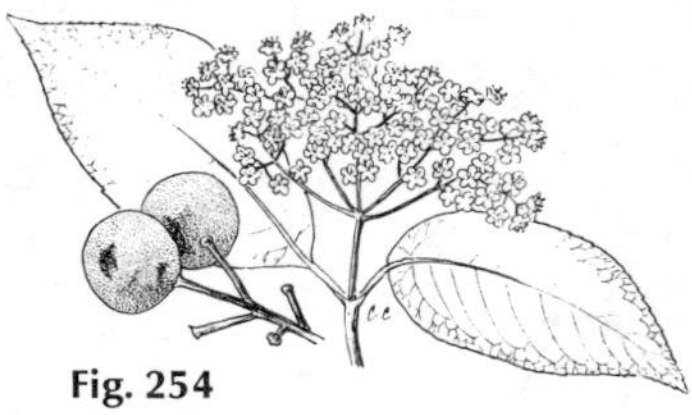

Fig. 254

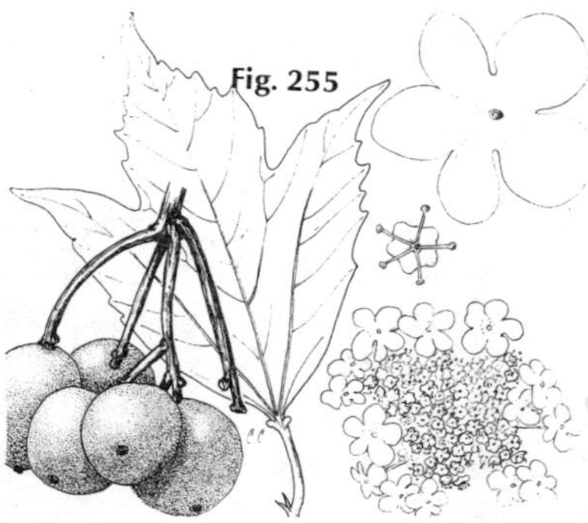

Fig. 255

Highbush Cranberry. *V. trilobum. Fig. 255.* Handsome bold shrub to 12′. Leaves palmately 3-5-ribbed, maplelike, with 3 long lobes and coarse teeth; 2-4″ long; petioles with persistent stipules at the base, and high convex glands near the leaf blade (a feature that distinguishes this native species from the similar European *V. opulus* with its saucerlike concave glands). Flower cluster flat, 2-4″ across with outer ring of large, pure-white sterile florets; pedicels on a long peduncle. Fruits bright red, translucent, shiny, juicy, and acidic; desirable for jelly if not confused with the bitter acrid *V. opulus;* drooping clusters persist until spring. Low moist thickets, woods, shores; throughout, except lower Appalachians. Late spring.

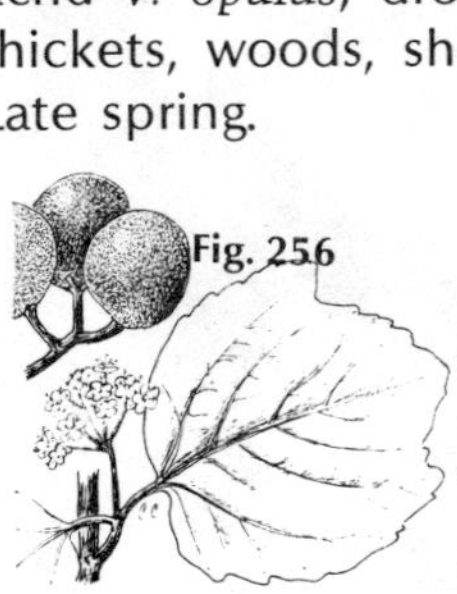

Fig. 256

Squashberry. *V. edule. Fig. 256.* Smooth, 2-6′. Leaves mostly palmately 3-5-ribbed, with 3 short lobes and coarse teeth; 1-4″ long. Flower cluster few-flowered, compact, rounded, ¾-1½″ across, florets all alike; pedicels on a short peduncle at the end of short lateral 2-leaved branchlets. Fruits in small clusters, orange-red; hard and sharply acid before frost, soft and milder after frost; widely used for sauce and jelly. Moist porous soil in cold woods, thickets, shores, mountain slopes; throughout, except lower Appalachians. Late spring through summer.

Red-berried Elder. *Sambucus pubens. Fig. 257.* Large shrub 3-12′, older branches rough and warty, twigs hairy, pith brown. Leaves pinnately compound with 5-7 sharp-toothed leaflets, hairy below; petioles reddish. Flowers numerous in ovoid clusters, yellowish-white, with 4 reflexed lobes and 4 spreading stamens. Fruits bright red, with juicy, yellow, inedible flesh. Woods, openings, rocky ravines; throughout. Early spring.

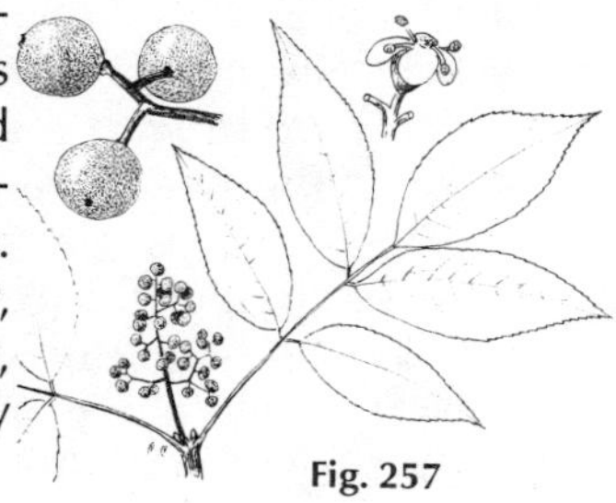

Fig. 257

Common Elder, *S. canadensis*, a more southern species, may be found in rich moist soil in southern parts of region. Pith is white. Large platelike flower clusters, to 8″ across, pure white and fragrant, appear in early summer. Heavy clusters of purple-black fruits, edible when fully ripe. Much used by birds.

BLUEBELL FAMILY. Herbs with milky juice, simple alternate leaves, and 5-lobed flowers.

Harebell. *Campanula rotundifolia. Fig. 258.* Smooth perennial 6-20″, of airy delicate mien but wiry stemmed and hardy. Stem leaves linear, sessile; basal rosette leaves with rounded coarse-toothed blades on long petioles, withering in summer. Flowers blue, bell-shaped, nodding from arched pedicels. Fruit a nodding capsule. Rocky crevices, sandy openings, mountain meadows; throughout, except lower Appalachians. Summer.

Fig. 258

Water Lobelia. *Lobelia Dortmanna. Fig. 259.* Aquatic perennial with submersed rosette of fleshy hollow flattened leaves, firmly anchored in sand of pond bottom. Flowers 2-lipped, pale violet to white, 1-few in a loose terminal raceme, usually lifted above the water on a long naked stalk. Margins of sandy ponds and lakes to depth of 3′; throughout except lower Appalachians. Late summer through fall.

Fig. 259

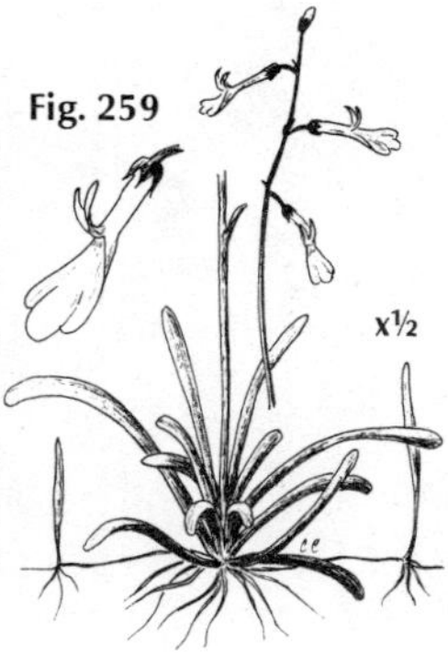

COMPOSITE FAMILY. Herbs whose "flowers" are composed of many small florets assembled on a common base called a *receptacle*, all enclosed by rows of bracts called an *involucre*, in a structure called a *head*. Florets are of two forms: 1) those with a slim 5-lobed tube, grouped at the center of the head, are *disk florets*; 2) those with a single straplike petal, usually encircling the disk, are *ray florets*. Heads of composites like asters contain both forms, while other kinds contain only rays or only disks.

Each fertile ovary in the head produces a one-seeded fruit bearing at its summit a whorl of hairs, bristles, or scales, called a *pappus*. In most species the fruiting head becomes dandelionlike at maturity as the involucre curves back and the pappus hairs spread out.

Identification, based on the above features, is difficult in this worldwide family of more than 15,000 highly variable species. In this book, only the most common species native in this region are detailed, and, as an aid to identification, the family is divided into three groups according to the form of florets in the head.

GROUP I. Heads composed entirely of disk florets.

Joe-Pye-weed. *Eupatorium maculatum. Fig. 260a.* A stout perennial 2-7'. Leaves plaited, toothed, in whorls of 4-5. Heads pink or purplish, long cylindric with pistils and stamens projecting, in a large fuzzy terminal cluster. Damp calcareous shores, meadows, thickets; throughout. Summer.

Two white-flowered species occur southward. Boneset, *E. perfoliatum, Fig. 260b*, of low damp habitats, has a dull white terminal inflorescence and opposite veiny leaves with broad bases joined around the stem. White Snakeroot, *E. rugosum, Fig. 260c*, of woods,

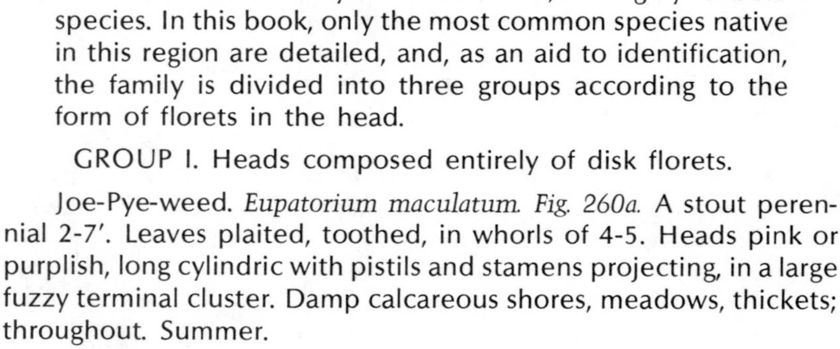

Fig. 260

has a bright white branched inflorescence and opposite leaves with slender petioles. Both late summer through fall.

Fig. 261

Pussy-toes. *Antennaria* sp. *Fig. 261.* Perennials, 4-16″. Species are highly variable, but plants are easily recognized as a genus. Stems and leaves may be green and smooth, or whitened with wool. Fluffy white heads are clustered atop tall stems rising from basal rosettes of paddled-shaped leaves. Often seen as mats of rosettes with few or no flowering stems. Dry open woods, barrens, and gravelly openings; throughout. Spring through summer.

Fig. 262

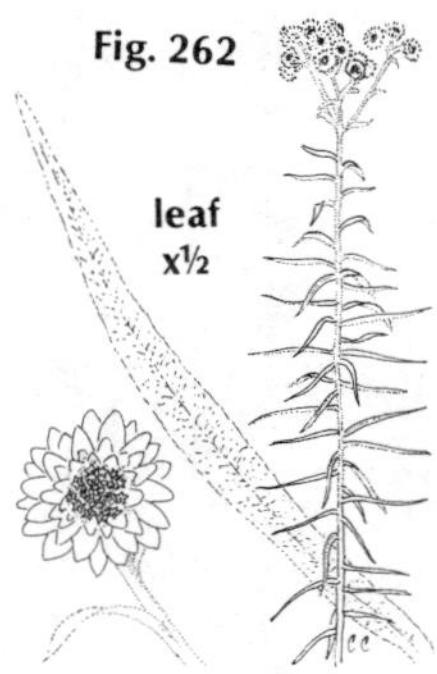

Pearly Everlasting. *Anaphalis margaritacea. Fig. 262.* Perennial 1-3′. Stems white woolly; leaves gray-green woolly, alternate. Heads with bright white bracts that spread outward petal-like around the yellow disks, so that each head looks like a many-petaled single flower. Openings, shores; throughout. May be dried for winter bouquets. Late summer through fall.

Sweet Everlasting, *Gnaphalium uliginosum*, is similar to above but has branched stems and creamy, ovoid heads whose bracts do not spread out until seeds are ripe.

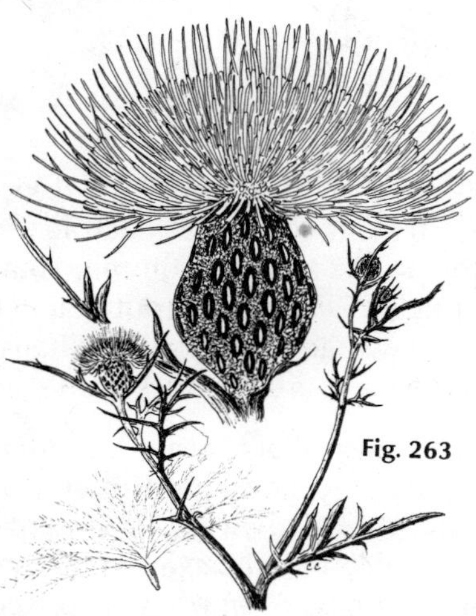

Fig. 263

Swamp Thistle. *Cirsium muticum. Fig. 263.* Biennial 3-9′. Stems growing the second year from a large circular rosette produced the previous year. Leaves of rosette to 8″ long, stem leaves smaller; very deeply cut, with prickles on the margins and weak spines at tips of lobes; hairy beneath. Flowers magenta-pink to rosy-purple; few heads, in axils of upper leaves; involucres sticky, spineless; bracts glossy green with cobwebby, white wool between, which makes the involucre appear gray. Pappus bristles featherlike. Low moist places; throughout. Late summer.

GROUP II. Heads composed of both disk and ray flowers.

Goldenrods. *Solidago. Fig. 264.* Flowers all yellow; heads small, very numerous in showy inflorescences of various forms. Perennials, with alternate leaves on slender erect stems which are most often solitary and unbranched, but tend to grow in colonies. A difficult group, tending to hybridize. Of about 50 species in this region, the following are fairly easily recognized, and illustrate the different forms of inflorescence.

Fig. 264

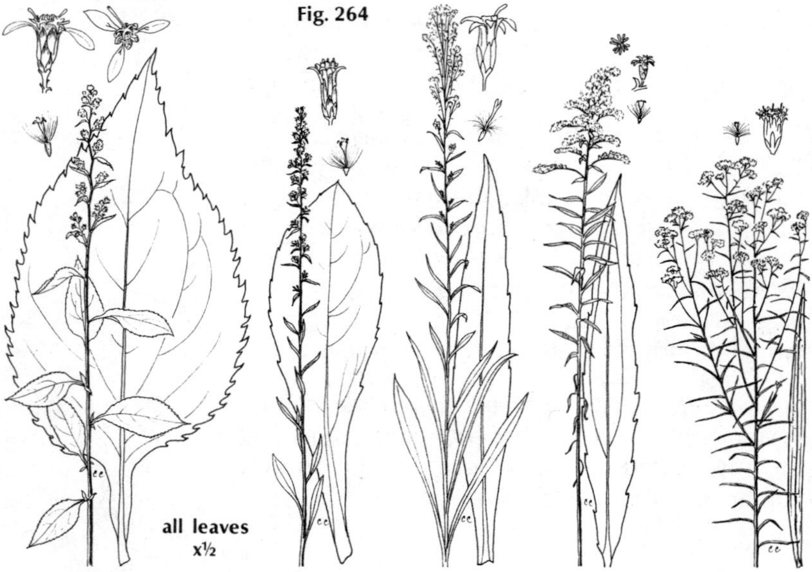

Zigzag Goldenrod. *S. flexicaulis. Fig. 264a.* 1-3′. Upperpart of stem bent slightly at each leaf axil, with small clusters of heads at the angles and the summit. Heads few-flowered, with only 3-4 rays. Principal leaves all about equal; broad, with coarse sharp teeth and a short winged petiole; soft-hairy beneath. Woods; throughout the hardwood area. Late summer.

Hairy Goldenrod. *S. hispida. Fig. 264b.* 1-3′. Inflorescence slenderly cylindric at the end of stems that may be hairy or nearly smooth. Heads with 7-14 deep-yellow rays, in small clusters in the axils of leafy bracts, alternate around the stem. Leaves more or less hairy, margins smooth or obscurely toothed. Upper leaves much smaller than lower, becoming sessile toward the top of stem; lowermost and basal leaves to 8″ long, with evident petioles.

Woods' edges, rocky (mainly calcareous) openings and shores; throughout. Summer through fall.

Stout Goldenrod, *S. squarrosa*, an eastern species of similar form, differs in being larger and smoother, with larger heads of 10-17 well-formed rays, and stiff, recurved bracts.

Bog (or Marsh) Goldenrod. *S. Purshii. Fig. 264c.* 2-5′. Inflorescence a terminal panicle of long-stalked heads loosely arranged around ascending branches, giving the whole an open graceful look. Heads with 4-6 rays. Plant smooth. Leaves somewhat fleshy, reduced in size toward top of stem; lower and basal leaves to 12″ or more long, with long petioles. Marshy or damp peaty places; throughout. Late summer.

This species should not be confused with *S. uliginosa* of most books, a more southern form of bog goldenrod, which has heads arranged on the upper side of spreading branches. Where ranges overlap, the two species tend to hybridize.

Canada Goldenrod. *S. canadensis. Fig. 264d.* 2-4′. Classic goldenrod inflorescence, with showy pyramidal clusters formed of arched, spreading branches crowded with tiny bright yellow heads all turned upward. Heads with 10-17 minute rays and few disk flowers. Leaves all about equal, with 3 prominent parallel veins; upper leaves sessile, crowded around the stem; lower leaves wither early. Upperpart of stem hairy or downy. Stems solitary or clustered, spreading by rhizomes to form colonies. Openings and roadsides; throughout. Late summer.

Rough Goldenrod, *S. rugosa*, abundant northeastward, is similar in general form, but differs in having feather-veined leaves, and only 6-11 small rays in the slightly larger heads.

Grass-leaved Goldenrod. *S. graminifolia. Fig. 264e.* 1-4′. Stems branching above the middle into a broad open inflorescence composed of many compact clusters of small heads at the ends of the leafy branches. Leaves very slender, rough edged. Moist open thickets, shores; throughout. Summer through early fall.

The genus *Aster*, like the goldenrods, is a large group, very freely hybridizing. Even expert botanists have difficulty identifying them closely. Of the 24 species identified in this region, this book lists only those common ones with fairly clear features. Asters are perennials with numerous heads and conspicuous rays, in showy clusters at the ends of branched leafy stems.

Large-leaved Aster. *A. macrophyllus. Fig. 265.* 1-3½'. Variable, but easily recognized by the large heart-shaped, long petioled, rough-textured leaves at the base of the stem. Tufts of these large leaves, spreading by rhizomes, cover broad areas of the forest floor, only occasionally sending up flowering stems. Heads relatively few in a flat-topped or rounded cluster, with sticky glandular branches; rays 9-20, blue-violet or, rarely, white. Woods in the hardwood area. Summer through fall.

Heart-leaved Aster. *A. cordifolius. Fig. 266.* 1-5'. Heads numerous in a tall leafy-bracted panicle; rays 10-20, pale blue-violet to white. Leaves heart-shaped, petioled, relatively thin textured, sharply-toothed. Open woods in the hardwood area from Wisconsin eastward. Late summer through fall.

Redstem Aster. *A. puniceus. Fig. 267.* To 6' or more. Highly variable. Many heads in a large leafy inflorescence; rays 20-40, blue-violet, pink, or white; disk flowers numerous; bracts of the involucre loose. Leaves lance shaped, to 8" long, tapered from a sessile base clasping the stem. Stems reddish; hairy or bristly. Damp thickets, openings, shores; throughout. Fall.

Panicled Aster. *A. simplex. Fig. 268.* 2-7'. Conspicuous, with a large twice-branched, leafy panicle of brilliant white flowers. Numerous heads, with 20-40 narrow rays; bracts of involucre show a central green longitudinal band. Leaves numerous, slenderly lance-shaped, 4-8" long, becoming progressively larger toward the base of the plant. Spreads by rhizomes to form localized colonies. Shores, damp meadows; throughout the hardwood area. Late summer through fall.

Calico Aster. *A. lateriflorus. Fig. 269.* 1-4'. Very distinctive with small heads of 9-15 white rays and pink-to-purple disk flowers carried on the upper side of nearly-horizontal, leafy branches arising from the axils of lancelike stem leaves on the upper half of the plant. Openings, woods edges, shores; throughout the hardwood area. Late summer through fall.

Bog Aster. *A. nemoralis. Fig. 270.* 4-24". Heads few or solitary at the ends of simple stems; rays lilac to purple; bracts of involucre long tapered and often tinged with purple. Leaves 40-100, with rough inrolled margins, crowded on slightly sticky, rough-hairy stems. Spreads by rhizomes. Acid bogs in coniferous forest area from Michigan eastward. Late summer.

Fig. 266

Fig. 265

Fig. 267

Fig. 269

Fig. 268

Fig. 270

Fig. 271

all leaves
x½

Flat-topped Aster. *A. umbellatus. Fig. 271.* 2-6′. Easily identified by its bold arc of creamy white flowers at the ends of stout leafy stems. Heads numerous on a flattened branched cluster; rays few and unevenly spaced. Leaves broadly lance-shaped, to 6″ long; margins bristly, not toothed. Forest edges, moist thickets, in hardwood areas. Late summer.

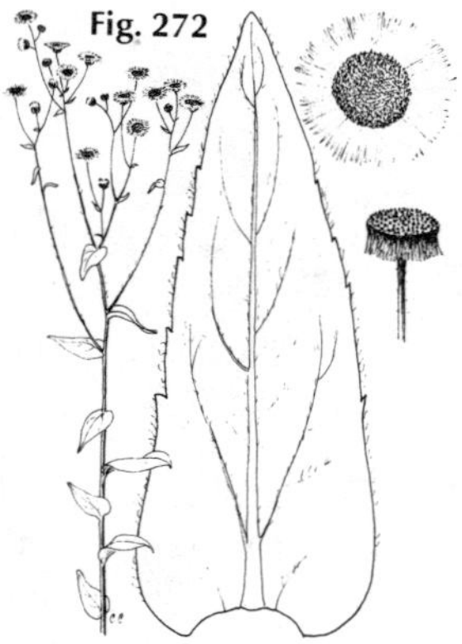
Fig. 272

Fleabane. *Erigeron philadelphicus. Fig.* 272. 1-3′. Annual or short-lived perennial, superficially resembling an aster, but with 100-150 very delicate pink to white rays encircling a bright yellow disk. Heads few to many in an open, branched, terminal cluster. Leaves and stems clothed with long soft hairs. The leaves sessile, with clasping bases. Seeds are quickly deciduous, leaving a brown papillose receptacle. Found in moist places throughout the hardwood forest area. Spring through summer.

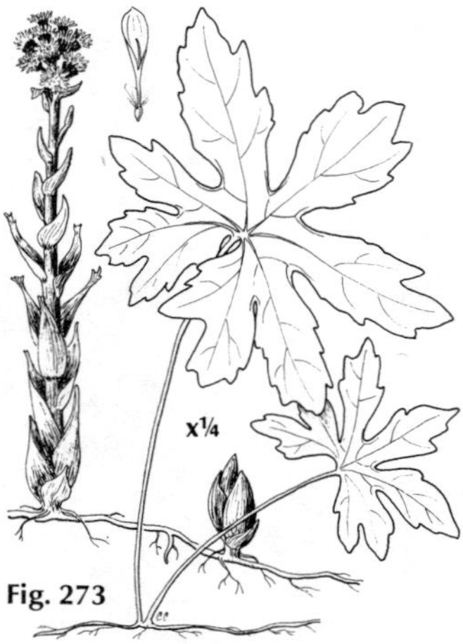

Fig. 273

Sweet Coltsfoot. *Petasites palmatus. Fig.* 273. 4-18″. Perennial with stout flowering stalks from creeping rhizomes before the leaves appear. Heads of fragrant creamy white flowers, some without rays, in a large terminal cluster. Stalk sheathed by leaflike bracts with parallel veins. Leaves arising from rhizome; long-petioled, with blades 2-10″ broad, palmately cut into several coarse-toothed lobes; white-woolly beneath. In patches in conifer woods and cold boggy meadows; throughout, except lower Appalachians. Spring.

Fig. 274

Ragwort. *Senecio pauperculus. Fig.* 274. 4-16″. A small perennial with few heads in a terminal cluster; rays and disk yellow; involucre a single series of slender bracts. Flowering stems bear pinnately-lobed leaves, smaller and sessile toward the inflorescence. Plants usually in colonies, with many sterile tufts of rosette leaves with long petioles and simple elliptic blades. Wet rocks, gravels, shores, in limestone areas; throughout. Summer.

Variety *Balsamitae* is larger, with as many as 40 heads in a cluster.

GROUP III. Heads composed entirely of ray flowers.

Blue Lettuce. *Lactuca biennis. Fig. 275.* 3-12′. Striking, tall, leafy-stemmed biennial with milky juice. Distinctive lobed leaves coarsely- and sharply-toothed, 4-16″ long. Heads very numerous in a massive many-branched inflorescence in all stages of development; smoky-blue or dingy-yellow rays rarely seen in full bloom; the involucre bright green with purple tipped bracts, slender in flower, becoming bulbous at base in fruit. Pappus gray-brown, bristles ephemeral, falling one by one. Damp openings and thickets; throughout hardwood area. Summer.

Fig. 275

Canada Hawkweed. *Hieracium canadense. Fig. 276.* 1-5′. Leafy stemmed perennial, sometimes hairy at base. Leaves sessile, coarse-toothed, smooth or slightly hairy. Showy yellow flowers in an open cluster of relatively few heads. Rays 40-100, neatly arranged in concentric series, with 5 teeth on each square-ended ray. Pappus bristles tan, in spherical long-lasting heads. Sandy openings, woods, shores, rocks; throughout except lower Appalachians. Summer.

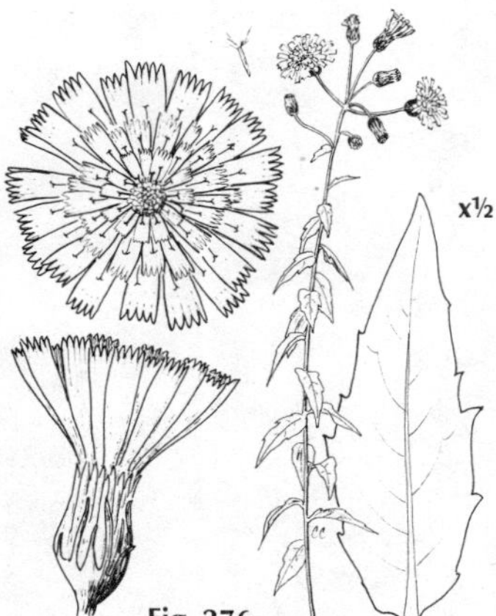

Fig. 276

Rough Hawkweed, *H. scabrum*, can be distinguished from the above species by the following features: stems reddish and bristly; flower stalks and involucres rough with bristles and dark glands; leaves more or less rough-hairy, with glandular margins; heads more numerous in a stiff somewhat cylindric flower cluster. Dry sandy woods and openings throughout the hardwood areas. Summer.

Fig. 277. In this Northwoods scene, no animals are visible. Yet, close observation over a period of time would reveal a large number of mammals, birds, and cold-blooded vertebrates here. The following pages are designed to help you discover those "invisible" creatures which may be underground, overhead, or hidden in the vegetation.

Mammals of the Northwoods

Every type of habitat in the Northwoods Region is occupied by one or more species of mammal. The animal may have its den or nest in the area, it may be seeking food there, or simply passing through. Some mammals are restricted to one type of habitat while others may be found in several different habitats. Some need a territory many miles in extent, but others live out their lives in a fraction of an acre.

Good places to look for mammals are streamsides and lake shores, edges of forests and thickets, openings, and back roads. Look for their signs: runways, dens, nests on the ground or in trees, remains of food or food caches, tracks, and droppings.

There are many bird watchers, but few good mammal watchers; however, observing mammals can be just as rewarding, albeit often more difficult. Most mammals in the wild are wary. Many are active only during the hours from dusk to early morning. Most are secretive, showing themselves rarely, and those that do come into view seldom stand still long enough to give us a good look at them. In order to see more than the most common and fearless mammals, knowledge of their haunts and habits is required.

The more knowledgeable one becomes about the wildlife of an area, the more enjoyable it can be to live or visit there. The purpose of the following pages is to help you become better acquainted with the native animals that inhabit the Northwoods, so that you can appreciate them for their fascinating variety, and understand them as essential elements of the complex fabric of the region. Understanding of the animals and their ways can help us to adapt our reactions to their behavior, so that we see them not as antagonists to be fought (and, all too often, killed), but rather as fellow inhabitants with a rightful place on an earth of infinite diversity. On better acquaintance, some will be discovered to be not only interesting and beautiful, but also charming neighbors around the home, cabin, or campsite.

As with the plants, the descriptions and illustrations below are designed to complement each other. Features clearly shown in the figures are not repeated in the text unless they have a special significance that adds to understanding the animal.

Body length in the descriptions is the combined length of head and torso, excluding the tail, for this is the dimension which gives the visual impression of an animal's size.

Mammal color cannot always be described in simple terms. In many species, the fur is not a single color; it may vary through two or more hues in bands from base to tip of hair. This variation can be further complicated by the presence of guard hairs of still another hue intermixed with the underfur. In addition, some mammals vary their color with the seasons.

Since this book is written for field observation, the descriptions of species do not include morphological details that would require an animal to be captured for examination. Rather, those features that can be seen with the naked eye or field glasses, as the animals move about their habitats, are described here.

INSECT-EATING MAMMALS. A group of small plantigrade animals with 5 toes on both front and back feet, small eyes and ears, long snouts, and short dark, velvety fur.

MOLE FAMILY. Broad powerful front legs and feet, very small eyes buried in fur, and absence of external ears adapt these mammals for tunneling through the ground.

Hairytail Mole. *Parascalops breweri. Fig. 278*. Body 5-6″; tail 1″. Fur is velvety soft, dark slate to blackish. Soles of the front feet face outward. Tail bristly. Found in sandy areas in the east and south of this region.

Fig. 278

Fig. 279

Starnose Mole. *Condylura cristata. Fig. 279*. Body 5″; tail 2½″. Fur is dark brown to black, dense and silky. Tail thickened near the body, tapering to a long point. Snout has 22 pink fleshy projections around the nostrils. A good swimmer, found in wet areas, bogs, and swamps; throughout.

SHREW FAMILY. *Fig. 280*. Superficially resemble long-nosed mice. Includes the smallest of all our mammals.

Masked Shrew. *Sorex cinereus.* Body 2-2½"; tail 1½". Fur dull black or brownish-black, grayish beneath. Found under leaves and plant debris in woodlands, and in brushy or grassy areas near water; throughout.

Smoky Shrew. *S. fumeus*. Body 3"; tail 2". Fur brownish-gray, lighter beneath. Found locally under duff on the floor of mixed forest; above the Great Lakes and eastward.

Arctic Shrew. *S. arcticus*. Body 2½"; tail 1½". Upperparts dark brown; sides and face lighter brownish; underparts grayish. Found in spruce, tamarack, or open sphagnum bogs; throughout except southeast and Appalachians.

Northern Water Shrew. *S. palustris. Fig. 280b*. Body 3½"; tail 2½". Fur dull blackish-brown, lighter beneath. Long tail; large hind feet bordered with stiff hairs. Aquatic; found along streams, ponds, lakes, and bogs. This shrew will run over the surface of the water, swim beneath, or run on the bottom, feeding on aquatic insects. Throughout, but not common.

Pigmy Shrew. *Microsorex hoyi. Fig. 280a*. Body 2½"; tail 1". The smallest of our mammals. Fur light brown above, paler beneath. Found in wooded areas and grassy edges, but rarely seen; throughout.

Fig. 280

Short-tailed Shrew. *Blarina brevicauda. Fig. 280c*. Body 4½"; tail 1". Largest of the shrews of this region, about the size of a small meadow mouse. Fur gray or lead gray. The bite of this shrew is considered poisonous, but not dangerous. Found in all habitats; especially common in deep forest and swampy areas; throughout.

BATS. *Fig. 281*. Mammals adapted for true flight by a leathery winglike membrane stretched between the greatly elongated digits of the front feet, to the hind legs and tail. Food consists entirely of insects. All bats in this region belong to a single family characterized by plain unmodified muzzles. Body length of the bats below *includes* the tail.

Fig. 281

Little Brown Bat. *Myotis lucifugus*. 3½"; wingspread to 11". Body brown with an olive or yellowish tinge; shoulders darker; ears and wings dark brown to black. Ears not noticeably long. Nests in hollow trees, outbuildings, and under eaves; flies over lakes in forested areas; throughout.

The Eastern Long-eared Bat, *M. keeni*, is very similar to the little brown bat, and has similar habits, but differs in having longer, more pointed ears.

Silver-haired Bat. *Lasionycteris noctivagans*. 4"; wingspread to 12". Body blackish-brown, hairs tipped with silvery white. Solitary. Rests in hollow trees and dense foliage; flies late in the evening. Found in forested areas near water; throughout.

Big Brown Bat. *Eptesicus fuscus*. 4½"; wingspread to 12¾". Heavier bodied than the preceding species. Body uniform dark brown; ears and wings black. Solitary. Rests in hollow trees, caves, rock crevices, and buildings; flies late evening, often near the ground; throughout.

Hoary Bat. *Lasiurus cinereus*. 5½"; wingspread to 16". Fur of the back is colored in 4 bands from base to tip: dark brown, to golden yellow, to dark brown, to white. These colors appear as a mottled surface pattern of frosted yellowish-brown. Fur of the throat is yellowish. One of the largest bats of North America, but one of the least likely to be seen. Solitary. Nocturnal, but may sometimes be seen flying among forest trees in daylight. Found among conifers; throughout.

Red Bat. *L. borealis.* 4½"; wingspread to 12½". Fur is always reddish without any tinge of black; faintly white-tipped hairs give a slight frosty appearance. Solitary. Rests in trees. Found mainly in deciduous forest, open woodland, farmland, and parks, usually near water; throughout.

CARNIVORES. Flesh-eating mammals, with specially modified canine teeth and well developed brains. The value of these highly intelligent mammals in the plan of the earth is becoming better appreciated as mankind attains maturity and greater wisdom.

BEAR FAMILY. Plantigrade, virtually tailless carnivores that have lost much of their flesh-eating adaptation. The single species in this region eats mainly fruits, acorns and seeds, insects, and some small mammals.

Black Bear. *Ursus americanus. Fig. 282*. Body 4-6'; tail 4-6"; height 2-3'; 300-400 lbs. Exceedingly silent and agile despite its size. Fur is dark brown to black. Mostly solitary. Does not den, but seeks a sheltered place to rest. Dormant in winter. May seem friendly, but should not be trusted. Found in dense woods, swamps, brushy areas, and in dumps around human habitations within forested areas; throughout.

Fig. 282

Fig. 283

RACCOON FAMILY. A small family of semi-arboreal carnivores which, like the bears, have lost much of their flesh-eating habits. The diet of the single species in this region is similar to the bear's, but includes also frogs and crayfish.

Raccoon. *Procyon lotor. Fig. 283*. Body 18-28"; tail 9-11". Looks bulky because of its long fur. Color varies among individuals from yellowish-gray to nearly black. Plantigrade; walks with a swaying gait like a bear. Dens in hollow trees. Inactive in very cold weather. Found near lakes and streams in woods where large den trees are available; throughout.

WEASEL FAMILY. A diversified group of carnivores whose common characteristic is the possession of musk glands. Most have elongate bodies and short legs. Sizes range from the smallest of the American carnivores, the least weasel, to the large wolverine, formerly of this region but now found only in the far north.

Marten. *Martes americana. Fig. 284.* Body 16-18″; tail 8-9″. Upperparts yellowish-brown; underparts darker, but with a light buff throat and chest; legs and bushy tail dark brown to nearly black; ears prominent. Dens in hollow trees. Found in heavy conifer forest; north of Lake Superior and eastward.

Fisher. *M. pennanti. Fig. 285.* Body 22-26″; tail 13-15″. Fur dark brown to nearly black; whitish bands on guard hairs give back, shoulders, and head a grayed appearance. Dens in hollow trees or logs. Found in dense, mixed forests near water; north of Lake Superior and eastward; rarely in northern U.S.

Short-tailed Weasel. *Mustela erminea. Fig. 286.* Body 9″; tail 3½″. Summer fur dark brown above; underparts and inside of legs creamy- or yellowish-white; toes white; end of tail black. Winter fur white except for black tail-tip. Nests and runways underground beneath logs or stumps. Found in woodland and brushy open areas, or wherever mice are plentiful; throughout except lower Appalachians.

Long-tailed Weasel. *M. frenata. Fig. 287.* Body 10-12″; tail 5-6″. In all features similar to the above species, except that toes usually are not white in summer, and tail is proportionately longer. Uses runways of moles and chipmunks. Found in woodlands and brushy areas near water; southern half.

Least Weasel. *M. rixosa. Fig. 288.* Body 6″; tail 1½″. Summer fur dark brown above; underparts white; short tail not black-tipped. Winter fur entirely white. Uses nests of mice or other small mammals. Found in marshy areas, low woodlands, and meadows; west of the St. Lawrence River, and Appalachians; not common anywhere.

Mink. *M. vison. Fig. 289.* Body 16-18″; tail 8-9″. Fur uniformly dark brown, except for whitish chin, and black tail-tip. Inquisitive; a good swimmer. Dens in any available hole or crevice near water. Found along shores of lakes or streams in shrubby or forested areas; throughout.

River Otter. *Lutra canadensis. Fig. 290*. Body 24-30"; tail 12-18". Fur dark brown, glossy, and dense; grayish on throat and around mouth. Head broad and flattened; tail thick at base, tapering to the tip; feet webbed. Agile, graceful, and playful; active day or night, summer and winter. Watch for slides down muddy banks, or snowbanks, along watercourses. Feeds mainly on crayfish and non-game fish. Dens under banks, usually with entrance below water; or in abandoned beaver lodges. Found along rivers, streams, and lake shores; throughout.

Striped Skunk. *Mephitis mephitis. Fig. 291*. Body 16-19"; tail 9-11". Fur glossy black and white. Omnivorous; consumes many insects and mice. Dens in burrows, caves, or rock crevices. Inactive in winter, usually denning in groups. Found in broken woodland and grassy openings, usually near water; throughout.

DOG FAMILY. Carnivores with long muzzles, and long legs adapted for running. These handsome animals have long held an undeserved place on man's enemy list. More recently, the value of these and other carnivores is being reevaluated; they are becoming recognized as ecologically beneficial.

Coyote. *Canis latrans. Fig. 292*. Body 32-36"; tail 12-15". Fur yellowish-gray; hairs on back black-tipped; underparts whitish or light gray; bushy tail blackish above. Muzzle slim; ears large and pointed, directed forward; tail carried down when running. Sociable and playful. Feeds mainly on rodents, rabbits, and carrion. Dens in burrows or rock crevices, well concealed. Found at forest edges, cutover land, second growth hardwood, and shrubby areas; westward from New York and the St. Lawrence River.

Gray Wolf. *C. lupus. Fig. 293*. Body 43-46"; tail 15-19". Distinguished from the coyote by its grayer to nearly-black upperparts, its larger size, broader muzzle, relatively shorter ears, and the horizontal bearing of the tail when running. Dens in natural cavities, or under stumps or windfalls. Found in forest wilderness and openings within the forest; west from the St. Lawrence Valley.

Red Fox. *Vulpes fulva. Fig. 294*. Body 22-25"; tail 13-16". Upperparts bright yellowish-red, darker on back; underparts whitish; legs, feet, and back of ears black, tail tipped with white. Feeds largely on mice, and on insects and fruit in summer. Dens in burrows; often in one abandoned by another animal, usually on an open hillside. Found in woods interspersed with open areas, along streams, lakes, marshes, and farmlands; throughout.

The Gray Fox, *Urocyon cinereoargenteus*, is rare in woodland areas along the southern border of this region.

CAT FAMILY. Carnivores with highly specialized teeth in short broad skulls, and relatively large feet with retractile claws. The two species in this region feed largely on hares.

Lynx. *Lynx canadensis. Fig. 295*. Body 2½-3'; tail 4". Upperparts yellowish-gray, unevenly darker along the back due to black-tipped guard hairs; legs lighter, with scarcely any spotting; underparts white or grayish. Distinguished from the bobcat by the black tip of the tail, very large feet, long black ear tufts, and longer more pronounced ruff. Dens in hollow trees, or under logs or windfalls; throughout, wherever there is secluded dense forest.

Fig. 292

Fig. 294

Fig. 293

Fig. 295

Fig. 296

Bobcat. *L. rufus. Fig. 296*. Body 2-2½′; tail 6″. Fur color similar to the lynx, but distinguished by more distinct spotting on legs and underparts, and tail marked with black only on the upper side; feet smaller, ear tufts and ruff shorter than lynx's. Found in swampy or rocky woodlands with brush cover; throughout southern half of region.

RODENTS. Gnawing mammals having a pair of chisellike incisor teeth in each jaw, specialized for cutting into hard-shelled nuts and seeds, or slicing woody stems. Five families in this region.

SQUIRREL FAMILY. Mammals with bushy, well-furred tails. The tails of tree dwellers are long, with long hairs, and serve as balancers.

Woodchuck. *Marmota monax. Fig. 297*. Body 15-17"; tail 5-6". Largest of the squirrel family, of stocky build, with short strong legs. The northern form has upperparts brown; underparts with a reddish tone; coarse multi-hued guard hairs give the fur a salt-and-pepper appearance. The southern form is more gray-brown. Dens in extensive burrows which may start under a stump or tree root, in a cliff opening, under an old building, or on a hillside. Hibernates. May be seen in summer along edges of forest and thicket, never far from its home; throughout.

Least Chipmunk. *Eutamias minimus. Fig. 298*. Body 4-5"; tail 3-4". Slim build, sharp features. Upperparts yellow-brown overlaid with dark brown guard hairs; two conspicuous stripes on each side of the face; five dark brown stripes separated by four whitish stripes on the back, extending to the base of the tail; underparts creamy white. Sociable, active, and vocal; easily seen at midday from spring to fall. Nests in hollow trees or stumps. Hibernates. Found in areas of heavy ground cover and underbrush, usually near conifers; from Ontario westward.

Eastern Chipmunk. *Tamias striatus. Fig. 299*. Body 6-7"; tail 3-4". Slightly larger, more stocky than least chipmunk. Overall color more gray; facial stripes less distinct; back stripes end in a russet patch on the rump; central body stripes obscured by dark guard hairs. Solitary, and jealous of territory; but friendly with people, active, vocal, and easily seen. Nests in burrows. Hibernates. Found in mixed forest, open brushy areas, rock outcrops, and around habitations; throughout.

Red Squirrel. *Tamiasciurus hudsonicus. Fig. 300*. Body 7-8"; tail 5-6". A saucy, agile, and noisy little squirrel. Upperparts reddish-brown, brighter on the tail; underparts pure white, separated from the upper by a dark stripe; prominent white eye ring. Look for piles of cones and cone scales under conifer trees; or learn its rapid

Fig. 297 Fig. 298 Fig. 299 Fig. 300 Fig. 301 Fig. 302

chattering call and no other clue will be needed. Like all tree squirrels, it is charming and interesting to watch, and often comical. Nests in tree holes if available, or builds leaf nests on branches. Found mainly in forests where there are conifers; throughout.

Gray Squirrel. *Sciurus carolinensis. Fig. 301*. Body 9-11″; tail 8-10″. Upperparts gray with a yellowish-brown tinge; underparts white or dull white; hair of tail dark, tipped with white. Some individuals may be more brown than gray, with underparts yellowish-brown; and some, rarely, may be entirely black. Nests preferably in tree holes, but if necessary in leaf nests on branches. Found in hardwood forests, and in city parks and farm woodlots; southern half of the region.

Northern Flying Squirrel. *Glaucomys sabrinus. Fig. 302*. Body 6-7″; tail 5-6″. A nocturnal squirrel that "flies" by means of a furred membrane between wrist and ankle, which, when stretched out, enables the animal to glide from tree to tree. Upperparts yellowish-brown, toned grayish by the gray base of the hairs; flying membrane dark above, with a blackish edge; underparts entirely white. Gentle and sociable; nests in groups in hollow trees or old woodpecker holes. Found in mature conifer or mixed forest; throughout.

The Southern Flying Squirrel, *G. volans*, smaller and lighter colored, may be seen along the southern edges of this region.

BEAVER FAMILY. A single genus in the family, represented in this region by the following single species. Distinguished by its stocky body; broad, flattened, furless tail; and webbed hind feet.

Beaver. *Castor canadensis. Fig. 303*. Body 24-29"; tail 12-17", the terminal 9-12" flattened and scaly. Fur is deep brown; dense. Feeds on aquatic and shore plants in summer, and stored twigs in winter. Its dams and ponds, large lodges, and signs of its logging activity are frequent sights in the Northwoods. Found in water habitats in forest areas, among aspen, birch, willow, and maple; throughout.

MOUSE FAMILY. A diverse family with two groups here.

The first includes the *Peromyscus* mice. These have prominent eyes and ears, slender bodies and legs, white feet and underparts, and long bicolored tails.

The second includes the lemming, voles, and muskrat. These have small eyes and ears more or less concealed by the fur; compact rounded bodies with gray underparts; short legs; and shorter tails. The small ones are difficult to identify, for they live at a hectic pace and rarely pause to allow a good look. Best identified by habitat coupled with the descriptions.

Woodland Deer Mouse. *Peromyscus maniculatus gracilis. Fig. 304*. Body 3½-4"; tail 3-4". Upperparts reddish-brown; underparts pure white. Tail brownish above, white beneath, tipped with a small tuft of long hairs. Internal cheek pouches enable these mice to carry seeds and nuts (like chipmunks) to store in small caches. Feed mainly on seeds, nuts, and insects. Nest usually in cavities in or near the ground; but these climbers sometimes roof over an abandoned bird nest for a snug home. Handsome and lively; friendly neighbors around camp or summer cottage. Found in forested areas where undergrowth is plentiful; throughout.

The Northern White-footed Mouse, *P. leucopus*, closely resembles the above, and occurs along the southern edge of this region.

Southern Bog Lemming. *Synaptomys cooperi*. Body 4"; tail 1" or less. Upperparts gray-brown; underparts dull white or gray. Feeds on grass and sedges. Runways and nests at or near ground surface under grass thatch, fallen logs, or shrub roots. Found locally in low or boggy, grassy areas; throughout.

Fig. 303

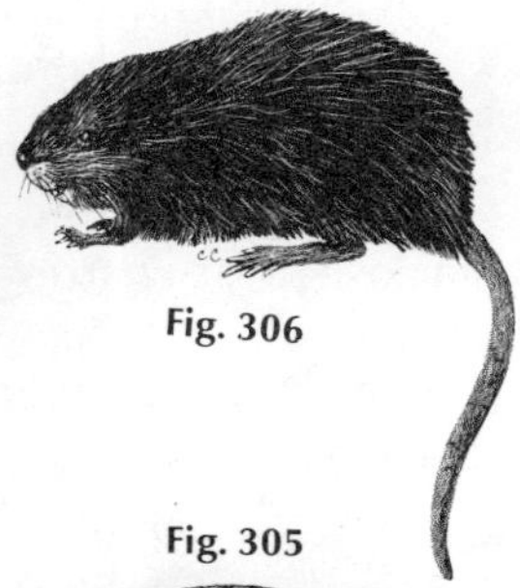

Fig. 306

Fig. 305

Fig. 304

Heather Vole. *Phenacomys intermedius.* Body 4″; tail 1-1½″. Upperparts gray; yellowish on face and nose; underparts light gray. Found in dry wild areas under good ground cover; uncommon; northward above the Great Lakes.

Boreal Red-backed Vole. *Clethrionomys gapperi.* Body 4″; tail 1-1½″. Upperparts yellowish-gray with a broad band of reddish-brown from top of head to tail; underparts gray. Found in coniferous swamps and moist coniferous or deciduous forest, principally where there are decaying moss-covered logs and stumps for nest sites; throughout.

Meadow Vole. *Microtus pennsylvanicus. Fig. 305.* Body 5″; tail 2″. Upperparts dark brown to nearly black; underparts tend toward brownish-gray and silvery. Eats mainly grass and sedge. Runways and nests under grass. Found wherever grass cover is heavy, in both upland and lowland; throughout.

Yellownose Vole. *M. chrotorrhinus.* Body 3½-4½″; tail 2″. Upperparts dark gray; nose and face reddish-orange; underparts light gray sprinkled with white. Found in areas of rocky outcrops; above the Canadian border, and down the Appalachians.

Muskrat. *Ondatra zibethica. Fig. 306.* Body 11-14″; tail 8-11″, compressed from side to side, scaly, and sparsely furred. Fur is dense; upperparts brown, with scattered glossy black guard hairs over the back; underparts grayish. Feeds on aquatic plants. Inhabits quiet waters, where it builds domed houses in the water, using cattails and other aquatic plants; throughout.

JUMPING MOUSE FAMILY. Small mice with large hind feet adapted for jumping, and very long bicolored tails.

Woodland Jumping Mouse. *Napaeozapus insignis. Fig. 307*. Body 4″; tail 5½-6″, tipped with white. Upperparts brownish with a broad blackish central stripe; sides bright yellow-brown; underparts pure white. Eats insects, berries, and seeds. Hibernates. A beautiful mouse found at woods' edges, and grassy brushland bordering streams; throughout.

The Meadow Jumping Mouse, *Zapus hudsonius*, is similar, but lacks the white tail-tip and clearly delineated color pattern. Similar habitat and range, but often in more open places.

Fig. 308

Fig. 307

Fig. 309

PORCUPINE FAMILY. A single species in North America, characterized by long barbed quills on lower back and tail.

Porcupine. *Erethizon dorsatum. Fig. 308*. Body 23-33″; tail 6-7″. The yellowish-white guard hairs and quills of this large rodent stand up above the dark brown soft body fur. Dens in hollow trees or logs, or rock crevices. Found in forested areas, preferably where there are conifers; throughout.

HARES AND RABBITS. Characterized by an upper pair of large chisel incisors for cutting, and directly behind them on the same jaw, a second small pair for grinding. Two species of a single family occur in the Northwoods Region.

Snowshoe Hare. *Lepus americanus. Fig. 309*. Body 14-19″; tail 1-2″. Fur is light brown in summer, white in winter. Very large hind feet densely furred; long ears. Does not make a nest, but has favorite sheltered spots where it rests. Found in mixed forest and swamps, where there is good daytime cover of brush and down logs; throughout.

The Cottontail, *Sylvilagus floridanus*, found in the southern parts of this region, retains its gray-brown color all year.

HOOFED MAMMALS. The third and fourth toes have become modified into a strong two-parted hoof. Represented in this region by a single family.

DEER FAMILY. Males of this family (and female caribou, also) have antlers which are shed each year.

Fig. 310 Fig. 311 Fig. 312

White-tailed Deer. *Odocoileus virginianus. Fig. 310*. Body 5-6′; tail 12-14″; height 3-3½′; 240 lbs. average weight. Upperparts reddish-brown in summer, and more gray in winter; underparts white. Watch for the flash of white under the raised tail as a deer takes flight. Found in border areas and openings of forests, thickets, farmlands, and occasionally cedar swamps; throughout.

Moose. *Alces alces. Fig. 311*. Body 8-9′; tail 3-4″; height 5½-6′; antler spread 4-6′; 850-1200 lbs. Fur dark brown to blackish. A strip of skin called the *bell*, 8-10″ or more long, hangs below the throat; more prominent in males. Nose rounded, upper lip overhanging. Antlers flattened and broad. Found in forested areas near swamps, lakes, and rivers, where it may be seen wading near shore feeding on aquatic plants; throughout, excepting the southernmost areas.

Woodland Caribou. *Rangifer caribou. Fig. 312*. Body 6-7′; tail 4-6″; height 4′; 350-400 lbs. Fur brownish or dark gray; head, neck, shoulders, and rump whitish. Hooves broad. Antlers flattened, and usually with prongs projecting forward over the brow. A wanderer, ranging through forests, swamps, and upland bogs; north above a line from Lake Superior to Newfoundland.

Fig. 313. Black tern in flight.

Birds of the Northwoods

Birds are the most mobile of all the wildlife discussed in this book, but over the long term most of them can be found during the breeding season within fairly well defined habitats in the Northwoods Region. Environmental conditions, however, can cause alterations in populations from year to year. Among the conditions having the most serious effect on bird presence are changes in food supply, destruction of habitat, and, more recently, the widespread use of highly toxic insecticides.

In the case of poisoning and habitat loss, species may be completely eliminated from an area; and in the case of failure or reduction of food supply, marked shifts in numbers can occur. At the same time, if population pressure is high in a favorable area, many kinds of birds will take up residence in less desirable situations, going unconcernedly about their activities in places we would not normally expect to find them.

Sensitive as they are to their surroundings, birds often seem to disregard human definitions of range and habitat, making the study of birds in the field a less than perfect science. But it is this very uncertainty that gives bird observation its interest and challenge.

In this book, ranges have been noted only for those species limited to a certain part of the region. The species included are those that normally nest here. Those that appear only during spring and fall migrations are not included, since they are not characteristic residents of the region.

Color descriptions are for adult males in breeding plumage, the plumage the birds will show during most of their stay in the Northwoods. (Females generally are more subdued in color, often without the characteristic patterns that mark the males.) Colors are described as they would appear to an observer in the field, aided by field glasses. Technical terminology and unfamiliar color terms have been eliminated as much as possible.

LOON FAMILY. Large diving birds with straight sharp bills. They can dive to great depths and swim fast and far under water. Dive or submerge when feeding or alarmed. Feed on non-game fish, frogs, and aquatic invertebrates.

Common Loon. *Gavia immer. Fig. 314*. 28-36". Head irridescent greenish-black; body black and white. Found on medium to large lakes in spring and summer; along coast and Great Lakes in winter. Nest on ground at edge of water.

GREBE FAMILY. Small diving birds of dainty appearance, often floating high, but able to submerge and dive like the loon. Feed on aquatic invertebrates and some small fish.

Horned Grebe. *Podiceps auritus. Fig. 315*. 12-15". Head black, with tan ear tufts; back dark gray-brown; neck, upper breast and sides reddish-brown. In winter, neck and cheeks white. Found on ponds, small lakes and bays of larger lakes in summer; along coast and Great Lakes in winter. Nests on a floating mat among reeds or cattails near open water.

Pied-billed Grebe. *Podilymbus podiceps. Fig. 316.* 13-15". Body gray-brown, black throat patch and ring on bill; white undertail. Very shy, more often heard than seen. Found on marshy ponds and small lakes where there are emergent plants for shelter. Nests on a floating mat among marsh plants near open water.

HERON FAMILY. Tall wading birds with long straight bills. In flight, the neck is folded back over the shoulders.

Great Blue Heron. *Ardea herodias. Fig. 317.* 43-50". Body slate blue; head white with blue-black plumes. Found at edges of water and in marshes. Builds large, stick platform nests in trees or shrubs near water; colonial. Feeds on insects, frogs and fish, mostly non-game; feeds alone.

The Green Heron, *Butorides striatus*, and the Black-crowned Night Heron, *Nicticorax nycticorax*, might be seen in southernmost parts.

American Bittern. *Botaurus lentiginosus. Fig. 318*. 24-34". Large brown bird with streaked breast; black wing-tips seen in flight; throat white with black patch at side. Found in meadows and marshes. Nests usually on ground. Feeds on insects, crayfish, frogs, and small rodents.

Fig. 314

Fig. 315

Fig. 316

Fig. 317

Fig. 318

WATERFOWL. Includes several families of waterbirds with heavy, somewhat flattened bodies; short legs; webbed feet; and, excepting the mergansers, broad flattened bills.

Canada Goose. *Branta canadensis. Fig. 319.* 36-42". Identified by its black head, and neck with white band. Found in marshes in extreme north. Nests on ground near water. Feeds on aquatic and marsh plants.

Fig. 319

DUCKS. The ducks in this region are divided into three groups according to their behavior and manner of feeding.

GROUP I. Pond Ducks, also called surface-feeding or river ducks, feed by skimming the surface of the water with the bill, or by "tipping and dabbling"; rarely dive. In rising to flight, they spring directly from the surface. Feed on water plants, roots, and some invertebrates.

Mallard. *Anas platyrhynchos. Fig. 320.* 22-24". Head and upper neck glossy green, with white neck ring; upper back gray-brown; tail black and white, with the black upper tail feathers recurved; wing speculum violet bordered with black and white; breast reddish-brown. Found in marshes and swamps, mostly westward. Nests on dry land near water.

Black Duck. *Anas rubripes. Fig. 321.* 22-24". Dark gray-brown, neck lighter than body; purple speculum without white borders; white beneath wings seen in flight. Found on streams, ponds, and in marshes. Nests same as mallard.

Pintail. *Anas acuta. Fig. 322.* 25-30". Gray above, whitish beneath. Distinguished by its small brown head poised on a slender neck and by very long pointed tail with the central black feathers 5-9" long; white of the breast runs up the front of the neck onto the side of the head. Found on ponds and marshes. Nests in grass away from water.

Green-winged Teal. *Anas crecca. Fig. 323.* 13-15". Small dark gray-bodied duck with a pinkish-tan breast; bright brown head with a contrasting glossy green band on each side; green speculum; white crescent in front of wing. Found in marshes and marshy edges of ponds and lakes. Nests in grass or willow thickets.

Blue-winged Teal. *Anas discors. Fig. 324.* 14-16". Small brown-bodied duck with spotted underparts; large white crescent between bill and eye; blue-gray on forepart of wings. Found in marshes, small shallow ponds, and bogs, along the southern parts of the Maritime Provinces. Nests in marsh grasses very near water.

Wood Duck. *Aix sponsa. Fig. 325.* 18-24". The familiar bright irridescent plumage of the male is absent in the summer, but the unique white throat pattern distinguishes this duck during all seasons. Found on woodland streams and ponds from the east end of Lake Superior to the St. Lawrence Valley and southward. Nests in hollow trees.

Fig. 320

Fig. 321

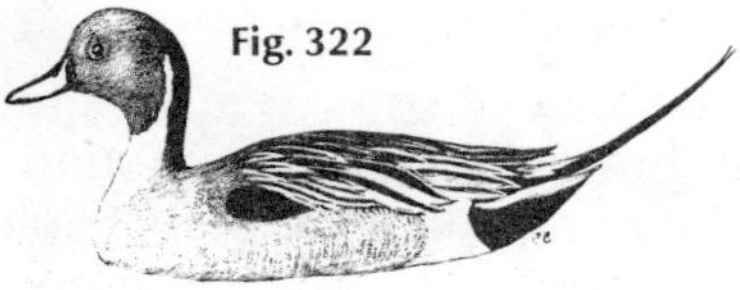

Fig. 322

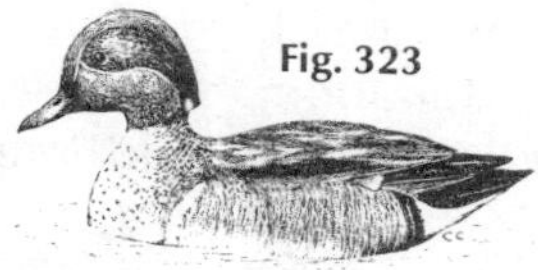

Fig. 323

Fig. 325

Fig. 324

Fig. 326

Fig. 327

GROUP II. Diving Ducks, also called bay ducks, feed by diving and swimming under water. In rising to flight, they patter along the surface before taking to the air. Birds of open water; rarely on land except for nesting. Feed on mollusks, crustaceans, and some deep water plants.

Ring-necked Duck. *Aythya collaris. Fig. 326.* 16-18". Head, breast, and back black; head with short puffy crest; arc of white in front of wing; sides pale gray. Found on small lakes, sloughs, and rivers; less often on broad open water than other diving ducks, and rises to flight more quickly.

Common Goldeneye. *Bucephala clangula. Fig. 327.* 18-22". Large dark green head with rounded white cheek spot; stocky black and white body. Found on forest lakes and rivers. Nests in hollow trees near or over water.

GROUP III. Mergansers are proficient divers and fast swimmers. They have slender cylindrical bills with saw-toothed edges. Females of all species have brown crests. Feed on fish, shellfish, frogs, and insects.

Hooded Merganser. *Lophodytes cucullatus. Fig. 328.* 16-19″. Upperparts glossy-black, except for the large white somewhat triangular patch on each side of the arced crest; sides rusty-brown, separated from the white breast by two black bars. Found on woodland ponds and streams in southern parts. Nests in hollow trees.

Fig. 328

Fig. 329

Fig. 330

Common Merganser. *Mergus merganser. Fig. 329.* 22-27″. Head greenish-black; back black; throat, wings, and underparts white, shading to salmon-tinged white on sides; bill and feet red. Found on woodland lakes and rivers. Nests in holes in trees or cliffs, or on the ground.

Red-breasted Merganser. *Mergus serrator. Fig. 330.* 20-25″. Somewhat similar to common merganser, but with a distinctive horizontal crest and rusty-brown chest below the white throat; sides gray. Found on lakes, rivers, and ponds. Nests on ground among tree roots or brush, or in rock crevices.

HAWKS AND ALLIES. Includes several families of diurnal birds of prey. In this book, they are divided into six groups according to their structure and manner of flying. All but the harrier and falcons build twig nests high above ground in trees, and most of them add to the same nest year after year until it becomes very large.

GROUP I. Accipiters, *Fig. 331,* have short, rounded wings and long tails. They are swift and direct in flight, and seldom soar in the open, but keep to forest shelter.

Goshawk. *Accipiter gentilis. Fig. 331a.* 20-26". Back light blue-gray; breast finely-barred gray and white; white stripe over eye. Found in conifer forests.

Sharp-shinned Hawk. *Accipiter striatus. Fig. 331b.* 10-14". Back dark blue-gray; breast finely-barred red-brown and white; tail-tip straight or notched. Found in conifer forests.

Cooper's Hawk, *Accipiter cooperii,* 14-20", is similar but larger than sharp-shinned hawk, and with rounded tail tip. The Cooper's hawk is secretive and rarely seen. Mostly in hardwood forest areas.

Fig. 331

Fig. 333

Fig. 332

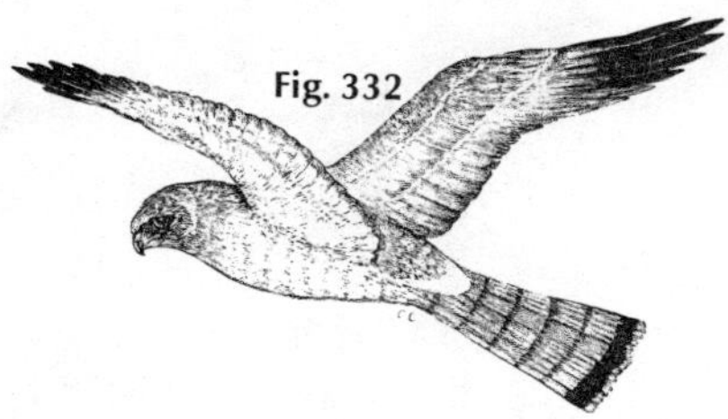

GROUP II. Harrier has long, narrow, rounded wings, long tail, and slender body. It sails close to the ground, veering from side to side, with wings held in a broad V. A single American species, the northern harrier, or marsh hawk.

Marsh Hawk. *Circus cyaneus. Fig. 332.* 18-24". Light gray above; white below; black wing-tips; conspicuous white rump. Nearly always on wing in daylight hours. Found over marshes and fields. Nests on ground among vegetation.

GROUP III. Osprey has long, slender wings held with a backward bend at the wrists. Hovers, and plunges feet first to capture its aquatic prey. Feeds on fish.

Osprey. *Pandion haliaetus. Fig. 333.* 21-24". Nearly black above; entirely white below except for light chest streaks. Found near bodies of clear water. Nests often on dead trees or poles.

GROUP IV. Buteos, *Fig. 334,* have broad, rounded wings, broad tails, and robust bodies. Soar in wide circles high in the air, and perch in the open. Feed almost entirely on rodents and insects.

Fig. 334

Red-tailed Hawk. *Buteo jamaicensis. Fig. 334a.* 18-25″. The plain rust-red tail distinguishes this buteo from others; body, brown and white. Found in upland hardwood forest edges near openings.

Red-shouldered Hawk. *Buteo lineatus. Fig. 334b.* 18-24″. Tail with *narrow* white bands; underparts barred red-brown. In flight, shows a light spot near end of wing. Found in lowland woods in southern part of region.

Broad-winged Hawk. *Buteo platypterus. Fig. 334c.* 14-18″. Tail with *broad* white bands; underparts barred red-brown. A quiet, gentle hawk, rather easily approached. Found in hillside forests, mainly deciduous.

Rough-legged Hawk. *Buteo lagopus. Fig. 334d.* 20-24″. White at base of tail; black on belly, wrists, wing borders, and tail-tip. Often hovers like an osprey; perches on topmost twigs of trees. Found in marshes, far north in summer, and southernmost parts in winter.

GROUP V. Eagles have heavy bodies, long narrow wings, and very large bills. Soar high in wide circles, wings held flat.

Bald Eagle. *Haliaeetus leucocephalus. Fig. 335.* 30″; wingspread to 7½′. Nearly black, with white head and tail. Found in forested areas near large bodies of water. Nests high in tall trees or on cliffs.

Fig. 335

Fig. 336

GROUP VI. Falcons, *Fig. 336*, have slim, pointed wings and slender tails. They fly with rapid wing-beats. Build no nests, but deposit eggs on bare nest sites.

Merlin. *Falco columbarius. Fig. 336a.* 10-14″. Dark gray above; streaked gray below; tail prominently banded. Found in conifer forests. Nests on rock ledges or in tree holes.

Peregrine Falcon. *Falco peregrinus. Fig. 336b.* 15-21″. Back slate gray; barred gray below; prominent black patch below the eye. Said to be the swiftest of all birds. Found on mountain crags near broad open stretches. Formerly nested on tall buildings in cities and preyed on starlings, English sparrows, and pigeons. Among those most severely affected by pesticides, now rare or absent from all but the most remote areas.

American Kestrel. *Falco sparverius. Fig. 336c.* 9-12″. Smallest and most colorful of the falcons. Back and crown rusty-brown; breast paler, wings blue-gray; tail bright rusty-colored with a terminal black band; distinctive black and white face pattern. Hovers and plunges like a tiny osprey. Found in open country. Nests in cavities in trees or rocks, bird houses, or on buildings. Feeds almost entirely on insects.

GROUSE FAMILY. Ground birds with plump bodies and short tails. Feed by browsing on leaves, buds, and fruits.

Spruce Grouse. *Canachites canadensis. Fig. 337.* 15-17″. Upperparts slate gray, barred with black; tail black, tipped with reddish-brown; bright reddish comb over each eye; underparts black, marked with white. Found in spruce forests. Nests on ground under spruces. Feeds mainly on conifer needles.

Ruffed Grouse. *Bonasa umbellus. Fig. 338.* 16-19″. Body gray-brown, streaked and barred; tail banded, with a broader black subterminal band; head with a slight crest; glossy-black shoulder ruff. Found in forests, rocky uplands, and brushy edges of streams and swamps. Nests on ground under shrubs.

Fig. 337

Fig. 338

Fig. 339

Fig. 340

Fig. 341

RAIL FAMILY. Small plump marsh birds. Except for the sociable American coot, they are of retiring habit, seldom seen. Feed on marsh and pond vegetation, and nest among marsh plants.

Virginia Rail. *Rallus limicola. Fig. 339.* 9-11″. Reddish-brown mottled with black; sides of head gray; long reddish bill; neck and breast chestnut; lower sides banded.

Sora. *Porzana carolina. Fig. 340.* 8-10″. Gray-brown above, gray beneath; lower sides banded; black behind short yellow bill.

American Coot. *Fulica americana. Fig. 341.* 14-16″. Slate gray, darker on head and neck; conspicuous ivory-white bill. More aquatic than the rails, resembling a small rotund duck. Found on quiet marsh-edged waters.

PLOVER AND SANDPIPER FAMILIES. Most are birds of shoreland, having relatively long legs, and slender bills to probe for insects, worms, and crustaceans. Plovers' bills are short, sandpipers' long. Those of open shores run, with intermittent short runs and pauses.

Piping Plover. *Charadrius melodus. Fig. 342*. 6-7". A dainty bird, very pale ashy-gray above, white beneath, with black collar. Found on gravelly or sandy lake shores in hardwood areas. Nests in depressions on bare sand; somewhat colonial.

Killdeer. *Charadrius vociferus. Fig. 343*. 10-11". Olive-brown above, white beneath, with two black bands across breast. Vociferous and conspicuous. Found in open grassy areas, fields, and lake shores. Nests on bare, gravelly ground.

Fig. 342 **Fig. 344** **Fig. 346** **Fig. 343** **Fig. 345**

Spotted Sandpiper. *Actitis macularia. Fig. 344*. 7-8". Back olive-brown, spotted and streaked with black, underparts white, prominently spotted; white line through eye. Sometimes called teeter-tail from its habit of teetering between runs. Ubiquitous on shores. Nests on ground.

Solitary Sandpiper. *Tringa solitaria. Fig. 345*. 7½-9". Back dark olive-brown with whitish spots; head and neck streaked; underparts white; prominent eye ring. Found along ponds, bogs, and swamps in conifer forests. Nests in abandoned bird nests in trees.

Greater Yellowlegs. *Tringa melanoleuca. Fig. 346*. 14-15". Upperparts dark brownish-gray, streaked and spotted with white; head and neck streaked; breast spotted, belly white; long legs bright yellow. Found in conifer forests in wet openings and shores of lakes and ponds. Nests on open ground.

Common Snipe. *Capella gallinago. Fig. 347*. 10-12". Upperparts mottled reddish and blackish-brown, with lighter streaks; head and neck streaked; underparts white. Found on shores of marshes, bogs, and marsh-edged ponds. Nests on grassy hummocks.

Woodcock. *Philohela minor. Fig. 348*. 11-12". Differs from others in this group in having compact body with very short neck, stubby tail, and very short legs. Color of the back a medley of gray, brown, and black; top of large head barred; eyes large; bill very long; underparts light orange-brown. Frequents muddy shores and wet areas where it probes for worms. Nests in dry upland woods near water, where its colors provide perfect camouflage.

Fig. 347

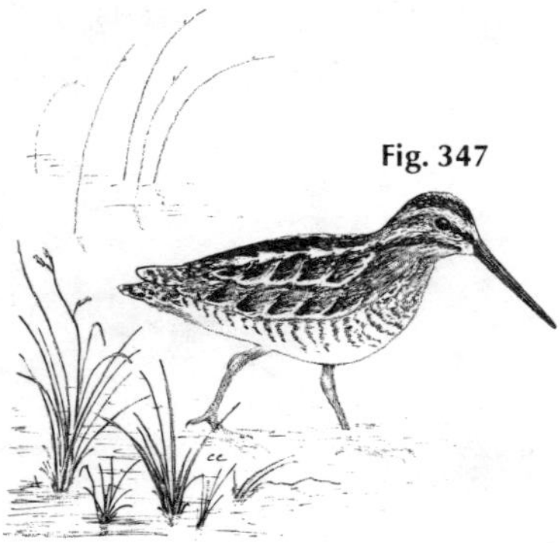

Fig. 348

GULLS AND TERNS. Strong-flying, colonial water birds, with webbed feet. Gulls are large bodied, with rounded or square-ended tails. Terns are slender, with forked tails.

Herring Gull. *Larus argentatus. Fig. 349a*. 24-26". Head, neck, and underparts white, back and wings blue-gray; wing-tips black, bill clear yellow. Seen along shores of large lakes and rivers. A scavenger, feeding also on aquatic animals, and berries. Nests on ground or cliffs, usually on islands.

The Ring-billed Gull, *L. delawarensis, Fig. 349b*, is almost identical to the herring gull except that it is about 6" smaller and has a black ring near the end of the yellow bill.

Common Tern. *Sterna hirundo. Fig. 350*. 14-16". White, shading to pale gray on back and wings; shining greenish-black cap, feet and bill coral-red, the bill tipped with black, tail prominently forked. Found along sandy shores. Nests on beaches or exposed rocks, usually on islands.

Black Tern. *Chlidonias niger. Fig. 351*. 9-10". Head and underparts of body black; back and wings gray, wings paler beneath; white beneath tail. Found in marshes and sloughs of inland lakes and rivers. Feeds on insects. Nests on a floating mat of aquatic vegetation.

Fig. 349

Fig. 350

Fig. 351

Fig. 352

DOVE FAMILY. Represented here by a single species.

Mourning Dove. *Zenaida macroura. Fig. 352*. 11-12". Back and wings soft gray, with a few large black spots; head and underparts pale fawn, underside of wings pale Dresden blue; tail long and pointed, outer feathers white-tipped. Wings whistle in flight. The head seems disproportionately small for the size of the body. Found in open areas in southern parts. Builds a loose twig nest in shrubs or low in trees, in woods, usually near water.

OWL FAMILY. Nocturnal birds of prey, superbly adjusted to their role by large eyes adapted for night vision, and a unique feather structure that enables them to fly on silent wings. Most nest in hollow trees, on cliffs, or in abandoned nests of other birds, and roost in trees during the day. Look for lime streaks and disgorged pellets under roosts. Species can be recognized by size, presence or absence of ear tufts, color of facial disks, and the streaked or barred pattern of the underparts, coupled with the overall color effect. Except for the barred owl, all Northwoods owls have yellow eyes.

Screech Owl. *Otus asio. Fig. 353*. 7-10". Occurs in two color phases, the one bright reddish-brown, the other brownish-gray; facial disks same color as body; underparts streaked and cross-barred. Noticeable ear tufts. Found in open woods. Will nest in boxes put up for them.

Long-eared Owl. *Asio otus. Fig. 354*. 14-16". Mottled dark brown with contrasting bright reddish-brown facial disks; underparts boldly streaked and cross-barred. Long ear tufts. Prefers dense conifer forests.

Great Horned Owl. *Bubo virginianus. Fig. 355*. 19-24". Dark brown, with contrasting light brown facial disks; underparts with narrow wavy bars; white collar on throat. Noticeable ear tufts. Found in most habitats in this region.

Short-eared Owl. *Asio flammeus. Fig. 356*. 14-16". Yellow-brown, boldly streaked; color of facial disks similar. Ear tufts very short, rarely visible. Found in marshes, bogs, and moist openings. A ground dweller, nests and roosts on or near ground in deep marsh grasses or low conifers. Sometimes flies in daytime, therefore more often seen than other owls.

Great Gray Owl. *Strix nebulosa. Fig. 357*. 26-32"; wingspread 5'. Very densely feathered. Gray-brown; facial disks same color, large, with concentric rings; underparts irregularly streaked and mottled. Ear tufts absent. Found in dense conifer forests and open bogs.

Barred Owl. *Strix varia. Fig. 358*. 17-23". Brown; underparts boldly streaked; facial disks same color, with concentric rings encircling the discs and extending down the neck in a kind of collar. Ear tufts absent. Eyes brown. Found in lowland woods and swamps.

Boreal Owl. *Aegolius funereus. Fig. 359*. 9-12". Dark brown, underparts streaked and cross-barred; crown spotted; facial disks pale whitish. Ear tufts absent. Bill yellow. Found in conifer forests and bogs.

Saw-whet Owl. *Aegolius acadicus. Fig. 360*. 7-8". Reddish-brown; underparts streaked; crown faintly streaked; facial disks pale whitish. Ear tufts absent. Bill black. Found in moist conifer forests.

Fig. 353

Fig. 354

Fig. 355

Fig. 356

Fig. 357

Fig. 358

Fig. 359

Fig. 360

NIGHTJAR FAMILY. Insect-eaters with very small bills, but large gaping mouths adapted for capturing food on the wing while flying in the evening or night.

Whip-poor-will. *Caprimulgus vociferus. Fig. 361*. 9-10″. Reddish-brown, with gray-black and dull white mottling in a broken camouflage pattern; narrow white band on throat, and white patch on outer tail feathers. Found in deciduous woodland in the southern part of the region. Sleeps during the day in the duff on the woods' floor; very difficult to see because of its protective coloring. If this bird is in the area, you will likely hear it calling its name at night.

Common Nighthawk. *Chordeiles minor. Fig. 362*. 8-10″. Gray-black, with brown and yellowish-white mottling in a broken camouflage pattern; white band on neck and tail, and a conspicuous white patch on each wing clearly visible in flight. Found in open areas, flying at dusk, occasionally in daylight. Nests on gravel patches in fields, on rocks or gravel knobs in woods, or on gravelled rooftops.

Fig. 361

Fig. 362

Fig. 363

SWIFT FAMILY. Insect-eaters that feed on the wing, flying during the day. Feet adapted for clinging to vertical surfaces rather than perching.

Chimney Swift. *Chaetura pelagica. Fig. 363*. 5-5½″. Gray-brown to sooty-black. Look for this fast flier on the wing; listen for its chippering call as it passes overhead. Easily recognized as it soars, by the long arc of its slender pointed wings, and the very short blunt tail. Found in mature forests with large hollow trees, or in urban areas where it fastens its nests inside chimneys.

HUMMINGBIRD FAMILY. A large family, but with a single species in this region. Feathers are irridescent, and the color shows full only in certain angles of light. These tiny birds feed on insects and on nectar obtained while hovering before flowers. Their quick flight and darting motion to and from flowers identifies them.

Ruby-throated Hummingbird. *Archilochus colubris. Fig. 364*. 3-4". Upperparts bronze-green; breast whitish; ruby throat only on male, bill long and thin for reaching into tubular flowers. Found in woods and openings in southernmost parts of the region. Nests on tree branches. Watch for it perching on the ends of tree twigs, or on telephone wires.

Fig. 364

Fig. 365

KINGFISHER FAMILY. Fish-eating birds that nest at the end of long tunnels bored into river banks, bluffs, or cutbanks.

Belted Kingfisher. *Megaceryle alcyon. Fig. 365*. 11-14". Blue-gray and white. Bill and crested head very large in proportion to body. The female has an additional rusty band on the chest. Found along streams and lakes where they sit on branches overhanging the water. The loud rattling call is often heard before the bird is seen. Feeds on small fish and aquatic invertebrates.

WOODPECKER FAMILY. Birds with sharp strong bills for digging insects out of bark and for cutting nest holes in trees. Their sharp claws and spine-tipped tail feathers are further adaptations for these purposes. One or another species of woodpecker can be expected wherever there are large trees suitable for excavating nest holes.

Common Flicker. *Colaptes auratus. Fig. 366*. 12-14". Upperparts grayish-brown, barred with black; red stripe across back of head; white patch on rump; underparts whitish spotted with brown; black band across chest; yellow beneath wings shows in flight. Found in open woodland. Unlike others of its family, this woodpecker is a ground feeder, hunting ground-dwelling insects; often seen feeding on ants at anthills.

Pileated Woodpecker. *Dryocopus pileatus. Fig. 367*. 16-19". Black, with white pattern on head and neck, and a large bright red crest; white beneath wings shows in flight. Found in deep forest and forest edges in southern parts. Look for large, somewhat-rectangular excavations in trees.

Yellow-bellied Sapsucker. *Sphyrapicus varius. Fig. 368*. 8-9". Black and yellowish-white; back barred; bright red on throat and forehead; a noticeable long longitudinal white bar on the black wing. Found in open woodland.

Hairy Woodpecker. *Picoides villosus. Fig. 369*. 8-10". Black and very white; back white; short broken white cross-bars on the black wings appear more like spots than bars; short red band on back of head; often appearing as two spots. Found in deciduous forests.

The small Downy Woodpecker, *P. pubescens*, is identical except for size. Found in open woodlands. Very abundant, and easily approached.

Black-backed Three-toed Woodpecker. *Picoides arcticus. Fig. 370*. 9-10". Black and white; back entirely black; crown bright yellow or orange; sides barred. Found in spruce forests, favoring cutover or burned areas with dead or dying trees. Not common, but somewhat easily approached.

Northern Three-toed Woodpecker. *Picoides tridactylus. Fig. 371*. 8-9". Similar to the above species except for the barred back. Found in the same kind of habitats. Both are far-northern species.

Fig. 366

Fig. 368

Fig. 367

Fig. 369

Fig. 370

Fig. 371

FLYCATCHER FAMILY. Characterized by the habit of sitting perfectly still and alert on an exposed branch or other perch, then darting out at intervals to capture a passing insect, and returning at once to the same perch.

Eastern Kingbird. *Tyrannus tyrannus. Fig. 372*. 8-9″. Head and tail black, back slate gray; tail with a terminal white band, head with a rarely-visible, small, red topknot; underparts white. Found in open country, near lakes and streams; often seen on roadside fence posts. Nests in bushes or trees.

Great-crested Flycatcher. *Myriarchus crinitus. Fig. 373.* 9″. Head and back gray-brown, head with a slight crest; tail conspicuous brownish-red; throat and chest gray; belly yellow. Found in open forests where there are large trees with cavities for nest sites. Will nest in bird boxes.

Eastern Phoebe. *Sayornis phoebe. Fig. 374*. 6-7″. Upperparts grayish-brown with an olive-green cast, without any pattern marks; underparts dull whitish. Feathers of the crown can be raised. Habitually moves its tail from side to side as it perches quite erect. Found in woods near water in southern parts. Often nests beneath bridges.

The following three small flycatchers, *Fig. 375*, are so similar that field identification by color and pattern in all but impossible. All have dark greenish-brown to gray upperparts, whitish underparts (except the yellow-bellied flycatcher), two wing bars, and an eye ring. The best guide to their identity is their habitats.

Yellow-bellied Flycatcher. *Empidonax flaviventris. Fig. 375*. 5-6″. Distinguished from the following species by its yellow underparts. Found in lowland thickets in conifer forests. Nests on or near ground, in mossy areas.

Alder Flycatcher. *Empidonax alnorum. Fig. 375*. 5-6″. Found in alder thickets along streams or lakes. Nests low in bushes or small trees.

Least Flycatcher. *Empidonax minimus. Fig. 375*. 5-6″. Found in the southern part of the region in open woodland, edges and roadsides, and orchards and shade trees in towns. Nests in tree crotches. Most easily identified by its *che-BEK* call, uttered repeatedly through the day.

Fig. 372

Fig. 373

Fig. 374

Fig. 375

Fig. 376

Fig. 377

Eastern Pewee. *Contopus virens. Fig. 376.* 6½″. A slightly larger version of the preceding three species, similar except that it lacks the eye ring. Found in the same kind of habitats as the least flycatcher. Best identified by its soft *pee-a-wee* call, on an ascending tone.

Olive-sided Flycatcher. *Nuttallornis borealis. Fig. 377.* 7½″. Upperparts dark olive-gray; sides of breast and belly lighter brownish-gray; throat and central longitudinal band on belly white. Tuft of white feathers sometimes visible on rump. Found in conifer forests, near burned or cutover tracts. Perches on the topmost branches, from which you can hear its loud two- or three-syllabled call. Nests high in trees.

SWALLOW FAMILY. Small birds with long, pointed wings, short bills, and small feet. Strong fliers, they feed on the wing and are commonly seen soaring and swooping over lakes, marshes, and openings.

Fig. 378 Fig. 380 Fig. 379 Fig. 381

Tree Swallow. *Iridoprocne bicolor. Fig. 378*. 5-6″. Lustrous dark blue-green above; pure white below. Found in open woods near lakes, streams, and marshes. Nests in hollow trees or bird houses.

Bank Swallow. *Riparia riparia. Fig. 379*. 5-5½″. Gray-brown above, with a band of the same color crossing the white of the underparts. Found near streams or other sites with vertical sandy banks, such as highway cutbanks. Nest, at the end of tunnels excavated in the banks. Colonial.

Cliff Swallow. *Petrochelidon pyrrhonota. Fig. 380*. 5-6″. Upperparts steel blue, separated by a pale gray-brown collar extending to the upper chest, with a chestnut band above it on throat and sides of head; forehead white; belly white; conspicuous light rusty rump. Found near cliffs in open areas. Mud nests fastened to cliff faces, in colonies.

Barn Swallow. *Hirundo rustica. Fig. 381*. 6-8″. Upperparts metallic dark blue; forehead, chin, and throat chestnut; breast and belly light tan. Tail deeply forked. Found near marshes and lake shores, and around habitations. Nests on ledges in the wild, or on rafters of buildings.

The Purple Martin, *Progne subis*, 7-8½", of overall deep metallic blue, might be seen in open woodland near water in southern parts as far north as Nova Scotia. These colonial birds most often seek bird houses erected for them by man.

CROWS AND JAYS. Medium to large perching birds of omnivorous food habits.

Fig. 382

Fig. 383

Fig. 384

Gray Jay. *Perisoreus canadensis. Fig. 382*. 10-12". Upperparts gray; eye stripe and back of head black; forehead and throat white; underparts light gray. Found in conifer forests. Nests in dense conifers. Very tame, familiar around campsites.

Blue Jay. *Cyanocitta cristata. Fig. 383*. 12". Light amethyst-blue above, with bright blue wings and tail boldly marked with black and white; rather prominent crest; face and throat bordered with black; white below. Found in deciduous forests, particularly where there are oaks. Acorns are a staple food. Nests in trees, preferably conifers.

Northern Raven. *Corvus corax. Fig. 384*. 22-26". Large, entirely black bird with bluish reflections from the feathers. Throat feathers appear loose and ruffled. End of tail is not squared off, but tapers to a rounded point. Voice is a low-toned *cr-r-uck*. Found in rather remote forest and mountain areas.

The American Crow, *C. brachyrhynchos*, is about 5″ smaller than the raven, lacks the loose throat feathers, and has a truncated tail. Found farther south in settled and agricultural areas.

TITMOUSE FAMILY. Small, active insect-eaters. Those in this region nest in tree holes or other natural cavities.

Black-capped Chickadee. *Parus atricapillus Fig. 385*. 4½-5½″. Upperparts gray; underparts dull whitish, with pale rusty sides. The black cap and throat, and white cheeks, distinguish this bird, together with its quick flitting activity and cheery call. Found in mixed forest, open woods, and near habitations. Will nest in bird boxes.

Boreal Chicakadee. *Parus hudsonicus.* 5-5½″. Similar to the black-capped chickadee except that the coloring is brown rather than black and gray, and the rusty side color is more prominent. Found in dense spruce forests.

NUTHATCH FAMILY. Small tree climbers. Any bird seen crawling head downward on a tree belongs to this family.

Red-breasted Nuthatch. *Sitta canadensis. Fig. 386*. 4½-5″. Upperparts blue-gray; head black, with a black stripe through the eye across the white cheek; underparts soft rust color. Found in conifer forests. Feeds on seeds and small insects.

The White-breasted Nuthatch, *S. carolinensis,* is similar except that it lacks the black eye stripe and is slightly larger. Found in southern parts in deciduous forests, and near habitations. Both species nest in cavities.

CREEPER FAMILY. Small tree climbers. The single species in North America feeds on insects and spiders in tree bark.

Brown Creeper. *Certhia familiaris. Fig. 387*. 5-5½″. Brown, streaked with dull white, with white underparts. Bill long and sharp, downward curved. Moves spirally upward on tree trunk, then flies back to the base of the same or a different tree to begin the upward search again. Found in mixed woodlands. Nests behind loose bark on trees.

WREN FAMILY. Small, active brown birds with plump bodies, slender bills, and small tails which they tend to tip at an upward angle. The three species described below are difficult to see because they remain so closely concealed within their habitats. But a fourth species, the familiar

House Wren, *Troglodytes aedon,* is not at all secretive. It has adapted so well to man that it has taken up residence around human habitations, and in the nesting season is more often seen and heard in city and farm gardens than in the wild. All species feed on insects.

Fig. 385 Fig. 386 Fig. 387 Fig. 388 Fig. 389

Winter Wren. *Troglodytes troglodytes. Fig. 388*. 4-4½". Dark brown above, obscurely streaked and barred; somewhat lighter beneath, with prominent dark bars on the sides of the belly. Tail very short. Found in conifer or mixed forests, among tangles of brush and twigs on forest floor. Nests, extremely well concealed on or near the ground.

Marsh Wren. *Cistothorus palustris. Fig. 389*. 4-5". Brown above, with black and white streaks on upper back; prominent white line above eye; underparts pale brown to dull white, not barred; tail banded. Found in cattail, sedge, or bulrush marshes. Nests amidst marsh vegetation.

Sedge Wren. *Cistothorus platensis*. 4-4½". Similar to the marsh wren, but smaller, color more gray-brown with a streaked crown, but less conspicuous streaking on the back, and no white line above the eye. Found in grassy meadows and sedge marshes. Nests in vegetation.

MOCKINGBIRD FAMILY. Long-tailed, medium-sized birds with strong singing voices, tending often to mimic other bird sounds. Two species in the southern part of the Northwoods Region.

Brown Thrasher. *Toxostoma rufum. Fig. 390*. 10-11″. Upperparts reddish brown; underparts white, with bold elongated brown spots in streaks. Found in thickets and second growth woodland. Nests in bushes, close to ground.

Gray Catbird. *Dumetella carolinensis. Fig. 391*. 8-9″. Smooth medium gray, with nearly black crown and tail, and rusty under base of tail. Found in brushy woodlands, and near habitations. Nests well concealed in bushes.

THRUSH FAMILY. A large family of medium-sized birds noted for their melodious singing.

American Robin. *Turdus migratorius. Fig. 392.* 9-10″. Dark gray above, with a clear rusty-red breast. This dooryard bird, familiar to everyone, is also found in remote forest areas as well as in woodlands near habitations. Nests in trees or on ledges.

Eastern Bluebird. *Sialia sialis. Fig. 393*. 6-7″. Clear rusty-red breast, like the American robin, but the upperparts are uniformly bright blue. Found in deciduous woodland openings, and near habitations. Nests in old woodpecker holes, and in bird boxes.

THRUSHES. *Fig. 394*. The features that distinguish the four thrushes of this region from each other are not obvious. Their feather patterns are very similar, differing only in the warmth of color on the upperparts and the degree of spotting on the whitish breast. All but the veery are found in conifer forests and build tidy cup nests low in branches of shrubs or conifer trees. Their echoing calls in the forest, or across a northern lake, have a most haunting quality.

Hermit Thrush. *Catharus guttatus. Fig. 394*. 6-8″. Warm brown above, with a reddish-brown tail noticeably brighter than the back; sides of breast moderately spotted. Has the habit of flipping the tail slightly upward after coming to rest on a perch.

Swainson's Thrush. *Catharus ustulatus*. 6-7″. Uniformly dull gray-brown above; cheeks yellowish or buff, with a light eye ring; breast moderately spotted.

Gray-cheeked Thrush. *Catharus minimus*. 6-8″. Coloring same as the Swainson's thrush, except that the cheeks are grayish, and the eye ring is not noticeable.

Veery. *Catharus fuscescens*. 6-7″. Uniformly reddish-brown above, with very faint spotting on upper breast. Found in deciduous forests and brushy areas. Bulky nest on or near ground.

Fig. 390

Fig. 391

Fig. 395

Fig. 392

Fig. 394

Fig. 393

KINGLET FAMILY. *Fig. 395*. Among the smallest of all birds. Feed on insects and spiders. The two species in this region are found in dense conifer forests, and build large nests of mosses and lichens in thick conifer trees.

Golden-crowned Kinglet. *Regulus satrapa. Fig. 395a*. 3½-4″. Upperparts olive-green; crown bright orange, bordered by a series of yellow, black, and white stripes; wings dark with two inconspicuous, dull white bars; underparts yellowish white.

Ruby-crowned Kinglet. *Regulus calendula. Fig. 395b*. 4-4½″. Feather pattern similar to the golden-crowned kinglet, except that the crown has only one small central tuft of red feathers, not always visible.

WAXWING FAMILY. A family of only three species, with a single species in this region. Tame and sociable birds, feeding on insects and berries.

Cedar Waxwing. *Bombycilla cedrorum. Fig. 396*. 7-8". Very sleek smooth-colored bird, light pinkish brown above, shading to gray on wings and tail; black eye mask narrowly bordered with white; waxy red tips on wing feathers; yellow terminal band on tail. Found in the southern part of the region in open woods and near habitations. Nests in trees.

Fig. 396

Fig. 397

SHRIKE FAMILY. Solitary birds of open country, feeding principally on insects and rodents.

Northern Shrike. *Lanius excubitor. Fig. 397*. 9-10". Blue-gray above, white below, with black mask, wings, and tail, and hawk-like bill. A far northern bird whose breeding range touches only the northernmost part of this region, but may be seen throughout in winter. Nests in conifers. The smaller Loggerhead, *L. ludovicianus*, occurs in southern parts.

VIREO FAMILY. Small insect-eaters resembling warblers, but without bold pattern, and more deliberate in action. Those in this region all have upperparts grayish-olive, and underparts white with more or less yellowish sides. All but one build hanging nests from forks of tree twigs.

Solitary Vireo. *Vireo solitarius. Fig. 398*. 5-6". Wings slightly darker than the back, with two white bars; head dark blue-gray, with white eye ring. Found in conifer or mixed forests.

Red-eyed Vireo. *Vireo olivaceus. Fig. 399*. 5½-6½". Crown slate gray; conspicuous black-bordered white line above the eye; no wing bars. Found in deciduous forests, and shade trees near habitations. Sings throughout the day.

Warbling Vireo. *Vireo gilvus.* 5½-6″. Differs from the red-eyed vireo only in its slightly smaller size, slightly darker wings, and plain white stripe above the black eye. Found in the southern part of the region in deciduous woodlands, in the tops of mature trees near streams.

Philadelphia Vireo. *Vireo philadelphicus.* 4½-5½″. Differs from the warbling vireo only in its more decidedly yellow underparts and less conspicuous stripe above the eye. Found in mixed forests and brushy clearings near streams and lakes. Nests on tree branches, preferably conifers.

Fig. 398

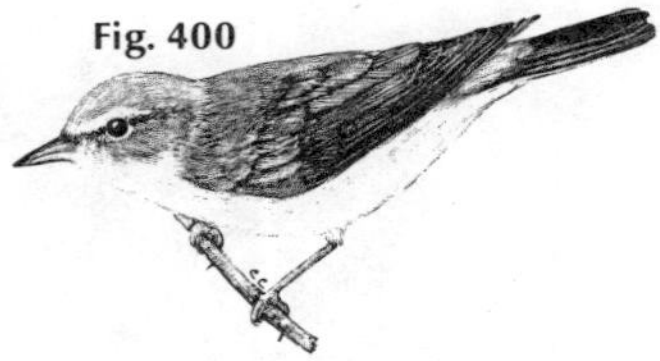

Fig. 400

Fig. 399

Fig. 401

WOOD WARBLER FAMILY. Tiny, very active, insect-eating birds, with bright and varied feather patterns. If any bird could be called characteristic of the Northwoods it would be these bits of feathered energy. Twenty-four species breed in the region, with one or more species found in nearly every habitat. A few are absent from the Appalachians.

Tennessee Warbler. *Vermivora peregrina. Fig. 400.* 5″. Resembles a vireo. Plain olive-green above; gray crown with a black line through the eye and white stripe above; underparts white. Found in mixed forests, edges, swamps, and bogs. Nests on the ground under bushes or mosses, well concealed.

Parula Warbler. *Parula americana. Fig. 401.* 4¾″. Gray-blue above, with a wash of olive-green on center back; two conspicuous white wing bars; throat and breast yellow, crossed by a brownish band; belly white. Found in southern parts in moist coniferous areas where Usnea lichen grows. Nests concealed in the Usnea.

Black-and-White Warbler. *Mniotilta varia. Fig. 402*. 5-5½″. The only purely black-and-white warbler that creeps on trees. Found in deciduous forests and woodlands. Nests on ground at the base of a stump or other protection.

Blackpoll Warbler. *Dendroica striata. Fig. 403*. 5-5½″. Could be confused with the black-and-white warbler except that the crown is entirely black, the cheeks white, and the upperparts olive-tinged gray. Found in conifer forests, and mixed forests with spruce. Nests in conifers.

Fig. 402

Fig. 405

Fig. 404

Fig. 403

Fig. 406

Yellow Warbler. *Dendroica petechia. Fig. 404*. 4½-5″. Greenish-yellow above; underparts bright yellow streaked with light reddish-brown. From a distance, appears all yellow. Found in brushy edges of streams and lakes. Nests in small trees.

Pine Warbler. *Dendroica pinus. Fig. 405*. 5½″. Plain grayish-olive above, with two white wingbars; throat and breast bright yellow, with inconspicuous streaks; belly white. Found in pine woods. Nests at end of branches, high in pine trees.

Palm Warbler. *Dendroica palmarum. Fig. 406*. 5-5½″. Brownish-olive above, with inconspicuous streaks on back; light olive rump; crown bright brownish-red; yellowish over entire underparts, with inconspicuous streaks on sides. Found on or near ground, in spruce and tamarack bogs, and edges of fields and roads. Nests on the ground. Habitually flips its tail up and down.

Yellow-rumped Warbler. *Dendroica coronata. Fig. 407*. 5-6". Upperparts blue-gray, streaked with black; crown and rump yellow, two white wingbars; underparts white, with upper chest and sides black, and yellow blaze at side of breast. Found in mixed forests. Prefers to nest in conifer trees.

Magnolia Warbler. *Dendroica magnolia. Fig. 408*. 4½-5". Upperparts slate gray to black; crown gray; rump yellow; broad white patch on wings, and wide band on tail; underparts bright yellow, with heavy black streaks on breast and sides. Found in conifer forests. Nests low in small conifers.

Fig. 407

Fig. 409

Fig. 408

Fig. 410

Cape May Warbler. *Dendroica tigrina. Fig. 409*. 4¾-5½". Back olive-green streaked with black; crown black; cheeks reddish-brown; rump yellow; broad white patch on wing; underparts bright yellow, the yellow carried up behind the chestnut cheek patch; boldly streaked with black on sides. Found in conifer forests and edges of spruce bogs. Nests high in tall conifer trees.

Chestnut-sided Warbler. *Dendroica pensylvanica. Fig. 410*. 5-6". Upperparts blackish, streaked with yellowish-white; crown yellow; two inconspicuous wingbars; underparts white, with reddish-brown sides. Found in shrubby and second growth areas. Nests low in bushes.

Bay-breasted Warbler. *Dendroica castanea. Fig. 411.* 5-6". Crown, throat, chest, and sides reddish-brown; face black; sides of throat pale tan; upperparts otherwise grayish-olive streaked with black; belly white. Found in conifer and mixed forests. Nests usually high in conifer trees.

Black-throated Green Warbler. *Dendroica virens. Fig. 412.* 4½-5½". Yellowish-olive-green above, with bright yellow face; wings darker, with two white wingbars; throat and sides black; chest and belly white. Found in coniferous woodlands. Nests from near ground to high in trees, usually conifers.

Black-throated Blue Warbler. *Dendroica caerulescens. Fig. 413.* 4¾-5½". Clear gray-blue above, with a small white patch on the wing; face, throat, and sides black; chest and belly, white. Found in deciduous and mixed woodland. Nests in tangled undergrowth.

Fig. 411

Fig. 412

Fig. 414

Fig. 413

Fig. 415

Blackburnian Warbler. *Dendroica fusca. Fig. 414.* 5-5¼". Black above, streaked with white; center of crown, sides of head, throat, and upper chest bright orange, with a black cheek mark; underparts pale yellow, streaked with black on sides. Found in conifer forests, or on deciduous forest ridges in the mountains. Nests in conifers or oaks.

American Redstart. *Setophaga ruticilla. Fig. 415.* 4½-5½". A black warbler with conspicuous reddish-orange bands on tail, wings, and sides of breast; belly white. Found in mixed or deciduous woodlands, brushy edges, and thickets near water. Nests in deciduous trees or bushes.

Nashville Warbler. *Vermivora ruficapilla. Fig. 416*. 4-5". Olive-green above; head blue-gray with an inconspicuous reddish-brown spot on crown; white eye ring; underparts clear yellow. Found in second growth woodland, thickets, and bog edges. Nests on ground, concealed in moss or woodland debris.

Connecticut Warbler. *Oporornis agilis. Fig. 417*. 5½-6". Similar to the Nashville warbler, except that the blue-gray color extends over the throat and upper chest. Found in bogs and tamarack swamps in shrubby undergrowth, in the western part of the region. Nests on ground in moss.

Mourning Warbler. *Oporornis philadelphia. Fig. 418*. 5½-6". Similar to the Connecticut warbler except that the throat and upper chest are black, and there is no eye ring. Found in undergrowth in deciduous woodland. Nests on or near the ground.

Fig. 416 **Fig. 418** **Fig. 419** **Fig. 417** **Fig. 420**

Common Yellowthroat. *Geothlypis trichas. Fig. 419*. 4½-5¾". Greenish-brown above; black mask edged with white; underparts yellow fading to white on belly, and suffused with brown on sides. Found in brushy undergrowth beside water and swamps; occasionally in drier edges of openings. Nests on or near the ground, well concealed in vegetation.

Wilson's Warbler. *Wilsonia pusilla. Fig. 420*. 4½-5". Olive-green above, with a small black crown patch; underparts bright yellow. Found in swamps, bogs, thickets, and second growth within coniferous areas. Nests on ground at the base of trees or shrubs.

Canada Warbler. *Wilsonia canadensis. Fig. 421*. 5-5¾". Gray above; bright yellow below, with a semicircle of short black streaks across the upper breast; yellow eye ring. Found in small moist glades in mixed forests, and along streams. Nests on or near ground in natural cavities or clumps of plants.

Ovenbird. *Seiurus aurocapillus. Fig. 422*. 5½-6". Brownish-olive-green above, with a narrow orange crown bordered with black; white below, with prominent black streaks on chest and sides. A ground dweller that walks rather than hops. Found in open, dry woodlands with plentiful forest debris on the ground. Named for the ovenlike shape of its nest, a depression in the ground roofed over with woods' litter, with an entrance hole on the side.

Northern Waterthrush. *Seiurus noveboracensis. Fig. 423*. 5¾-6". Similar to the ovenbird, but lacks the orange crown, and has a yellowish line above the eye and pale yellow underparts. Found in forests along shores of ponds and bogs, where it can be seen walking on fallen timber at the water's edge, constantly teetering its body and tipping its tail. Nests on ground amidst fallen timber or in natural cavities.

BLACKBIRD FAMILY. A diverse family of medium-sized birds. The five species in this region inhabit fields, marshes, and other open areas, feeding mainly on insects and seeds.

Bobolink. *Dolichonyx oryzivorus. Fig. 424*. 6-8". Black, with a distinctive pattern of light yellow on back of head; yellow stripes on back and wings; white rump, lower back, and upper wing feathers. Found in southern parts in meadows and grassy fields. Nests on ground.

Fig. 424

Fig. 425

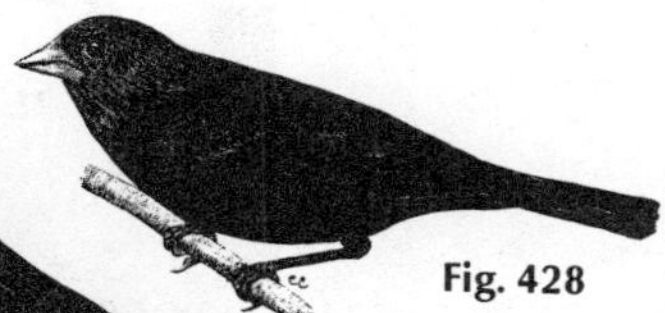

Fig. 428

Fig. 426

Fig. 427

Northern Oriole. *Icterus galbula. Fig. 425*. 7-8″. Glossy-black and flame-orange, with white wingbar. Found in southern parts in deciduous woods with large trees. Builds long pendant nests from ends of branches high in trees.

Red-winged Blackbird. *Agelaius phoeniceus. Fig. 426*. 7-9½″. Jet black, brightened by yellow-bordered scarlet wing patches not always fully visible. Found in marshes and on marshy lake shores. Nests in cattails or marsh shrubs. Somewhat colonial.

Rusty Blackbird. *Euphagus carolinus*. 8½-9″. Entirely glossy blue-black; similar to the red-winged blackbird, but without the red wing patches. Eyes pale yellow. Found in bogs, swamps, and forest ponds in wet woods. Nests in shrubs or low trees beside water.

Common Grackle. *Quiscalus quiscula. Fig. 427*. 12-13″. Entirely black, with irridescent feathers; yellow eyes. May be found in marshes and fields in southern parts; nests in trees or shrubs, preferably conifers. Somewhat colonial.

Brown-headed Cowbird. *Molothrus ater. Fig. 428*. 6-8″. Small black bird with brown head and short bill. Found at edges of woods, mostly near farms and settlements.

TANAGER FAMILY. Tropical, brightly-colored birds, with one species reaching into the southernmost parts here.

Fig. 429

Scarlet Tanager. *Piranga olivacea. Fig. 429.* 6½-7". Brilliant clear scarlet, with black wings and tail. Found in mature oak and pine forests, usually high in treetops. Nests on tree branches.

GROSBEAKS, FINCHES, AND SPARROWS. The world's largest bird family, characterized by short strong bills adapted for breaking seeds.

Rose-breasted Grosbeak. *Pheucticus ludovicianus. Fig. 430.* 8". Black above and on throat, with white rump and two bold white wingbars; breast patch and underside of wings rose-red; rest of underparts white; thick whitish bill. Found in moist deciduous woods near openings. Nests in low tree branches.

Evening Grosbeak. *Hesperiphona vespertina. Fig. 431.* 7½-8½". Yellow-brown, brightening to yellow on lower back, rump, and belly; wings and tail black, with large white wing patches. Found in conifer forests. Nests in conifer trees.

Purple Finch. *Carpodacus purpureus. Fig. 432.* 6-6½". Rose-red, with bright rose crown and rump; back streaked with the same brownish color as the wings; two indistinct wingbars; white belly. Found in conifer forests in openings, burned and cutover areas, and pond edges. Nests in conifers.

Pine Grosbeak. *Pinicola enucleator. Fig. 433.* 9-10". Like a magnified version of the purple finch, but with darker wings and tail, more distinct wingbars, and light gray belly. Found in conifer forests. Nests in conifers.

Red Crossbill. *Loxia curvirostra. Fig. 434.* 5½-6½". Subdued red, with brownish streaks on back; wings and tail brownish-black, without bars. Bill crossed at tip.

The White-winged Crossbill, *L. leucoptera*, has the same kind of bill, but is more like a small version of the pine grosbeak in color; has two wide conspicuous white wingbars.

Both crossbills are found in spruce and fir forests, feeding exclusively on conifer seeds. Both are noted as wanderers. They nest in conifer trees.

Fig. 430

Fig. 431

Fig. 432

Fig. 434

Fig. 435

Fig. 436

Fig. 433

Pine Siskin. *Carduelis pinus. Fig. 435*. 4½-5″. A little brown bird with heavy gray and brown streaks, and small splashes of yellow on dark wings and tail. Found in conifer forests, alder and birch thickets, and openings. Nests in conifers.

American Goldfinch. *Carduelis tristis. Fig. 436*. 4½-5″. Bright yellow, with black forehead, wings, and tail. Found in openings, edges of mixed woodland, and shores of streams and marshes. Nests in bushes or small trees.

Rufous-sided Towhee. *Pipilo erythrophthalmus. Fig. 437.* 7-9". Black above and on throat and chest; sides reddish-brown; wing and tail feathers tipped with white; belly white; eyes red. Found in southernmost parts, in open woods and brushy edges. Nests on or near the ground, in dense brush.

Northern Junco. *Junco hyemalis. Fig. 438.* 6". Slate gray, with white belly, white outer tail feathers, and whitish bill. Found in conifer and mixed forests. Nests on or near the ground.

White-throated Sparrow. *Zonotrichia albicollis. Fig. 439.* 7". Upperparts reddish-brown streaked with black; head striped white and black, with a bright yellow spot behind the bill; throat white; underparts gray. Found in spruce forests with brushy undergrowth. Nests in brush on or near the ground.

The similar White-crowned Sparrow, *Z. leucophrys,* might be seen in the extreme north of this region. It differs only in that it lacks the white throat and yellow spot behind the bill.

Chipping Sparrow. *Spizella passerina. Fig. 440.* 5-5½". Small brown and gray bird with light brown back streaked with grayish black; crown rich reddish-brown bordered by white; black stripe through the eye; clear light gray underparts. Found in woodland edges and roadsides. Nests in shrubby underbrush.

Swamp Sparrow. *Melospiza georgiana.* 5-6". Similar to the chipping sparrow, but with the reddish crown bordered with gray instead of white; somewhat grayer below, with faintly streaked sides, and a more definite white throat. Found in swamps and marshes. Nests on ground or in marsh grasses.

Song Sparrow. *Melospiza melodia. Fig. 441.* 6-7". Upperparts streaked brown and black; underparts whitish, heavily streaked with dark brown, the streaks running to a prominent dark spot on the breast. Found in mixed or deciduous woodland, in shrubby areas near water. Nests on ground or low in shrubs.

Lincoln's Sparrow. *Melospiza lincolnii.* 5-6". Like a smaller version of the song sparrow, but its markings are more delicate, the breast is pale tan, and the breast streaks do not run to the central spot. Found in conifer forests, heath bogs, and shrubby edges of streams and ponds. Nests in underbrush.

Savannah Sparrow. *Passerculus sandwichensis.* 5-6". Small brown-streaked bird similar to the three above in general appearance, but

with a yellow stripe above the eye. Found in openings and grassy fields. Nests on the ground in grass.

Vesper Sparrow. *Pooecetes gramineus. Fig. 442*. 5-6". Small brown-streaked bird similar to the two above, but with white outer tail feathers, a narrow whitish eye ring, and a brownish-red patch at the shoulder. Found in southern parts in openings, fields, and roadsides. Nests on the ground in grass.

Fox Sparrow. *Passerella iliaca. Fig. 443*. 7-7½". Largest and most brightly colored of the sparrows here, like a larger, brighter song sparrow. Upperparts rich reddish-brown, streaked; tail brighter; underparts white, heavily spotted with reddish-brown, the spots running in streaks, and confluent to a more or less solid spot on breast. Found in conifer forest undergrowth. Nests on or near the ground in brush.

Reptiles and Amphibians of the Northwoods

Reptiles and amphibians are "cold-blooded" animals in the sense that their body temperatures are not constant like that of mammals and birds, but rise and fall with the temperature of their environment. For this reason, when the cold Northwoods winter descends, these animals disappear from the scene, retreating under water, below ground, into deep rock crevices, or similar places of hibernation where they are protected from freezing and become more or less dormant until spring.

Two kinds of reptiles and three kinds of amphibians are found in the Northwoods.

TURTLES

Turtles are unique among reptiles in having their bodies sandwiched between two bony shells covered with horny plates of varying shapes and textures. The upper shell is called the carapace; the lower, the plastron. In some species the plastron is hinged so it can be closed against the carapace. Whether wholly or partially aquatic, all turtles lay eggs on land near water, in a shallow hole dug by the female. The rounded or ellipsoidal, usually leathery, white or pinkish eggs are then covered over with earth and left to hatch.

Snapping Turtle. *Chelydra serpentina. Fig. 444*. 12" or more. Carapace black to light brown, more or less rough, especially when young; keeled. Tail long, the upper edge saw-toothed. Plastron small. These turtles are short-tempered and should be treated with caution. Found in rivers, lakes, and ponds. Southern half.

Painted Turtle. *Chrysemys picta. Fig. 445*. 4-7". Carapace smooth, not keeled; boldly or lightly colored around the edge with red marks. These are the turtles most commonly seen basking on logs in the water. Found in ponds, marshes, lake edges, and quiet waters along streams. Southern edge of the Northwoods Region.

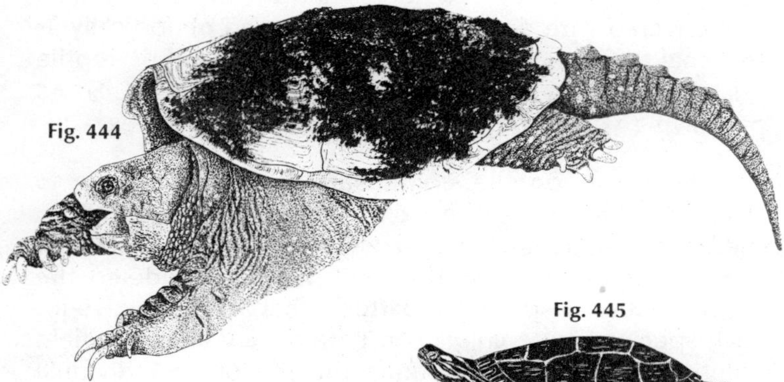

Fig. 444

Fig. 445

Fig. 446

Fig. 447

Wood Turtle. *Clemmys insculpta. Fig. 446.* 5-7". Carapace with a sculptured surface due to the ridging and somewhat pyramidal relief on each large plate. Prominent orange streaks on legs and neck. Found in woods and openings, some distance from water. Southern half, and southward along the mountain highlands.

Blandings Turtle. *Emydoidea blandingi. Fig. 447.* 5-8". Carapace dark gray-brown, spotted with many whitish dots and streaks; throat and chin bright yellow. Plastron is hinged, but shell cannot be closed entirely. Found in marshes, streams, ponds, and lakes; wanders about on land, but is never very far from water. Great Lakes area.

SNAKES

Snakes have long sinuous bodies and the typical reptilian skin covered with dry scales, which is shed periodically as the snake grows. Snakes differ from their other reptile relatives in being without legs or movable eyelids. Some bear living young; others lay ellipsoidal, leathery eggs.

The scales on the upper surface of a snake lie in longitudinal rows and may be smooth or keeled. Those on the lower surface are wide, each scale—called a plate or scute—extending across the belly from one side to the other. Scales are colored in patterns that are distinctive for each species. These colors and patterns are an aid to field identification. However, during the life of an individual snake there can be much variation. In younger snakes, and particularly just after molting, colors are brighter and patterns more distinct. As the snake ages, colors tend to become darker and the patterns less distinct or absent.

In the descriptions below, a basic color is first indicated, followed by the colors, form, and placement of the pattern. These patterns may consist of longitudinal stripes, crossbands of varying widths, and small spots or large blotches.

Poisonous snakes generally are not considered part of the Northwoods fauna. Nevertheless, one should be cautious, particularly in that small area of the region where it is possible to encounter the venomous eastern massasauga. It is wise policy at all times not to put a hand in a hole or crevice into which you cannot see, for a non-poisonous snake—or even a mouse, for that matter—can inflict a nasty bite. Some of the harmless snakes, even if not inclined to bite, give off an offensive odor if handled.

Northern Water Snake. *Natrix sipedon. Fig. 448*. 20-40″. Heavy bodied, the only large water snake in this region. Basic color varies from gray to tan or brown. Pattern colors vary from black to reddish-brown, with broad crossbands on the forepart, and a row of large closely spaced blotches along the rest of the back, alternating with slightly smaller blotches on the sides. The pattern may disappear in older individuals, leaving them plain dark brown or nearly black. Live bearers. Found in all kinds of water habitats. Extreme southern part, eastward from Wisconsin, excluding upper Michigan.

Red-bellied Snake. *Storeria occipitomaculata. Fig. 449*. 8-12″. A small, faintly-striped snake. Basic color of upperparts varies from dark gray or brown to nearly black, patterned with a slightly lighter stripe bordered with black lines the length of the back, and a dark stripe lower on each side; light spots in a broken band behind the head. Underside uniformly red, orange, or yellowish. Live bearer. Feeds mainly on slugs. Found beneath logs and bark in woods, and in sphagnum bogs. Southern half; abundant in mountain areas.

Fig. 448

Fig. 449

Fig. 450

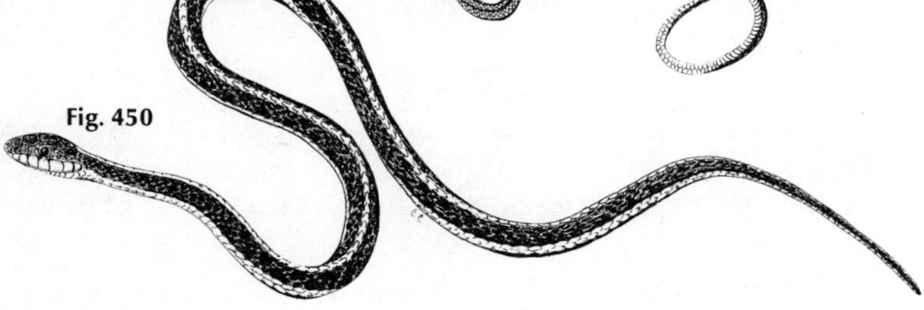

Eastern Garter Snake. *Thamnophis sirtalis. Fig. 450*. 18-24″. Variable, but usually distinctly striped and checkered. Basic color greenish, dark brown, or blackish, patterned with three light stripes; these stripes are usually yellowish but may be blue, green, or tan, and they usually have two rows of alternating dark spots between them. Underside yellowish or greenish, with a row of indistinct dark spots on each side. Live bearer. Feeds on earthworms and amphibians. Found in nearly all habitats except deep forests. Throughout.

Northern Ringneck Snake. *Diadophis punctatus Fig. 451*. 12-14". A small, slender snake without pattern except for a yellow collar. Upperparts uniformly gray, brownish, or black, sometimes with a bluish tinge. Underside mostly uniform yellow or orange, sometimes showing a faint central row of spots. Egg layer. Feeds on small amphibians, earthworms, and insects. Found in open woods and cutover areas, under woods' debris. Southern half, eastward from Wisconsin.

Smooth Green Snake. *Opheodrys vernalis*. 15-20". Slender, without pattern. The only green snake in this region. Upperparts uniformly bright green; underside white or yellowish. Egg layer. Feeds on insects and spiders. Found in openings, marshes, and mountain meadows. Southern half eastward from Wisconsin.

Eastern Milk Snake. *Lampropeltis doliata triangulum. Fig. 452*. 24-36". Large, boldly-blotched and checkered. Basic color gray or yellow-gray, patterned with three or five rows of blotches: a central row of large, *black-bordered*, brown or reddish blotches; and one or two rows of smaller blotches on each side. Underside white, somewhat checkered with black spots. Egg layer. Feeds on small rodents. Found in nearly all kinds of environments except strictly water habitats. Southernmost parts eastward from the east end of Lake Superior.

Eastern Massasauga. *Sistrurus catanatus. Fig. 453*. 20-30". Venomous. A heavy bodied, dark to nearly black "swamp rattler." Basic color brownish-gray, patterned with five to seven rows of blotches: a central row of large, faintly *light-bordered*, dark brown to black blotches; and two or three rows of smaller, lighter blotches on each side. Underside black with irregular whitish marks. Some adult individuals may be entirely black, with no pattern. The young have distinct lighter-colored pattern. Rattles are small. Live bearers. Feed mainly on mice. Found primarily in bogs and swamps, occasionally in dry woodlands. Around the Great Lakes, east of Lake Superior.

These small rattlers are reputed to be mild mannered, and my own experience seems to bear this out. But take no chances! Wild animals in general should be observed and enjoyed in their natural settings, and left strictly alone.

Fig. 451

Fig. 452

Fig. 453

AMPHIBIANS

Amphibians differ from reptiles in having soft skin without scales or shells. They lay gelatinous eggs, usually in water. Most spend their early life in water as tadpoles, and all but the mudpuppy become partially or wholly land dwellers in adult life.

Salamanders have elongate bodies with tails, short, rather weak legs of nearly equal size, and smooth slippery skin. Frogs have short bodies without tails as adults, long, well-developed hind legs suitable for leaping, and rather smooth, moist skin. Toads are similar to frogs, but have somewhat shorter hind legs suitable for hopping, and dry, warty skin.

SALAMANDERS

Mudpuppy. *Necturus maculosus. Fig. 454.* 8-13″ or more. Generally gray to rusty-brown above, usually marked with scattered indistinct dark spots on the back. Underside paler, with dark spots. Gills permanent, plumelike, maroon-colored. Aquatic throughout all stages of life. Found in lakes, ponds, streams, and rivers. Southern half, except Maine and the Maritime Provinces.

Fig. 454

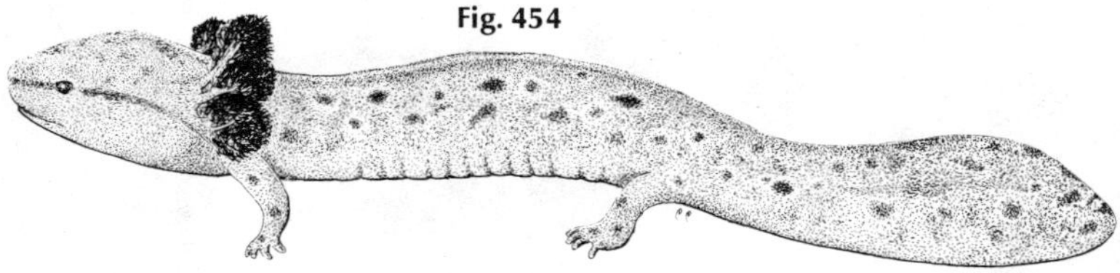

Jefferson Salamander. *Ambystoma jeffersonianum.* 4-7″. Slender; dark brown or gray above, with indistinct pattern of bluish flecks on sides and tail; underside lighter. Found in moist woodlands near water, but rarely seen because of its secretive and nocturnal habits. Mainly in eastern half of region.

Blue-spotted Salamander. *Ambystoma laterale. Fig. 455.* 4-6″. Resembles the Jefferson salamander, and where ranges overlap the two hybridize. Somewhat less slender; overall black or dark brown, with blue or bluish-white spots on back, and sometimes on sides and tail. Found in similar habitats. Mainly in western half of region.

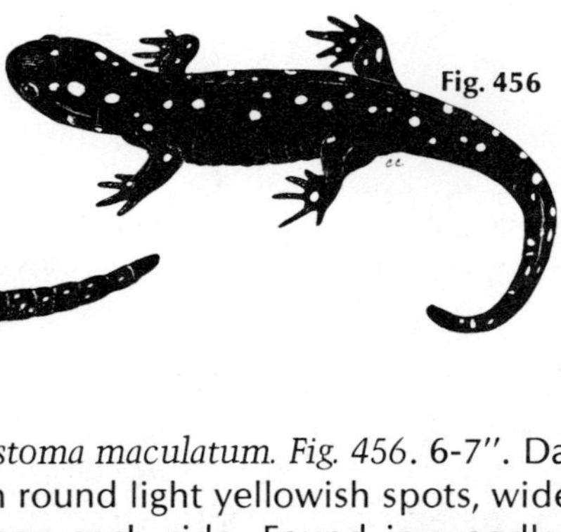

Fig. 456

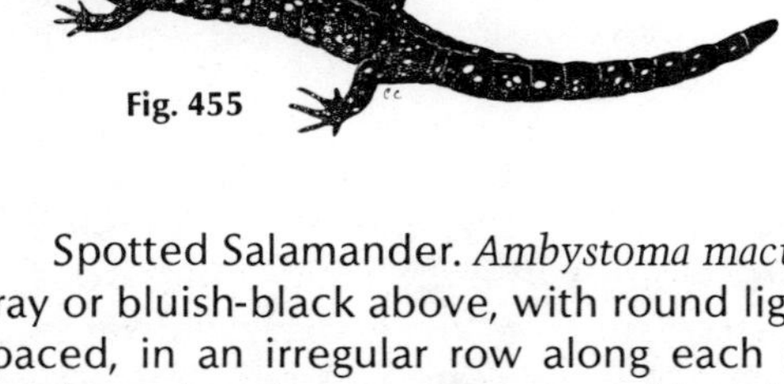

Fig. 455

Spotted Salamander. *Ambystoma maculatum. Fig. 456.* 6-7″. Dark gray or bluish-black above, with round light yellowish spots, widely spaced, in an irregular row along each side. Found in woodland ponds, and under stones or rotted logs in moist areas. Throughout except far north and west.

Red-spotted Newt. *Diemictylus viridescens. Fig. 457.* 3-4". The usual color is olive-green above, varying to shades of brown, with two rows of black-bordered, scarlet spots along the back; underside yellow, with small black spots. This species may pass through three stages of adult life: 1) an aquatic stage, when it is the usual olive-green color; 2) a land or "red eft" stage, when it is orange-red; 3) another aquatic stage, when it returns to the water to breed and regains its olive-green color. (A form without the characteristic scarlet spots sometimes occurs in Wisconsin and Michigan.) Only the aquatic stages should be expected in most areas of this region, where it inhabits shallow quiet lakes and permanent ponds. The red eft stage occurs most commonly in upland or mountain forests in the east, where it may be found in moist places near water; this stage is rarely, if ever, present in lowland areas.

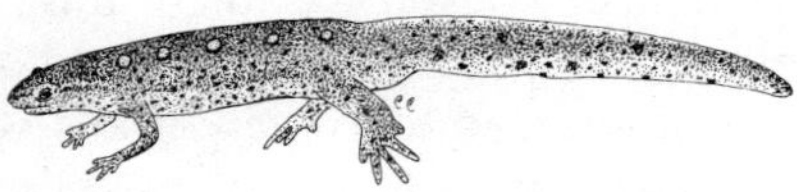

Fig. 457

Fig. 458

Fig. 459

Red-backed Salamander. *Plethodon cinereus. Fig. 458.* 2½-3¾". Occurs in two color phases: one, called lead-backed, is uniformly dark gray to nearly black; the other, called red-backed, is similarly colored on the sides, but has a central stripe from head to tail, usually red, but varies to orange or yellow. In both phases the underside is finely mottled black and white. Wholly terrestrial, with no aquatic tadpole stage. Found in wooded areas where its eggs are laid under moist logs, moss, or the like. Abundant throughout, excepting western Minnesota and southwestern Ontario.

Northern Two-lined Salamander. *Eurycea bislineata. Fig. 459.* 3-4". Upperparts somewhat bronzy-yellow, varying to brownish, greenish, or orange; trisected by narrow lines of black on each side of the back, with small black spots along the central section; sides finely-speckled; underside yellow. Found along shores of streams or near springs, and in adjacent woodlands. East from Lake Huron.

FROGS AND TOADS

American Toad. *Bufo americanus. Fig. 460.* 2½-4″. The only toad in the Northwoods. Color ranges from plain gray to brown, sometimes patterned with bright spots, especially on females; throat of males black. Found in moist woodlands and other habitats where there are insects for food and shallow water for egg laying. Throughout.

Spring Peeper. *Hyla crucifer. Fig. 461.* ¾-1¼″. A tiny treefrog, yellow-brown to dark brown, patterned with a shallow V between the eyes; a large, often imperfect, cross on the back; two narrow crossbands on the hind legs. Like all treefrogs, the ends of the toes are equipped with disks that allow them to climb into trees and bushes. Abundant in swamps, woodlands, and brushy areas with shallow pools. Throughout.

Gray Treefrog. *Hyla versicolor. Fig. 462.* 1¼-2″. This small treefrog can change its color from gray to green or nearly white. Camouflaged by a large irregular dark pattern on the back, and dark crossbands on legs and feet. Skin somewhat warty; toe disks large. Found on trees and bushes in moist woods and shrubby swamps. Southernmost parts.

Boreal Chorus Frog. *Pseudacris triseriata. Fig. 463.* 1-1½″. Color variable, light gray, brown, or greenish, with a pattern of three dark stripes on the back, and another on each side extending through the eye. Toe disks small; toes slightly webbed. These northern frogs have shorter legs than their southern counterparts, and tend to hop rather than leap. Found principally in marshy edges of ponds. West and north from upper Michigan.

Bullfrog. *Rana catesbeiana. Fig. 464.* 4-7″. Largest frog of this region. Color above varies from light to dark shades of green or greenish-brown, plain or lightly-spotted; legs spotted or barred; underside whitish, sometimes mottled. Lateral folds absent. Found on edges of large ponds, lakes, and slow-flowing rivers. Southern parts eastward from Wisconsin, interrupted in parts of Maine and the Maritime Provinces.

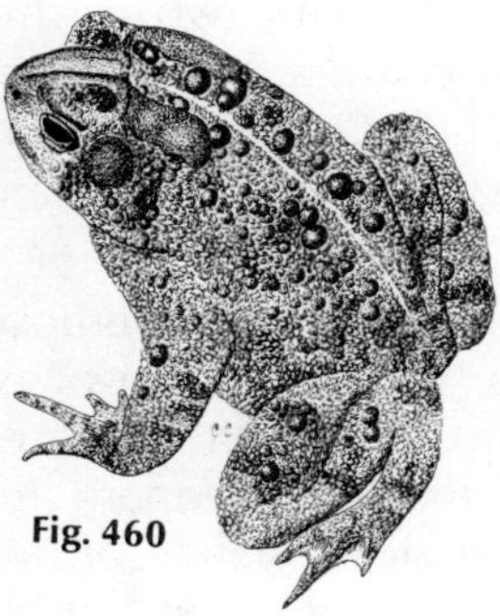

Fig. 460

Fig. 461

Fig. 462

Fig. 463

Fig. 466

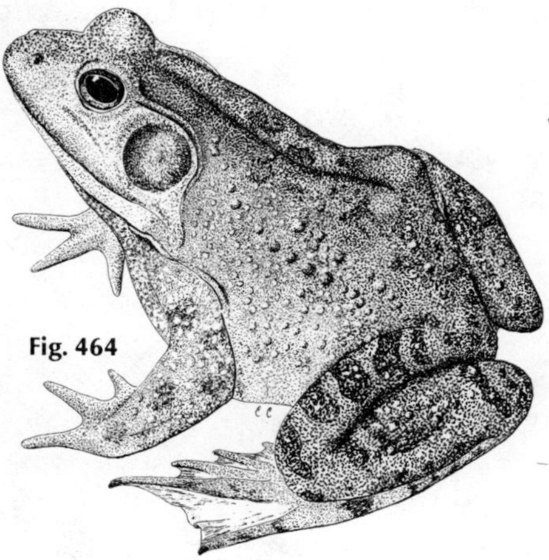

Fig. 464

Fig. 465

Mink Frog. *Rana septentrionalis. Fig. 465.* 2-3". Light olive above, usually more or less mottled with dark spots; legs spotted or banded; underside light yellowish without spots. Lateral folds usually absent. Emits a minklike odor if handled. Found on shores of rivers and streams, and edges of lakes among lily pads. Throughout except the Appalachians.

Green Frog. *Rana clamitans. Fig. 466.* 4-5". Color above variable and changeable, generally green on head and shoulders, and greenish-brown on back; underside white, with throat of male bright yellow. Lateral folds extend only to the rump. Found in nearly all shallow water habitats, and along shores of lakes and ponds. Throughout.

Northern Leopard Frog. *Rana pipiens. Fig. 467.* 2½-4″. Color above changeable, green or brown, patterned with two or three random rows of dark, light-bordered spots between the prominent lateral folds; sides similarly spotted; legs banded or spotted. Found in marshes, ponds, and adjacent drier areas, often some distance from water. Throughout.

Pickerel Frog. *Rana palustris. Fig. 468.* 2-3½″. Superficially resembles the leopard frog. Brown above, with a pattern of two rows of somewhat squared or oblong spots between the lateral folds; these spots in more regular rows than the leopard frog, and without light borders; similar spots on sides; bands on legs; underside white in front and bright orange-yellow under the hind legs. Found in cool spring-fed streams and ponds, sphagnum bogs and adjacent areas, often some distance from water. Eastward from Wisconsin.

Fig. 468

Fig. 467

Fig. 469

Wood Frog. *Rana sylvatica. Fig. 469.* 2-3″. Most northern of all frogs. Color changeable from light tan to dark chocolate-brown. Regardless of changes in color or variations in markings, this frog always wears a unique dark brown mask through and behind the eyes, and has prominent lateral folds. Found in moist woodlands, often far from water. Throughout.

Glossary

Alternate. Borne singly at different levels on a stem or axis, as leaves, flowers, or twigs.

Anther. The part of a stamen which produces pollen. See also *Stamen.*

Apetalous. Without petals.

Appressed. Lying flat against a surface.

Axil. The upper angle between the base of a leaf or twig and the stem to which it is attached.

Beard. Hairlike projections on a petal.

Benchland. A bench; a flat terracelike piece of land in a valley, above a stream, or along the shore of a lake.

Berry. A pulpy fruit with seeds embedded within the flesh.

Bilabiate. Two-lipped, referring to an irregular corolla or calyx which is symmetrical from side to side, but with dissimilar upper and lower divisions spreading above and below a throat or tube, as in the mints.

Bloom. A whitish powdery coating on the surface of some fruits or leaves.

Bract. A modified leaf, usually small, beneath a flower or an inflorescence, or sometimes on the floral stem.

Calyx. The outer ring of flower parts, usually green.

Canine teeth. The pointed teeth between the front incisors and the premolars.

Capsule. A dry fruit containing two or more seeds, which splits open when mature.

Catkin. An inflorescence called an ament; a dense spike or raceme composed of very many bracts and apetalous flowers.

Compound leaf. Composed of two or more separate leaflets.

Conglomerate. Rock composed of rounded rock fragments consolidated by hardened clay or the like.

Corm. An enlarged fleshy bulblike base of a stem; a solid bulb.

Corolla. The petals of a flower, either separate or fused, usually encircled by the calyx.

Decumbent. A stem or shoot with the basal portion horizontal, but with the tip ascending or upright.

Decurrent. Extending downward, as a leaf whose blade extends downward along the petiole.

Drumlin. A long, narrow or oval, smoothly rounded hill of unstratified glacial drift, the length running parallel to the path of the glacier.

Drupe. A fruit with a fleshy outer layer enclosing a hard woody seed-bearing stone.

Ear tufts. Erectile feathers on each side of the head or forehead of owls.

Emergent. Water plants whose apexes rise above the surface.

Entire. Having a continuous unbroken margin.

Ephemeral. Existing for a short time, as plants that complete their life cycle in spring before the trees leaf out.

Esker. A serpentine ridge composed of sand and gravel deposited by a stream flowing through or beneath glacial ice.

Facial disc. A circle of feathers around an owl's eye.

Filament. The stalk of the stamen which bears the anther. See also *Stamen.*

Gemma. A bud or budlike structure capable of producing a new plant.

Gland. A secreting structure in plants usually producing nectar or volatile oils; or a structure which looks like a gland.

Gneiss. A banded metamorphic rock, modified from either igneous or sedimentary rock, having a composition similar to granite, but coarser textured, and splitting more readily than granite.

Granite. A very hard igneous rock, strong, of crystalline texture, composed of quartz, feldspar, mica, and other minerals.

Guard hairs. Long hairs that protect the shorter, soft underfur.

Head. A dense cluster of flowers or fruit, sessile or nearly so, on a short axis.

Igneous. Rock produced under conditions of intense heat and pressure.

Incisor teeth. Flat, chisellike teeth in the front of the jaw, adapted for cutting.

Inflorescence. The manner in which flowers are arranged on the axis.

Involucre. Close-set bracts surrounding a flower, cluster, or head of flowers.

Keel. A prominent longitudinal ridge.

Lateral folds. Raised longitudinal folds of skin on the back of some frogs. Also referred to as dorsolateral folds.

Leaflet. One of the divisions of a compound leaf.

Lip. The upper or lower division of a bilabiate flower.

Moraine. Hills and ridges of sand, gravel, boulders, and earth deposited by a glacier.

Nut. A hard one-seeded fruit that does not split open.

Nutlet. A small nutlike seed.

Omnivorous. Not specialized in food preference.

Opposite. Borne directly across from each other at the same level, as leaves, flowers, or twigs.

Ovary. The part of the pistil in which seeds are produced. See also *Pistil.*

Palmate. Radiately lobed or divided, with the veins or divisions spreading from a common point.

Panicle. A loose compound flower cluster, the flower stems which branch from the axis having, themselves, two or more branches.

Papillose. A surface having short blunt, rounded, or cylindric projections.

Pedicel. The stem of a single flower in a compound inflorescence.

Peduncle. A part of the main stem that bears the inflorescence, whether a solitary flower or a cluster.

Perfect. Having both stamens and pistils.

Petiole. The stalklike portion of a leaf between the stem and the leaf blade.

Pinnate. Having leaflets arranged on each side of a common petiole, or veins arising from each side of a midvein.

Pistil. The female organ of a flower, consisting of the stigma, the style, and the seed-producing ovary.

Pistillate. Female flowers having pistils but no fertile stamens.

Plaited. Folded, or pleated, usually longitudinally.

Plantigrade. Walking on the sole of the foot with the heel touching the ground.

Pubescent. Covered with short soft or downy hairs.

Raceme. An inflorescence with stalked flowers arranged along an axis.

-ranked. The number of longitudinal rows in which leaves, etc., are arranged up an axis.

Regular. A flower in which the divisions within each ring of floral parts are more or less uniform, e.g., all the petals similar to each other in size and shape, etc.

Rhizome. An underground stem which produces roots on its lower side and leafy stems on its upper side.

Ruff. Longer and distinctly marked hairs or feathers on the neck of some species of mammals or birds.

Rump. The area of the lower back just above the tail.

Saccate. Shaped like a sac or pouch.

Samara. A dry, one-seeded, winged fruit.

Saprophyte. A plant without chlorophyl, which derives its nourishment from soil organic matter.

Scurf. Scalelike, or branlike particles.

Sedimentary. Rock resulting from the compacting and hardening or material deposited by wind or water, as limestone, sandstone, etc.

Sepal. One of the divisions of a calyx.

Sessile. Without a stalk, as a leaf lacking a petiole, the blade adjoining the stem.

Sheath. A tubular envelope surrounding a stem, as the lower part of a grass blade or the base of an angelica leaf.

Spadix. A flower spike having a fleshy axis.

Spathe. A large leaflike bract enclosing an inflorescence.

Speculum. A bright patch on the wing.

Spike. An inflorescence in which the flowers are sessile, or nearly so, on an elongated axis.

Spur. A hollow tubelike or saclike structure on some flowers, usually containing nectar.

Stamen. The male organ of a flower, consisting of a stalk or filament, and a pollen-producing anther at its tip.

Staminate. Male flowers having stamens but no pistils.

Stigma. The upperpart of the pistil which receives pollen. See also *Pistil.*

Stipe. An elongated stalk supporting a pistil at its summit.

Stipule. A small leaflike or bractlike structure at the base of some leaf petioles.

Stolon. A horizontal stem at the base of a plant, growing along the ground and taking root at the nodes or tip.

Streaked. Having narrow color markings running lengthwise of the body, as distinguished from bars which run crosswise of the body.

Style. The part of the pistil, usually short and narrowed, between the ovary and the stigma. See also *Pistil.*

Submersed. Growing entirely under water.

Tomentose. Having woolly, matted hairs.

Umbel. An inflorescence in which the flowers all grow from the same point and radiate out like the ribs of an umbrella.

Understory. Shrubs and small trees growing beneath the large dominant trees in a forest.

Whorl. Three or more leaves growing around a stem at the same node.

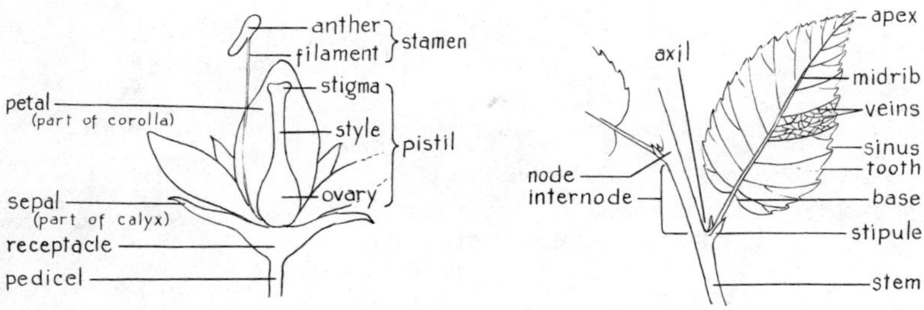

For convenience in identifying parts of a plant, the above diagrams are given; the diagram on the left shows the parts of a flower, while the drawing on the right details the parts of a leaf.

Index